The War of Our Childhood

The War

Memories of

# of Our

World War II

Childhood

Wolfgang W. E. Samuel

University Press of Mississippi / *Jackson*

www.upress.state.ms.us

Photograph on page ii: Goetz Oertel
leading family members on their flight west
from the Red Army, 1945

10 09 08 07 06 05 04 03 02   4 3 2 1

Library of Congress Cataloging-in-Publication Data

The war of our childhood : memories of World War II / [reported by] Wolfgang W. E.
Samuel.
   p. cm.
   Includes index.
   ISBN 1-57806-482-1 (cloth : alk. paper)
   1. World War, 1939–1945—Children—Germany. 2. Children and war—Germany.
3. World War, 1939–1945—Personal narratives, German. 4. Germany—Social conditions—1939–1945. 5. Children—Germany—Biography. I. Samuel, Wolfgang W. E.

D810.C4 W27 2002
940.53'161—dc21   2002006172

British Library Cataloging-in-Publication Data available

To my "little" sister, Ingrid

To everything there is a season,
and a time to every purpose under the heaven:
A time to be born, and a time to die;
a time to plant, and a time to pluck up that
which is planted;
A time to kill, and a time to heal;
a time to break down, and a time to build up;
A time to weep, and a time to laugh;
a time to mourn, and a time to dance;
A time to cast away stones,
and a time to gather stones together;
a time to embrace, and a time to refrain
from embracing;
A time to get, and a time to lose;
a time to keep, and a time to cast away;
A time to rend, and a time to sew;
a time to keep silence, and a time to speak;
A time to love, and a time to hate;
a time of war, and a time of peace.

—Ecclesiastes 3: 1–8

Contents

Preface and Acknowledgments   xi

Part I: War from the Sky   3

Ingrid Frohberg ~ *Dresden, Saxony*   6

Helga Schaefer ~ *Kassel, Hesse*   17

Hubertus Thiel ~ *Würzburg, Bavaria*   26

Wolf Stäglich ~ *Leuna, Saxony*   34

Rita and Ingrid Nille ~ *Arneburg, Saxony-Anhalt*   53

Christa Glowalla ~ *Berlin*   67

Siegrid Mayer ~ *Kaiserslautern, Rhineland-Palatinate*   80

Karl Kremer ~ *Köln, Northrhine-Westfalia*   91

Contents

Ina Hesse ~ *Westerburg, Rhineland-Palatinate* 101

Hans Herzmann ~ *Remagen, Rhineland-Palatinate* 112

Part II: War on the Ground   127

Annelies Sorofka ~ *Landau, Lower Silesia (Poland)* 130

Bernd Heinrich ~ *Gut Borowki, Wartheland (Poland)* 148

Karl Brach ~ *Domnau, East Prussia (Poland)* 161

Irmgard Broweleit ~ *Königsberg, East Prussia (Russia)* 177

Arnold Bieber ~ *Ortelsburg, East Prussia (Poland)* 194

Goetz Oertel ~ *Stuhm, East Prussia (Poland)* 206

Fred Rother ~ *Weisstein, Upper Silesia (Poland)* 223

Dieter Hahn ~ *Posen, Wartheland (Poland)* 238

Arnim Krüger ~ *Potsdam, Brandenburg* 250

Helgard Seifert ~ *Berlin* 263

Erich Abshoff ~ *Wuppertal, Northrhine-Westfalia* 278

Johann Koppe ~ *Wollup, Brandenburg* 285

Contents

Part III: Other Dimensions of War   299

Heinz Loquai ~ *Komotau, Czech Republic*   302

Hans-Peter Haupt ~ *Prague, Czech Republic*   314

Etta Krecker ~ *Eilenburg, Saxony-Anhalt*   329

Regina Demetrio ~ *Zwickau, Saxony*   335

Epilogue   343
Explanation of Terms   349
Index   353

Preface and
Acknowledgments

Early in May 1945, at the very end of World War II in Europe, there was precious little innocence left in what remained of a once proud country called Germany. Its reputation and cities lay in ruins. Millions of German men had died on hundreds of fields of battle. Over a million women and children perished or were injured in the devastating rain of Allied bombs and bullets visited upon the land like a biblical swarm of locusts. Millions more were driven from their homes east of the Oder-Neisse rivers and from the former Sudetenland. Many perished in the process. Few of the victors felt a need to extend humane treatment toward a people who themselves had shown so little humanity toward others. The Germans were defeated, let them suffer. They who sowed the wind shall reap the whirlwind.

In the four zones of occupation—American, British, French, and Russian—of this broken and humbled land, its traumatized survivors shivered in the wintry cold. Hunger, disease, despair, and hopelessness were their steadfast companions. Children held onto their mothers as if they were life preservers, as if holding on so tightly would bring back the lost security they longed for. The gloomy wintry skies of 1945 became even more depressing when the hungry and cold survivors learned of the death camps their former leader and his followers had left as their legacy. Germans dropped their eyes in shame, some refused to believe, and the word "German" became synonymous with evil. At the very end there was little innocence left in the war-ravaged land—except in the eyes and hearts of its young children.

The gaunt faces of Germany's children—mine among them—peeked out of the rubble, suffering, and heartbreak. The children offered a timid smile to anyone who cared to look. Dressed mostly in worn and patched clothing, our stomachs frequently empty, we looked at our world of chaos without comprehending—yet, it was home. Our eyes carried no hate, only recognition of what was. Peace was an abstraction. The world we *Kinder* knew nearly always had the word WAR appended to it. So we tried to make do with the world we lived in. We played *Krieg*. What else was there?

In September 2000 I published my childhood experiences in a book entitled *German Boy*. It took fifty years, nearly a lifetime, for me to be able to look back and re-create those days of darkness and terror. And once I had done so, I began to wonder what had happened to other children of my generation. I knew my own experience was only a small fragment of a much greater tragedy. How had other German children experienced the world of war we were born into? How did they cope in the postwar world?

My own ordeal ended in 1951 when my mother and I emigrated to the United States—a land where cities and towns knew no ruins, where there was ample food for everyone, where children attended school without worrying about *Tiefflieger* or the howl of a siren in the middle of the night. I soon forgot about my turbulent past; I tried to blend in and become just another American. I returned to school, went to work, married, and in time had children of my own. My children grew up knowing none of the terror and deprivation experienced by many in my generation of German children.

As I began my search for the children of '45, I discovered that the Germany of today was a very different society from the land I had known in 1945. It was no easy task to locate the children of '45 in a country where the greater part of the population was born after that year and a substantial number of the remainder are immigrants. I turned for help to friends I made while attending the *Führungsakademie der Bundeswehr* from 1973 to 1975 as a U.S. Air Force exchange officer. Some of my former classmates consented to share with me their own wartime experiences, and in turn provided names of others. An equally important source became Germans who had emigrated to the United States. I feel fortunate to have captured among my many interviewees a diversity of wartime experiences. I found people who came from various geographic areas of the Third Reich and whose social and economic backgrounds were as diverse as their places of origin.

Initially, I believed that in my interviews I would find little that was new, little that I had not experienced for myself, heard of, or read about. I was wrong. I found each story and each narrator to be unique and different. In many instances children survived by the thinnest of margins, with chance playing a large role in their survival—what some call fate, others the hand of God. As I explored with them their wartime and postwar experiences I was amazed to discover how well these children of '45 coped with troubled pasts, entering the future with confidence to fashion their own lives. This generation of wartime German children proved to be uniquely resilient. They built personal lives as successful as the new Germany they helped to create. In a number of cases their traumatic wartime and postwar lives became the basis for professional careers. The most dramatic example I found of this was in someone who as a boy had survived on birds and rodents in a remote German forest. In later life he became a respected American biologist, a chronicler of the New England woods and the life of ravens. To this day the forest which sustained this man as a youngster remains his friend and close companion.

I want to emphasize for the reader that *The War of Our Childhood* is not a book about politics or ideology. Nor is it a book about right or wrong, about war or blame. Rather, it is a connected narrative about the consequences of war visited upon children. Although many of the stories reflect the agony and the terror of the times, that is not my intended focus; it represents only the framework within which we children lived, played, and, if fortunate, survived. My focus is entirely on the young children, on their resilience under trying circumstances, on the critical role of mothers in their lives, and on the astounding ability of a generation of German children to emerge from debilitating circumstances as sane and productive human beings.

I present the stories in the principal manner in which war manifested itself to each child. War came to us children gradually, first from the sky. Initially war from the sky was no more than an annoyance; later it became a terrorizing experience. War on the ground, in both east and west Germany, came later in 1944. The final part of the book looks at children expelled from the Sudetenland, at the role of a bipolar Germany in their lives, and at the continuing absence of fathers years after war's end. Each chapter begins with the name and age in 1945 of the individual child, along with the place of his or her permanent residence in Germany at the time the story begins. For ease of location I have indicated in which *Land* (state) of the current *Bundesrepublik* a particular town or city is located. If the location is in territory which now is a part of Poland or Russia, it is so noted. Interviews have been edited for brevity and word choice.

I want to recognize the important contributions of Hannelore Fricke and Oberst (a.D.) Wulf Fricke to the completion of this project. Not only did Hannelore and Wulf locate people who might consent to being interviewed, but they also used their considerable persuasive powers to get these men and women to recall in detail experiences many of them had avoided recalling for a lifetime. For Hanne and Wulf a "no" was a challenge to try again and again until their efforts were crowned by success. In addition to the women and men whose stories appear in the book, I would like to recognize and thank the following for sharing their memories or providing assistance: Barbara Conrad, Helgard Gray, Ulla Hahn, Robert Hamill, Frederick Kailer, Joseph

Laufer, Brigitte Murdock, Charles Phillips, Dorothee Schupp, and Angela Ruhland. Finally, I want to express my appreciation and offer my humble thanks to the historian and author Stephen E. Ambrose for his continued inspiration and generous support of my efforts and to Craig W. Gill, editor in chief at the University Press of Mississippi, for sharing my belief that this is a book that needed to be written.

The War of Our Childhood

Part I

War from the Sky

The reply to the President's request of 24 August 1942 was designated AWPD-42 [Air War Plans Division plan developed in 1942]. In it the Air Offensive against Germany was described as a combined effort of the United States Army Air Forces and the British Royal Air Force. The former would concentrate on daylight bombing of precision objectives; the latter on night bombing of area objectives. . . .

—Major General Haywood S. Hansell, Jr., U.S. Air Force, The Air Plan That Defeated Hitler

The Federal Statistical Office in Wiesbaden computed after the war that 593,000 German civilians died and 3.37 million dwellings were destroyed from 1939 to 1945.

—Max Hastings, Bomber Command

When war began in September 1939 it meant little to us children. Our routines were not interrupted by an event most of us didn't even know was taking place, much less understand. War, when we thought of it at all, was something for adults, taking place in lands with strange-sounding names. War seemed heroic to many of us; at least that's how the adults spoke of it when we overheard them over Sunday afternoon Kaffee und Kuchen. We continued to play hide-and-seek, hopscotch, and Indianer, went to school, and in time simply added another game to our repertoire—Krieg.

By 1940 and 1941 the airwaves were filled with constant program interruptions of Sondermeldungen, special announcements of great victories won by the Wehrmacht. As a six-year-old I tried to listen closely to these announcements because they had about them the uplifting and raucous sound of the circus. But by 1943 there were no more Sondermeldungen. Instead, the drone of enemy aircraft overhead and the wail of the air raid siren began to define our lives. Sleeping through a night without being awakened by the wail of a siren or the thump of exploding bombs became a rarity for many German children. Next the Americans came in broad daylight with their fleets of four-engined bombers. Everything vibrated in our homes when the Americans flew over, leaving behind them a swath of destruction and a lingering fear of tomorrow. We clung to our mothers, and when Mutti said that everything would be all right, we tried to believe, holding on even more tightly as we were herded into house cellars and bunkers.

By 1944 war no longer was a game to us, nor was it heroic. Instead, we saw our houses burned, our friends buried under rubble. At school there were faces missing. The air raids became larger, more frequent, and more violent, resulting in firestorms rivaling the atomic bombs yet to be dropped on Japan. First Cologne, then Hamburg, Darmstadt, and Nürnberg perished in man-made firestorms. In February 1945 Dresden, the last of the cities to be erased in such a manner, became a funeral pyre my family escaped only by chance. Chance—fate or the hand of God—played an ever increasing role in the survival of us children. For still other children the war from the sky meant Tiefflieger, the low-flying fighter planes which seemed to fire at anything that moved below. They came upon us in an instant, and frequently only chance decided life or death. We were taught to get out of the street when hearing Tiefflieger, to hide behind anything nearby, throw ourselves on the ground if there was no shelter available, and never to run or remain standing.

The air raid siren became the ultimate sound of terror. The war from the sky—which would claim the lives of nearly six hundred thousand civilians, many of them children—remains a vivid memory for many of the German children of war.

Ingrid Frohberg

{Age 5}

Dresden, Saxony

The attacks on Dresden by Bomber Command and the American 8th Air Force between 13 and 15 February 1945 destroyed the city and killed a minimum of 30,000 and perhaps as many as 100,000 people. . . .

—Max Hastings, *Bomber Command*

Of all those people in that shelter, only two of us survived.

—Ingrid Frohberg

My father, Alexander Frohberg, was born in 1912 in Freiberg, a small university town in the province of Saxony, about thirty kilometers southwest of Dresden. He was the youngest of twelve children, ten boys and two girls. My grandparents owned a large dance and concert hall on Schützenstrasse in Freiberg, called the Tivoli Frohberg. The largest room seated as many as twelve hundred persons. After the war, I remember my father telling me that before the National Socialists came to power this large room in the Tivoli was often used for political rallies. My grandparents insisted that the rally sponsors have insurance to cover the frequent damage done to furnishings during their unruly meetings.

My grandfather kept what he called a Golden Book, which he asked every band leader, concert master, and political speaker to sign. There were the signatures of Ernst Tahlmann, the leader of the German Communist Party; Gustav Stresemann, who led the Social Democrats; and Adolf Hitler, the leader of the NSDAP, the Nazis. My father, who

---

Previous page: Ingrid and her mother Frieda, 1944

was only a youngster when Hitler came to speak, remembers him as a small man, entering through the rear door of the Tivoli, surrounded by his bodyguards. He was the only one to use the stage entrance; all others came in through the front door. Hitler's signature, my grandfather told me, was written in very small letters. After the Nazis came to power my grandparents carefully removed the page with Hitler's signature from the Golden Book, and reinserted it again after the war. The Golden Book is still in the possession of my family.

My father completed the eight compulsory years of school and then apprenticed as a pharmacist. He accepted a position in a drugstore in Dresden, Drogerie Lachmann, after completing his apprenticeship. While on vacation in Kiel in 1938, he met my mother, Frieda, an apprentice at the Bankhaus Wilhelm Ahlmann—the same bank where, many years later, I entered into my own apprenticeship and where I met my future husband. My parents fell in love and married on March 28, 1939. After the wedding and a brief honeymoon my father returned to Dresden, found an apartment, and my mother followed. She quickly found a job at the Dresdner Handelsbank. They both worked, not a common practice in Germany at that time. Drogerie Lachmann was a family-owned business. The owner, who took a liking to my father, didn't have children of his own and asked my father if he would consider taking over the store when the time came. Of course my father agreed to such a generous proposal. But soon the war started, on September 1, 1939, and Alexander Frohberg was drafted into the Wehrmacht as a *Sanitäter*, a medical corpsman. He served throughout the war on or just behind the immediate front lines, first in France, then in the east, until he was taken prisoner by the Americans in April 1945.

With my father suddenly gone, my mother continued to work, living alone in her new apartment, pregnant with her first child. In September 1940, in her ninth month of pregnancy, her family wrote and asked her to return to Kiel. You can have the child in Kiel, they wrote. You will not be alone, and we can help you. So my mother

moved to Kiel, where I was born on September 23, 1940. She stayed
for four to six weeks, I was told, and as soon as I was able to travel
she returned with me to Dresden. There we lived a quiet, uneventful life until February 1945, only rarely interrupted by the arrival of
my father on very brief military leaves.

In March 1945 my mother was to have her second child. Her relatives in Kiel again asked her to come and stay with them. They
could take care of me, they wrote, while she delivered the baby. This
time my mother said no. Kiel was frequently bombed because it was
a naval base, and she felt it was just too dangerous. Dresden had
never been bombed by either the English or the Americans. I understand that the residents of Dresden at the time believed that Dresden
was an "open city," a town which by tacit agreement with the Allies
was not to be bombed because of its cultural heritage and lack of
industry. Also, by now my mother had made many friends in Dresden
and no longer felt alone. So she stayed in Dresden. Frieda, her friends
said to her repeatedly, we will take care of Ingrid. You don't have to
go to Kiel to have the baby.

In February 1945 my mother was in her eighth month of pregnancy. Although only four years old then, I vaguely recall the first air raid
on the night of February 13. In my mind I can see a picture of my
mother pushing me somewhere in my baby buggy, the houses around
us on fire. The entire street was burning. I don't recall being afraid. On
the following night, the fourteenth of February, I clearly remember the
air raid warning and the siren going off. My mother hurriedly got me
out of bed. I wore only a nightshirt and stood on a chair while she tried
to dress me, pulling a pair of pants over my legs. After she got the pants
on, she pulled a pair of long stockings on my feet. Then she stuffed my
arms into an overcoat, buttoned it, and put a warm hat on my head. I
remember it all. I always said that hat was my 'larm mütze (air raid
warning cap), because every time there was an air raid warning my
mother pulled that hat over my head. It was a thick, padded hat, which
muffled the sound of the awful howling of the siren. The siren made a

very dreadful noise—huh-huh-huh-huh—up and down, on and on. It scared me. The sound was so awful that for many years afterward I went into a state of panic whenever I heard a siren wailing like that. I can still hear it today.

There I stood on the chair, finally dressed. Behind me, on the dresser, stood our *Volksempfänger*, a small radio. Over the radio I heard the announcer say, *Achtung, Achtung, Luftlagemeldung.* At four years of age I could already say that, having heard the announcement many times. Whenever I heard it I imitated the announcer, repeating in unison with him—*Achtung, Achtung Luftlagemeldung.* Then he would say what was happening—that enemy aircraft were approaching, and that all people should go into the air raid shelters. Of course I didn't understand the meaning of what the announcer was saying. I just thought it was fun to imitate him. And when he finished his announcement I raised my arm and said *Heil Hitler*, just like he said it on the radio. I imitated everything I heard. I was proud that I could do that.

When I think back on that night, I believe my mother was rather agitated. She said to me, "*Schnell, schnell, schnell, Ingrid*," while I stood on my chair imitating the radio announcer. We ran really fast to the shelter, three streets over, into the cellar of a large apartment house. I recall seeing benches on either side of the whitewashed cellar walls, and on those benches sat many people. Maybe fifty. Maybe sixty. Again, I don't remember being afraid, or being aware that something awful could happen to me. But I can recall that some people held towels or handkerchiefs in front of their mouths to filter the smoke that began to fill the shelter. Suddenly the people around me became very excited and rushed toward the steel door at one end of the cellar, which I know was an emergency exit connecting to the cellar of the adjacent apartment house. The door was level with the ground. It had a long steel arm which the people pushed down. When they opened the door all I could see was fire. Lots of fire. And I thought the people all jumped into the fire. That's what I thought at the time as a four-year-old child.

Ingrid Frohberg

At this point in her story Ingrid lost her composure. The tears ran down her face freely. She looked away and down, clearly wanting to hide her pain. After a long period of silence around the table where she sat with her father and me, she continued.

Later, I learned that the people didn't jump into the fire, that the suction of the fire pulled them into it. Still, I wasn't afraid at the time. I wasn't afraid of the fire. I didn't know it was dangerous, nor did I understand what was happening to the people and my mother.

I carry this picture in my mind of what the shelter looked like, and I can re-create the scene. The steel door leading to the neighboring cellar was to my left. There were stairs leading upstairs, but they were unusable because the house above us had burned and debris blocked the door. To the right of that door, near the ceiling of the cellar, were two small rectangular windows, maybe thirty by forty centimeters. But large enough for a small child to fit through. I sat still on my bench, waiting for my mother to return. I don't recall how long I sat there. Finally I could see people outside removing debris from the windows with their bare hands. They forced the windows open. Someone shouted for me to stand on the bench and to lift my hands. I did. They pulled me out through the narrow window opening by my outstretched hands. I lost a shoe and stocking in the process.

I believe it was a young soldier who saved me. He carried me onto a bus. The bus windows had shades which were pulled down. Inside of the bus there was light, I recall, and the bus didn't have seats like a regular bus, but rather long benches on either side. The soldier sat me on a bench, and then he knelt before me and wrapped a light blue scarf around my naked foot. It was cold that February night. Maybe I trembled. Maybe that's why he wrapped the shawl around my foot. The bus drove to a hospital.

My next clear recollection is being with a Frau Schmitt. Frau Schmitt was a nurse at the hospital. She took me home with her and put me into what I thought was a huge white bed. And as I looked into the light of the bedside lamp before going to sleep I marveled that I had never lain in such a huge bed before. Those are my memories. The next day when I awoke I don't recall that I cried, or that I called for my *Muschi*. Frau Schmitt questioned me about where I lived, and I was able to tell her. My mother had taught me to say Moritz-Kloss-Strasse 2. I also had a small leather pouch around my neck which held a card with my name and address. Frau Schmitt went to the Moritz-Kloss-Strasse to see what she could find. Everything there was totally destroyed except for a piece of fence, on which Frau Schmitt wrote in *weisse Kreide*, "Who knows Ingrid Frohberg? Please contact Schmitt, Coswiger Strasse 44." Soon, a friend of my mother's, Tante Graupner, came to Frau Schmitt's home and identified me. After the women talked I accompanied Tante Graupner home, and I lived with her for several days. She knew that the sister of my father, Tante Elfriede, lived in nearby Freiberg. She informed my aunt that I was alive and living with her. We knew nothing of my mother's fate.

Our Dresden apartment house had been totally destroyed with the exception of a small shack in our garden in back of the house. In this shack stood two suitcases with clothes and family photos which my aunt retrieved. She also attempted to find out through the authorities what may have happened to my mother. On the twelfth of March the police issued a certificate declaring that my mother was most likely dead—*voraussichtlich tot*. When in later years I read and understood the meaning of this brief sentence at the end of the certificate—"*Mutter des Kindes voraussichtlich tot. Vater beim Heer im Osten*" ("Mother of the child most likely dead. Father with the army in the east")—I cried. I still feel like crying for my mother when I read it today.

I really don't know how my mother died. She must have been one of the many people in the shelter who were sucked into the flames that night. I don't know why I survived. Another child was also saved. Of all those people in that shelter, only two of us survived. My aunt Elfriede came to Dresden, and I went with her to Freiberg. Tante Elfriede hung a picture of my mother over my bed, and she told me that my mother was in heaven. I believed her. I looked up into the night sky and at the stars above me, and I picked the largest star I saw, the planet Venus, and decided it was my mother. My *Muschi*. Every evening when I could see the sky I waved at my *Muschi* and told her that I was a brave child and that I was good. For many years afterward I did this and believed in this vision of my mother.

I lived in Freiberg with my aunt in the Tivoli Frohberg when the Russians entered town in April 1945. The Russians took over our large house and used it as an officers' club and dining facility. I can't remember anything about the Russians coming into town or what happened. It's a total blank for me. While the Russians used the lower level of the Tivoli, we were allowed to continue to live upstairs. My aunt worked as a cook in her own kitchen, cooking for the Russians. The advantage of this arrangement was that there was plenty of food for all of us. We never went hungry, as did so many others. I remember a Russian major who took a liking to me. He would have me sit on his lap while he played chess with my *Onkel*, my father's brother. In February 1946 my father was released from an American prisoner-of-war camp and returned to Kiel. He remarried in 1948, to a family friend of my mother's parents.

In May 1948 my father and my new stepmother came by train to Freiberg in the Russian zone of occupation to take me back to Kiel. At the time the Russians permitted a limited amount of family reunification, even though it was the beginning of the Berlin blockade, and relations with the West were none too good. I still remember the old, dark, and smelly office at the Russian *Kommandatura* where my parents had to take me to apply for a travel permit for me. I sat on my new mother's lap in this smoky waiting room filled with many people. My father thought we would have to wait many hours before our turn. But then a Russian soldier entered the room, saw us sitting there and said, "*Frau mit Kind zuerst*," woman with child first. I was the only child in the room. We were out of there within minutes.

My stepmother was very good to me, but of course I still missed my real mother. At eight years of age I began to have dreams. One awful dream recurred for many years. I lay in a street with many, many other people. They were all dead, and soldiers with rifles came around and shot those who moved. I knew that I was alive and lay very still and acted dead. This recurring dream stayed with me for years, as I lay amongst the dead people with my face turned down to the ground, lying dead quiet so I wouldn't be shot like the others. I don't believe I actually experienced that. But I must have seen something very disturbing, because the dream came to me so often.

At age twelve I began to believe that my mother was still alive. I looked for her in every brunette woman who resembled her. I constantly looked at women. I saw her in my mind. Is that her? I thought. And I would run to look at the woman's face. I was always disappointed. I wanted her to be alive. I didn't want to believe my mother was dead. At that age I desperately wanted my real mother, although my stepmother was very kind to me and tried hard to be my mother. But I thought that if I had my real mother things would be very different. Later in life I decided the facts are the facts. She was dead and I had to live with it.

I hope there never again is a war. I don't like anything about war, least of all war movies. Although at times I believe I am past it, at the most unexpected moments I find myself touched by my past. Sirens, fire, the sound of guns going off affect me deeply. It never disappears. I can only cover it up. Interestingly, I cannot ever recall being afraid as a young child. I didn't acquire fear until later in life, as I began to understand what really happened to me in Dresden.

As for my children, we seldom spoke of these things. When my three daughters were young and had no children of their own they were not interested. Later, when they had their own children, and were at an age where an interest in the lives of one's parents naturally arises, they didn't have the time. We never really talked about those days amongst ourselves. Only bits and pieces here and there. I have several pictures in my inner eye which stay with me. For example, the picture of my mother dressing me when the sirens went off and we hurried to the shelter. Or the picture in the dream where I act dead. But I don't know where that picture came from, and it bothers me. The picture in the air raid shelter I know is real. I know I didn't dream that. These pictures of my past are always there, and if I want to I can recall them at will. But I don't want to do that anymore. I have done it often enough, and it only brings sadness and grief. It's best to leave it alone. Not to touch it. But I still miss my mother.

As for my father?

Ingrid turned toward her father, age eighty-eight. His hair was white and his body frail, but his mind was as sharp as ever. Her eyes were warm and compassionate as she looked at him and spoke.

He loves my mother, Frieda, to this day, although his second marriage was very happy. For him it is inexplicable that he survived the war as a medical corpsman in combat, both in France and in Russia, and as a prisoner of war, while his wife, Frieda, whom he thought safe in Dresden, carrying their second child, died in a firestorm. He never got over that.

Ingrid took his hand in hers.

When he speaks of it I always try to get him to stop. It happened, I say to him. It's been so long ago, and you must come to terms with it. You only make life difficult for yourself. Still, it comes back all the time. At times I wonder if my mother had gone to Kiel to have her second child. . . .

After the Wall came down, I traveled with my father to Dresden. Together we visited the place where the house once stood where he lived with my mother and me. We also went to the cemetery and placed flowers on the mass graves, like many others do. Then we went to the Herzogin Garten Strasse, that's where the house stood with the air raid shelter. We found the place easily, but both houses of course are gone.

Ingrid, a banker by training, raised three beautiful daughters. She lives now in the windswept town of Kiel, a town where few reminders of war remain. She and her husband, Peter, enjoy taking trips around the world—the United States, China, Thailand, the Bahamas, the Holy Land. No place seems too distant. And as an accomplished and very active tourna-ment bridge player she fills her days while at home. Yet, now and then, against her will, her mind strays, and she becomes that little girl again— searching for her Muschi.

Helga Schaefer

{Age 7}

Kassel, Hesse

The most successful day for the Sturmgruppen was their 27th September slaughter of the wandering 445th Group; in three minutes they littered the countryside near Kassel with the burning wrecks of a score of Liberators. . . . [The 445th] lost 25 B-24s, the highest loss for a single group in any 8th Air Force operation.

—Roger A. Freeman, *Mighty Eighth War Diary*

I vividly recall the radio announcements warning of approaching enemy air-craft. They scared me terribly. *"Achtung, Achtung für Kurhessen. Feindliche Flieger sind im Anflug von England"*—enemy aircraft are approaching from England. I knew what followed—those awful stockings—and then we ran for the shelter.

—Helga Schaefer

We lived for a time in Kassel, before we moved out of town because of the air raids. My grandparents Schaefer cautioned us to move out of the city into the country before it was too late. "The cities," my grand-mother said, "are just too dangerous, and you will be killed if you stay." Somehow she didn't think it was going to happen to her, or maybe it didn't matter to her. We moved to a little village, Kleinropperhausen, near Kassel, where my father had worked as a forest ranger and game warden until he was drafted into the Wehrmacht. The *Forsthaus* sat on the edge of the forest with a large set of elk antlers over the front entrance, as it was proper for a German *Försterei*.

Previous page: Helga in front of Margarethe and sister Brigitte

Both my father, Wilhelm, and my mother, Margarethe, grew up in Kassel, where they met and married. I was born in 1938. My sister Brigitte was born in 1940, and Elisabeth in 1945. I was old enough near the end of the war to be very much aware of what war did to people. In Kassel, when we had to go into the air raid shelter, my mother always made me put on a pair of thick, knitted stockings which scratched my skin. I hated those stockings. For me as a five-year-old those coarse stockings were my personal nightmare, and they represented war. Not the bombing raids, but those awful stockings. I couldn't really imagine what a bombing raid was, or what its consequences were. That still lay in the future.

I vividly recall the radio announcements warning of approaching enemy aircraft. They scared me terribly. "*Achtung, Achtung für Kurhessen. Feindliche Flieger sind im Anflug von England*"—enemy aircraft are approaching from England. I knew what followed—those awful stockings—and then we ran for the shelter. Later, when we moved into our little *Forsthaus* in Kleinropperhausen, we still heard the announcements, but there was no place for us to run to. There were no shelters in the countryside. I could see the enemy planes flying overhead, but they didn't drop bombs on us, they dropped them on Kassel. Once I rode into Kassel on one of those foul-smelling trucks which had been converted to run on the gasses generated by a charcoal burner carried in back of the truck. My aunt Hildegard had a chemical factory in Kassel and was allowed to keep one truck. Occasionally the truck came out our way to get a load of wood for its burner, and one time I rode into town with my aunt. The sight of the bombed city was nightmarish. Kassel had been totally destroyed. It is a picture which I still carry in my inner eye.

Other than that the war passed us by. In our little village, life was relatively quiet and peaceful. My mother wrote letters for the farmers to their sons and husbands fighting at the front. There was no pastor or teacher living in our tiny village, so my father, the *Forstmeister*, was the person to whom the farmers turned for help. In his absence they turned to my mother. The farmers could read and write, but not well.

They were men and women who worked with their large calloused hands. They were uncomfortable holding a pen and preferred to dictate their simple letters about the weather, family, and work to someone like my mother who was educated and a good and willing writer.

Russian and French prisoners of war worked on the farms. They were quartered on one large farm, and in the morning they walked to the farms to which they were assigned. The prisoners received more or less good or bad treatment at those farms. Many German farmers treated these men like any other help they may have had before the war started. Some of these people maintained close contacts with each other after the war. But we had one farmer, he was our mayor, who didn't treat his workers well.

I entered school in the fall of 1944. I had a very nice, older teacher. We children loved him. He must have been in his sixties. He was drafted into the Volkssturm in January 1945 and was killed only two weeks later. That hit us children very hard when we heard that our wonderful teacher had been killed. Ours was a one-room schoolhouse, and our teacher was much more to us than just a teacher. We loved him, as children love kind and caring people. When I heard he had been killed I felt as if I had lost someone close and precious.

I remember April 1945 very clearly. Young German soldiers came through our village just before the Americans arrived. They were fourteen, fifteen, and sixteen years old, drafted only weeks earlier. I remember my mother hiding some of them overnight in our washhouse. These boys moved on the next morning. The following day the Americans came. It was Easter. We didn't have any sweets in those days, but it was customary for children to go from one farm to another and the farmers would give us colored, hard-boiled eggs. Then we would take the eggs out to a meadow, and there we threw them up in the air. The one who had the most unbroken eggs was the winner. We were playing our little game when the Americans came. Their tanks and trucks and jeeps rolled through our little village in what seemed to us a never-ending column. The minute we saw the Americans we forgot all about our eggs and ran to see the soldiers. The American soldiers were friendly and smiled at us. They handed us oranges, chewing gum, and Hershey bars. Things we had never seen or tasted before. Then they went through the village and searched every house for German soldiers.

A group of four Americans came to our house and politely asked if they could search it. My sister Brigitte, who was only five at the time, became so scared she locked herself in the toilet and wouldn't come out. "Tell your daughter she has nothing to fear. We won't do anything to harm her," one American soldier said to my mother, who spoke good school English. My mother finally convinced Brigitte to come out. She was afraid of soldiers. Any soldiers. The search was routine. The American soldiers were considerate and careful and did no damage. As a forest ranger my father of course had his uniforms. Some were simple work garments, others were to be worn on special occasions or on Sunday in church, and were accordingly fancy. The uniforms were a hunter green with cloth oak leaves sewn on the lapels and sleeves, and stag-horn buttons. I noticed that one of the soldiers spent a long time looking at the uniforms, stroking the sleeve of one of the coats. He was definitely interested in them. Maybe he was a hunter himself and had an eye for such things, I thought. My mother was more concerned about a briefcase in which she had placed her jewelry and silver and which she had hidden in the same *Schrank* where the uniforms hung.

The four soldiers left. We went somewhere that afternoon, and when we returned we saw that the door to the house had been broken open with a bayonet. We could see the marks the bayonet had made on the door and the door frame. The uniforms were gone. I suppose they ended up as souvenirs in America. The briefcase with the jewelry and silver still stood there, untouched.

The Americans moved on. In the small, nearby town of Neukirchen they established what we called a *Kommandantur*. It was a headquarters of sorts, and provided a police and administrative presence. Soon after the arrival of the Americans, one of the Russian workers, who now were free to go as they pleased, drove up to our house in a jeep driven by an American. He knew my mother by sight, and must have taken a liking to her, because he informed her that he was moving in with her. "I will take good care of your place," he assured my mother. "I will cut wood in the forest and keep the house warm."

"I am not going to let you do that," my mother protested firmly. "I am going to go to the American *Kommandantur* in Neukirchen, and I am going to check if they allow such things," she said loudly, nearly shouting. As the American driver heard her talking of going to the *Kommandantur*—maybe he spoke some German and understood the conversation between my mother and the Russian—he put his jeep in gear and hurriedly drove away, leaving his Russian friend behind. The next day my mother actually walked to the American *Kommandantur*, although she was pregnant and ill. Using all the school English she knew, she explained her situation—that she had two small school-age children and wondered if she had to take in a Russian laborer. The Americans informed her that she didn't have to do any such thing, and if that happened again she was to immediately report it. But nothing like it ever happened again.

A single rail line ran past our village not far from our house. A freight train appeared one day and stopped at our small station. The train was then loaded with hundreds of former Russian prisoners of war who now were free to return home. On the front of the engine the men mounted a huge, red Soviet star, and they planted red flags on the sides of the black engine. They cheered loudly as the train pulled away from the station. American soldiers operated the trains until they ran into trouble getting them up the hillside near our house. Then they reemployed German engineers and firemen. One day a train pulling open freight cars stacked with jerry cans filled with gasoline caught fire right beyond our house. Apparently sparks from the locomotive set off a fire in the first car. The train was near the top of the hill. The fireman jumped out of the cab and decoupled the cars behind the one that was burning and let them roll away from the fire, down the hill. Then, at the top of the hill, he decoupled the burning car and steamed out of danger. The burning car began to roll backwards, instead of down the other side of the hill. At first it rolled slowly, then faster and faster. Down the hill it went crashing into the stationary cars with their full loads of gasoline. They exploded and burned fiercely. The war was over, but strange things continued to happen.

My father was drafted early in the war in 1939. He was in Belgium first and then spent three years in Russia. There he was wounded in the arm and after nearly being captured by the Russians was returned to Germany where he filled a staff position in a headquarters in Kassel. He was only briefly interned by the Americans. Upon his return he reported to the American *Kommandantur* in Neukirchen and was immediately reappointed in his former position of game warden and forest ranger. But of course now he had no uniforms to wear. He eventually obtained a uniform from a war widow whose husband had been a forest ranger.

After the war ended our main focus became putting food on the table. My uncle Carl-Werner, my father's brother, came to live with us. Before the war he worked for a company in Vienna. Then he was drafted, and when he returned, along with other Germans, he was forced to leave Austria. His wife was Austrian and chose not to accompany him. With the help of my uncle Carl my father decided to farm the land that came with the *Försterei*. In the past he had let local farmers use the meadows and the fields. The farmers laughed at the city boys trying to become instant farmers. They didn't think my father and his brother could do it; they had never handled a team of horses. My father bought books and read up on how to raise pigs and cows. We ended up with two cows: Anna and Rosa, one black and white, the other red and white. Father farmed until the *Währungsreform* in June 1948. By then he had *die Nase voll*, as we say in German. He had his nose full of farming, and he sold everything. But for three years we lived the farm life, and it kept us alive. I remember threshing rye in the yard with a flail and cooking sugar beets in a large laundry kettle in our washhouse. The molasses we mixed into cream of wheat or oatmeal, which was our standard fare.

The Americans at the *Kommandantur* in Neukirchen kept to themselves. They turned most functions over to Germans and left soon thereafter. Things returned to normal for us rather quickly, other than not having much food to eat.

Nazis were not an item of conversation in my family. Of course my father was a party member. Every *Beamte*, civil servant, had to join the party or relinquish his job. But other than that our family was nonpolitical. I do remember my aunt and uncle who were good friends with a Jewish couple. They lived in Kassel. When we children visited my aunt we frequently accompanied her on visits for *Kaffee und Kuchen* to Onkel Fröhlich and Tante Fröhlich, as we affectionately called her Jewish friends. I can remember the day when they were no longer there. No one said anything to us children or told us where they had gone or why they left. My aunt was very upset when I asked her why we didn't visit them anymore. Both Onkel Fröhlich and Tante Fröhlich died in a concentration camp, we learned later. Being Jewish or not Jewish was not something we thought of as children. We thought of ourselves as ordinary people. Tante and Onkel Fröhlich were ordinary people. They were my aunt's friends, close friends whom we addressed as aunt and uncle. I missed them very much. Just like I missed my teacher.

My war experiences overall were limited and benign compared to those of others. Nevertheless, that incident with the American jeep driver and the Russian prisoner who wanted to move in with my mother—I dreamed about that for years afterward. There was an unexplained fear that had settled within me which I could not deal with and didn't totally understand. Well into my marriage I dreamed about soldiers coming into my village, about their tanks and trucks. And then they always wanted something, but I never knew what it was. It was a dream that stayed with me for twenty or more years. Soldiers were something to fear no matter what the color of their uniforms.

Helga Schaefer

My family lost a total of thirty-three men in the war. My father was one of the lucky ones to survive. He died quite young, in his mid sixties. I recall nights with him tossing in bed, moaning and crying out to men, his soldiers, who were long dead. Since he only had three daughters we couldn't save our family name of Schaefer. My family's name was exterminated as a result of the war. I cannot tell you how sad it makes me.

Hubertus Thiel

{Age 7}

Würzburg, Bavaria

In memory of the 350,000 airmen who served and in memory of the 47,742 combat crewmen killed or missing who paid the supreme sacrifice.

—Inscription on the 8th Air Force memorial in Arlington National Cemetery

As I turned on my back and looked up at the sky, I saw the contrails of German fighters attacking American bombers. I can still see them before my eyes. Straight lines and circles of contrails. Then slowly one of the bombers dropped out of the formation and fell behind a nearby hillside.

—Hubertus Thiel

What I remember most about the war are the air raids. In the fall of 1944 I entered the *Volksschule* in Würzburg. In the following months the town was nearly totally destroyed. Our school had a basement, but not an air raid shelter, so when an air raid warning was given, the teachers would send us children home. I was six years old then, in the first grade. Today I view such a procedure of sending young children out into the streets at a time of grave danger as totally irresponsible. But that was 1944, and people looked at things differently. The arrangement was for me to meet my sister, Waltraut, outside the school—she was a year older than I—and then we ran home together. It was about one kilometer to our house. Not too far, but for a little boy and girl of six and seven it was a long way.

Previous page: Hubertus, his mother Ilse, and sister Waltraut

War from the Sky

The teachers and our mothers had taught us when the bombs drop, and especially when *Tiefflieger* attack, to throw ourselves on the ground wherever we were. Don't stand up or keep running. Try to hide behind something. The first time we had an air raid warning, Waltraut and I ran as quickly as we could toward our house. We could hear the planes, then the bombs exploding. My sister jumped into the ditch to her right, me to the left. I had the great misfortune to thrust my face into the upturned spikes of a hedgehog. I never forgot this experience. My face was stung in numerous places. There was some blood. But I kept my face down in the grass until the danger passed. The hedgehog maintained its defensive position throughout my presence and never moved. My fear was of the attacking aircraft, and as a result the pain inflicted by the innocent hedgehog didn't really register until later. As I turned on my back and looked up at the sky, I saw the contrails of German fighters attacking American bombers. I can still see them before my eyes. Straight lines and circles of contrails. Then slowly one of the bombers dropped out of the formation and fell behind a nearby hillside. That was my first experience of the air war.

The air raids intensified to such a degree that my mother, Ilse, decided we should go to my grandparents in Berlin. My father was away in the war. Both my mother's and father's parents lived in Berlin. We took the train to Berlin and quickly discovered that we had jumped from the frying pan into the fire, because the air attacks against Berlin were even more frequent and more intense then what we had experienced in Würzburg. In Berlin I had a second frightening experience. It was customary when the air raid siren sounded for people to head for the nearest air raid shelter. There were signs in the streets showing which way to run. We lived in Berlin-Wilmersdorf, a normally quiet residential area of neatly kept villas. There were no shelters in Wilmersdorf, so we ran to seek shelter in the subway tunnels. That night when the alarm went off it was pitch black outside. My mother, Waltraut, and I ran for one of the subway entrances. My mother pushed a pram before her filled with a few things, and my sister carried a small suitcase. I believe it was her own in which she kept her doll clothes. I carried a large, black, patent leather hatbox. To me the box seemed gigantic, and it was heavy. We ran through the streets. Houses were on fire to our left and right. The five-story houses burned fiercely, flames shooting out of windows and doorways with hungry red tongues. Although the burning houses made an impression on me, it didn't scare me. What scared me was my fear that I couldn't keep up with my mother and sister. I couldn't see, carrying that huge hatbox before me, and I couldn't run as fast as they did. I can't keep up, I can't keep up, I thought, panic building within me. I was convinced I would lose them. We finally made it to the subway entrance where Red Cross nurses served hot tea, and I calmed down. That was war for me, direct and immediate. Deeply frightening for a young boy.

We returned to Würzburg again to escape the Berlin air raids, only to find that it wasn't much different in Würzburg. My mother decided to take us to her brother Werner who was a *Förster*, a forest and game warden, like my father had been before the war began. He had a small lodge in the country which she thought should be safe from air attacks. Once she had us safely deposited with her brother she took a small hand wagon and set off for Würzburg, nearly two hundred kilometers away. She took the train going down and walked all the way back pulling the little wagon. When she returned, the little wagon was filled not with treasure, but with common household items including a pair of chamber pots. She promptly turned around to make a second trip, but in the massive air raid the night of March 16, 1945, our house was destroyed. When she got there all she found was a still-smoking ruin. The house had been hit by phosphorous bombs.

We had a little dachshund, his name was Hurra. Hurra had long hair, not the short hair of the typical dachshund. For one reason or another my mother had left the little dog with an old couple who lived in an apartment above ours. Hurra died in the air raid. We missed him. The house had two basements. The first was for storage. Under this one was a second coal and coke cellar which was struck by a phosphorous bomb. The coke in the lower cellar glowed brightly for days. In the upper cellar my mother had stored a suitcase with our family silver. The suitcase of course had burned, but the silver had turned into a ball the size of a child's head. From this cellar she res-cued some of our fine Dresden china showing burn marks in places where it had been hand painted. I still have these pieces of porcelain, a reminder of those terrible days of war.

On Easter Sunday, 1945, the Americans came. We children, Waltraut and I and my three cousins, were busy playing our games with gaily colored hard-boiled eggs, throwing them up in the air and letting them drop in the grass. My uncle's lodge, the *Försterei*, was more like a small farmstead with barns and all that went with a farm. The entire farm was bounded by a sturdy stone wall. Across from the entrance to the *Försterei*, on the other side of the road, was the garden and a small meadow where we played our egg games. Suddenly there was a loud noise on the road and there came a group of fleeing German soldiers in small armored vehicles. Soon after they passed, only five hundred meters behind them, there came the first American tanks. I could see people sitting on the tanks. As they came closer I saw that they were not only soldiers, but some were women—German women the soldiers had picked up on the way. The tanks rolled past us, the soldiers and the women laughing, not paying attention to us. The American convoy seemed like it had no end—tanks, jeeps, armored vehicles of various types, trucks. It went on and on. The longer it took the more afraid we became. We were on one side of the road and our mothers were on the other, but we couldn't cross. Finally the column passed.

In the days that followed, the Americans requisitioned some hous-es for their soldiers, including the house of the village policeman. The policeman lived down the road from us. He was feared by all. As I passed his house one morning I saw his hat, his symbol of authority, lying in the chicken coop. I wanted the hat, but I didn't dare go in there because the Americans now lived in his house. The soldiers saw me looking into the chicken coop and asked me to come inside. Then they gave me oranges wrapped in red silky paper and Hershey candy bars. The Americans freely shared with all the children of our village. For them the war was over; they looked like they wanted to go home. They walked around the village with nothing to do, looking bored, glad to be able to share their chocolate and oranges with us children.

The Americans also seemed to have a surplus of cigarettes. I remember Chesterfield and Lucky Strike. German men smoked their cigarettes until they burned their fingers. The Americans took a few puffs and then threw away their cigarettes. We children, encouraged by adults, picked up the used American cigarettes, removed the paper and the blackened tobacco and then put the remaining tobacco into the red silky paper wrappers from the oranges. The paper was the size of a small handkerchief. When it was full, we tied the ends together and gave the tobacco to a man. I presume my mother got something in return for the tobacco that we children collected.

Even after the Americans arrived, small groups of German soldiers continued to pass through our area. They came at night, and my aunt would hide them during the day in one of her barns. It probably wasn't a smart thing to do because they were all supposed to turn themselves in. As a child I understood that what she was doing was something good and right, but at the same time I knew it was *verboten*. I worried about her, about them, and about right and wrong.

Four to six weeks after the Americans arrived, my mother was offered a position as teacher in a small town. There she was assigned an apartment which went with the job. But money of course didn't buy anything, and to feed ourselves we did what everybody else was doing, we went *stoppeln*. *Stoppeln* was to search harvested fields for dropped ears of wheat or rye, to look for undiscovered potatoes or whatever else may have been grown in a field. Stealing was accepted and practiced by nearly everyone as long as it was food and coal. Coal we gleaned from the nearby railroad tracks, and if a coal train passed through, I and others would climb on the cars and take all the coal we could carry. The coal trains were guarded, but we always managed to outsmart the guards. The railroad track ran only two hundred to three hundred meters from our house, which was convenient.

I recall one dark night when there was a tremendous explosion. The next morning we saw that it had been a train. An artillery shell in one of the cars may have set off others, and the chain reaction destroyed several of the railroad cars. The train also carried eggs. The word spread like wildfire, and hundreds of people converged on the wreckage. As a result of the explosion the eggs were not only scattered, but in the split-second heat of the explosion they were also hard-boiled, fried, or burned. People collected these cooked remnants of shattered eggs and carried them home as if it was gourmet food. Everything edible we ate. That was war as I experienced it, and what it did to people.

My father, Hans-Jürgen, was drafted in 1939. On military leave late in the war I recall him telling my mother, "If what I have heard about Jews is true, then God have mercy on us." At the end of the war he was in Berlin. He was in the Waffen-SS. The last we know of him was on the twenty-fifth of April 1945. During a lull in the fighting he went to visit an aunt who still lived in Berlin. She later told us that he was totally exhausted. He rested at her place. In the morning she said to him, "Stay with me. Take off your uniform. It's all without purpose." He answered, "I can't. My men need me." He left and was never heard from again. I never really had a father. The war took him from me.

For her day my mother was a tall woman, five feet, eight inches. She was educated, had made the *Abitur* at the *Konservatorium* in Berlin in the thirties, was extremely conservative in mind, and loved the German kaiser. For me my mother was the one person who assured our survival, that's how I saw her as a child. We had lost everything in the war. All we had left was each other. My father was gone for as long as I could remember. I have few memories of him. During the war we had enough food and few wants. The time after the war was the time of need. We had very hard winters in 1945, 1946, and 1947, but my mother coped, supported by an active imagination. We had no gloves, so she made my sister and me wear socks, woolen socks, to keep our hands from freezing on the way to school. Synthetic sugar sacks she unraveled, and then she knitted sweaters from the yarn; not very warm, but they covered our bodies. Rags were not thrown away. They were glued together and made into shoe soles and uppers and sewn together. That's how we and everybody else survived by using everything until it literally was worn away.

My mother never remarried. She remained one of millions of Germany's war widows. On *Totensonntag* she would wear a black armband on her coat in memory of my father. Until 1958 she taught school; then she finally had my father declared dead, and the government paid her a widow's pension. She retired in Würzburg, living alone in her own apartment until her death in 1990.

After graduating from the *Gymnasium* I went to the University of Würzburg to study law. My plan was to become a military judge, but the newly created *Bundeswehr* was not to have its own legal system, rather it would fall under the civil laws of the *Bundesrepublik*. So I decided to enter the Luftwaffe, from which I retired only recently in the rank of colonel.

Hubertus Thiel now lives with his wife in the greater Cologne area. While there I looked at the Dresden china his mother had saved in 1945 from their burned house in Würzburg. The china clearly showed the burn marks of long ago. I recall Hubertus cradling a cup carefully in his hands before passing it to me, as if it were irreplaceable treasure, which it was.

Wolf
Stäglich

{Age 9}

Leuna, Saxony

On May 12, 1944, bombers of the 8th Air Force attacked several synthetic fuel plants including the largest at Leuna. Leuna was a tangle of broken and twisted pipes. Our daily output of 5,850 metric tons of fuel dropped to 4,820. Subsequent attacks reduced production to only ten per cent of its peak. Without the production of aircraft fuel at Leuna there was no Luftwaffe.

—Albert Speer, *Inside the Third Reich*

Then the Americans began their daylight raids [on Leuna]. When their huge bomber formations passed overhead everything on the ground vibrated—the glass in our windows, the vase on the table, the furniture in the room, the house.

—Wolf Stäglich

Bad Dürrenberg, my hometown, lies between Halle and Leipzig. In those days a light rail, a streetcar-like train, ran between Bad Dürrenberg, Leuna, and Merseburg. In 1941, I was five years old then, my mother, Hildegard, and I were riding the streetcar to Merseburg when at one of the stops an army officer in full uniform boarded our car and sat down across from us. I remember looking at this officer with great curiosity. The hat he wore looked familiar to me. I thought I had seen a man wearing such a hat in a picture, and that man was called the Führer. In a voice audible to everyone in our car I said to my mother, "Mama, is that the Führer?" and I pointed at the man. I recall my mother answering in a stunned voice, "Of course not, Wolf, that man

Previous page: Wolf (left) with playmates in Leuna, 1941

is not the Führer." The innocent officer sitting across from me raised his hands as if trying to push something unpleasant away from him, and remonstrated, "In God's name, *nein, nein,* I am not the Führer." That was my first recollection of any political aspects of the times I lived in. Neither the Führer nor his party were topics of conversation in our household.

I remember quite well the Allied air attacks against the nearby synthetic petroleum refinery at Leuna. It was a huge complex about twelve kilometers long and two kilometers deep, visible from my home. We experienced twenty-eight major air attacks against the refinery by my count, as well as uncountable minor attacks and almost daily air raid alarms. The first attacks came at night. The entire refinery complex was protected by hundreds of antiaircraft batteries. Not individual guns, but batteries. Each battery consisted of six to eight guns. During these night attacks British pathfinder aircraft preceded the bomber stream and would drop numerous "Christmas trees" over the refinery to indicate to the bombers where to drop their bombs. Frequently the "Christmas trees" drifted outside the target area, and most of the bombs missed. When we had a northwesterly wind these parachute-borne flare devices drifted over our housing complex with the result that at least half of the bomb load intended for Leuna fell on us, the surrounding fields and forests.

We civilians had two options. Either we went into the above-ground reinforced concrete bunker, or we went into our own cellars which had provisionally been equipped to serve as air raid shelters. Every night starting at about eight in the evening, my mother listened to the radio where they gave detailed reports on detected enemy aircraft formations, their estimated numbers and heading. From that information she deduced if an air attack was imminent for us. My mother always tried to let me sleep as long as possible. She believed strongly that children needed their sleep to grow up properly. Starting in late 1943 our nights were nearly always interrupted by the threat of air attack. From then on I don't think there was a night when I slept all the way through, waking at least once to the sound of sirens, anti-aircraft guns, the drone of heavy bombers, or the rippling boom-boom of exploding bombs.

Every night my mother had to make the decision if we should stay in the house or go to the bunker. It was a life-or-death decision. Since she tried to give me the opportunity to sleep as long as possible, the decision most frequently was to stay in our house and to go down into our less-secure shelter. My father, Felix, was a division chief at Leuna and responsible for repairs to the refinery complex after each air attack. He was seldom home. I recall him talking about the monumental repair task that he faced after a major raid. Within twenty-four hours after a raid they were operating again. That was his job, keeping the gasoline flowing. I often thought it was magic how my father did it, because I had seen the fires burning in the refinery and found it nearly impossible to believe that he could restore its operation within such a short period of time. But he did. How did he do it? He had large numbers of Russian prisoners of war at his disposal who often had to risk their lives to work the magic to get the severely damaged refinery back into operation.

Then the Americans began their daylight raids. When their huge bomber formations passed overhead everything on the ground vibrated—the glass in our windows, the vase on the table, the furniture in the room, the house. It was difficult to hear anything other than the drone of the hundreds of bomber engines overhead. One Sunday I ran up to the rail embankment behind our house after the all clear was given. Below me I could see Leuna. Flames were shooting fifty meters into the air. It wasn't a good feeling I had watching the inferno, because I knew my father was right in the middle of it. After three or four hours the fires were out, and by the following day gasoline was again flowing into storage tanks. It was an incredible achievement. In later years when I was in the *Bundeswehr* simulating recovery efforts while under enemy attack, I recalled what people were capable of in a time of crisis and war when the stakes are very high.

Since my mother and I at most times chose to stay in the shelter of
our house, the time had to come when the house was hit—with us in
it. When it happened, fortunately, the house didn't collapse, but the
entry to our shelter was blocked by rubble. We lived in a single-family
house, very modern by the standards of the time. I don't recall exactly
how long we were buried under the rubble. At least seven or eight
hours. My father was at a meeting at another IG-Farben plant at the
time, and didn't know of our fate. The house next door was in worse
shape than ours. After my mother and I were freed we could hear the
people next door screaming in their shelter. The fear of dying was in
their voices. Of course I was scared during this episode, but not overly
so. We had air, so we wouldn't suffocate, and there was no fire. And it
wasn't the first time either that bombs had fallen nearby, although this
was closer than before. There was a certain automatic adjustment to
danger that took place within me and most other children. We got
used to it. What did get to me were the screams of the people from next
door who thought they were dying. They were eventually rescued.

We made some repairs to our house and continued to live in it. The
bomb had penetrated at an angle and then exploded in front of the
house. Therefore, the damage was not as bad as it could have been.
Our housing area was already severely damaged before the bomb
slashed through our house—not only by Allied bombs, but even more
so by the falling shrapnel from the hundreds of defending 88 mm or
larger antiaircraft guns. There was one huge rail gun which we boys on
Sundays frequently stopped to look at. It aimed for the center of an aircraft formation, bringing down more than one aircraft at one time if its
shell was on target. The residue from all the antiaircraft shells fell on
our houses and slowly pounded our roofs to pieces.

Another time we had a night attack. Not much happened to us
except for the usual broken windowpanes. Eventually we ran out of
glass and replaced the broken panes with cardboard. Then the cardboard was blown out of the windows, but we could reuse it. Behind our
housing development were private garden plots, a *Schrebergarten*. The

day after that night attack my friend and I explored the *Schrebergarten*. We found a huge crater which we decided to explore. In the middle of the crater we could see some metal parts sticking out of the dirt. We climbed into the crater and onto the innocent-looking metal protuberances. After completing our investigation we decided these things sticking out of the ground were the fins of a very large bomb. I told my mother about my find and that I was sure of what I had seen since I had examined it with my own hands. She reported my find to the *Luftschutzwarden*, who had a telephone, but she was aghast at what I had done. Soon the police appeared, and it was decided that my friend and I had in fact discovered a *Luftmine*, a bomb weighing several thousand pounds. Soon a small troop of bomb disposal experts arrived, led by an *Oberfeldwebel*, a master sergeant. The others were Russian POWs. The Russians were volunteers, I was told, to receive the better food and treatment that went with the bomb disposal job. They defused the bomb. It was loaded on a trailer and removed from our housing area. The *Herr Oberfeldwebel* then gave me a lecture on how to behave around things of this nature. Should I ever find a bomb again, he emphasized, "Please, do not touch it."

The Russian POWs stood around near our front door. My mother came outside and asked the *Oberfeldwebel*, "Can I give them something to eat?"

He said to her, "Listen carefully to what I am going to say. You know that's *verboten*. I'll be going behind your house for a while. I'll see nothing and hear nothing. I hope you are certain about your neighbors." My mother fed the prisoners. We didn't have much ourselves, but she shared the little we had. They were grateful and thanked her profusely for her kindness. It all took about fifteen minutes. Then the *Oberfeldwebel* returned and marched them off.

By early 1945 the air raids by high-flying bombers and *Tiefflieger* became more and more frequent and occurred at all hours of the day and night. I went to school as always. When I was in school a warning of an impending attack was given with three short up-and-down wails of the siren. Then we children grabbed our things, quickly stuffed them into our school bags and ran as fast as we could either toward the bunker or home. Every morning I talked with my mother, and we decided where I would meet her when the alarm was given. Usually we met at home. One early April morning the alarm was given too late. When we children ran out of the school building, the English *Tiefflieger* arrived from the opposite direction, flying down the street directly at us. I have never seen airplanes flying that low. They flew below the rooflines of our houses. The street was full of running children. They fired into us. We children reacted automatically, throwing ourselves to the ground, hiding behind anything nearby if there was time. I dove headfirst down the stairwell of a house. I was scuffed up pretty badly, but didn't break any bones. After the first firing pass the *Tiefflieger* turned around and came back to do it all over again. That was ugly— much more so than the time when I was buried for seven hours under the rubble of our house. When I came outside there was pure chaos in the street. School friends lay dead. Many more were wounded. There was blood all over the street. Screaming. Moaning. It was the worst experience of my life. But surprisingly I never dreamt of it, nor did it in any way inhibit me, or return in some fashion in later years. Although awful, it happened. And that was that.

I saw what happened to Allied air crews when they were shot down. Farmers often reacted brutally toward downed airmen. One day I saw an air crew abandon its bomber, six or eight parachutes. They came down not far from us in the fields. I saw farmers heading toward the landing site with pitchforks, or anything useable as a weapon they had been able to lay their hands on. At the last moment German military police arrived and kept the irate farmers at bay with their submachine guns. Often there was no military police to save the unlucky flyers. War, I later came to understand, awakens feelings in people which are at times uncontrollable.

As a child I developed a frightening rage against Allied flyers. I hated the planes and the bombs, the cannons of the *Tiefflieger* and what they did to us children. Our teachers actively supported our views and fanned our feelings of hate. Of course we were indoctrinated starting in the first grade. Even the games we boys played were war games. We wore steel helmets made from cardboard. We wore pieces of uniform purchased or received as presents, and carried wooden rifles. I too had a helmet like that and a wooden rifle. When there was an air attack we children watched it with wrath in our hearts, and we applauded enthusiastically when we saw a plane explode or fall to the ground.

Once we were on a nature outing with my class when we witnessed an air attack against Leuna. It was sometime in April 1945. We were too far away to feel threatened by the bombs, but because of the danger from antiaircraft shrapnel we sought shelter. I could see German fighters taking off from a nearby airfield. The sky darkened with explosions from the antiaircraft guns, and soon bombers began to fall from the sky. A frenzied cheer arose from us whenever a bomber was shot down. A Lancaster was hit. We yelled raucously as if Germany had won the soccer world championship in the last minute of a game. In terms of feelings that's about as excited as anyone can get. A few of the crew abandoned the plane. Fascinated, we watched the burning aircraft begin its slow descent. It got larger. Then it got even larger yet. And then suddenly it became very, very large. It was heading straight for our group. Our cheering died, and survival became my overriding interest. We had been walking along the Saale River. The plane crashed into the river, only about nine hundred feet away from us, its tail sticking out of the water, engines scattered about. Our teacher, a young woman, had dissolved in tears. We calmed her down, and then we ran to the river bank to gawk at the wreck. The wreck of that bomber remained there in the river for years. Every time I passed the wreck a certain satisfaction arose within me. After all, they were our tormentors. Those are my childhood recollections of the air war.

In late April 1945 the war was nearly over. The Americans were nearby. They took three days to get across the Saale River, but when they arrived they came in numbers of vehicles totally incomprehensible to me. Tanks, trucks, jeeps, things we couldn't even imagine rolled past us. Hour after hour, for two days. My friend and I had chosen this day to inspect a water tower which had served as an antiaircraft observation and direction center. This tower, which for us boys held so many secrets and which always had numerous guards at its entrance, now looked abandoned. The door stood open. There were no guards. We were curious and entered the forbidden tower. Up the stairs we went. In a room on the second floor lay a mass of military equipment—helmets, rifles, submachine guns, machine guns, pistols and various other military paraphernalia. No ammunition. At nine years of age we stood before our find with wide-open eyes, as if we had discovered an abandoned toy store.

My interest focused on one of the submachine guns. For years we had played soldier with our wooden guns. Now we had the real thing to play with. My friend and I each took a submachine gun and playfully aimed from our hips when the door opened and an American soldier entered, rifle at the ready. He looked at me. I lowered the barrel of my gun. He came over and took the guns away from us and tossed them on the floor. Then he gave us the unmistakable message to get out of there, which we promptly did. That's how I met my first American. When my mother learned of my expedition she reinforced her maternal lecture with a sound thrashing. The war ended and we children still played war, we didn't know anything else. Anyone who possessed a real ball was king of the street. He could decide who could play a game of street soccer and when and for how long. We had nothing but wooden guns for toys.

With the war ended, change came. For instance, we children only knew the greeting *Heil Hitler*. "Good morning" or "good day" were greetings we really weren't much aware of. Many of the adults, including my mother, didn't say *Heil Hitler*, but we children had learned that greeting in school and it had become second nature to us. Suddenly we were not to use it anymore. I found myself more than once starting to say *Heil. . .* , then remembering that this was a forbidden greeting; my hand was halfway up already and I diverted it to brush back my hair, or do something else. I just couldn't change from one day to the next. It took several months before "good morning" became something familiar and acceptable.

The American soldiers were friendly and approachable. Their generosity toward children was constant. For them to hand out chocolate bars and chewing gum was a common occurrence. Occasionally they even gave someone a can of coffee or other food items which enhanced our monotonous diet. My mother was pleased whenever I brought home something an American had given me. I especially remember the black American soldiers. I had never seen a *Neger* before. I wasn't even sure there were people like that with different skin color than my own. I wanted to see them up close and get to know them. When I did, the black American soldiers were especially friendly, always laughing, their white teeth showing prominently in their radiant faces.

First came the rumors that the Americans would leave and the Russians would take over. It encouraged many of the people who had lost everything either in a bombing raid or as refugees from the east to get ready and pack up to go west once the American troops actually began to move out. Soon the Americans departed with their huge motorized convoys, again handing out Hershey bars and chewing gum as they went. The Americans had no ideology that I became aware of. As a boy I went directly from one dictatorship to another, from the browns to the reds. I knew nothing but dictatorship.

We Germans had never feared the Americans. We feared the Russians. There was nothing sumptuous or opulent about their entry. The Russians had tanks, of course, but no seemingly endless motorized columns as the Americans had. What was most in evidence were long columns of *Panje* wagons, little wagons drawn by little shaggy horses. That's how they came to occupy our part of Germany. Little men from the east, Asians. The officers were Europeans, but the combat troops were from the steppes of Asia. There were no Hershey bars. No adult went near them. The women hid. No one wore a watch or a ring anymore. Men traveled home from work in groups, because individual Germans were frequently robbed by Russian soldiers of the little they carried. I saw no rapes or brutalities, but stories made their rounds, and we all feared our new occupiers. The Russian soldiers, Asian or European, were especially dangerous if they had been drinking. Alcohol made them unpredictable and capable of nearly anything. Soon the Asian troops were withdrawn and European Russians took their place, but their behavior when it came to drinking remained the same. Since they were nearly always armed, alcohol made all of the Russians very dangerous.

Leuna soon started up again producing fertilizer. Chemical fertilizer became a medium of exchange in our area. The fertilizer was loaded into open railroad cars in Bad Dürrenberg. Russian soldiers guarded the fertilizer trains and fired without warning if anyone approached. They had learned quickly that the *Volkspolizei*, which initially didn't have any weapons other than sticks, was unable to protect the trains. We boys stole the fertilizer and then traded it to farmers for anything edible. Fertilizer became de facto currency. In spite of Russian guards, inventive German boys managed to steal the fertilizer from under their noses. We crawled under a railroad car loaded with fertilizer. The Russian guard usually sat in a small brakeman's house attached to one of the cars, allowing him to look over the tops of the loaded cars. Not infrequently the guard fell asleep, aided by a little vodka. Once under a car I drilled a hole in its bottom with a large drill and drained the fertilizer into sacks which my companions quickly carried off into the night. When I finished, I plugged the hole. My father, for reasons of his own, didn't define this as stealing, something he forbade me to do. He took my share of the fertilizer, boarded a train to Thüringen, the province next to Sachsen, and traded the fertilizer to farmers for food.

Fertilizer was one way to obtain food; another was *stoppeln*, or the search for potatoes and loose heads of wheat and rye in already harvested fields. It was a difficult and time-consuming way to obtain very little food. So my friends and I developed more imaginative ways to steal potatoes from unharvested fields, in an unobtrusive manner of course. We didn't want the farmer to know because then he'd immediately begin to harvest his potatoes if he noticed anything amiss. We carefully pulled the potato stalks out of the ground, removed the potatoes, and then very carefully replaced the stalks and restored the ground to its near original condition. Although the farmer walked around his field two or three times a day, he never noticed. My father did. When he learned of my newest activity to supplement the family's food stocks, he took a dim view of it. There were two points of view when it came to stealing. Some boys got spanked and slapped around if they came home without anything; others, and I fell into the latter category, got taken behind the woodshed if we did bring something home. I am sure my father's point of view, reinforced by a willow branch, helped me in later life to differentiate between right and wrong. My mother viewed this matter quite differently. She was the one who actually put dinner on the table. She chose to ignore the source of our food. In spite of my father's efforts to discourage my foraging, our potato mound, kept in the cool of our basement, continued to grow. This, in spite of the fact that we ate potatoes every day.

Finally we turned the grassy areas in our development into gardens to plant vegetables. We also built a small chicken coup for five hens. My mother maintained in later years that the chickens saved our lives. The minute a chicken announced through its loud cackling that it had laid an egg, the egg was promptly removed. Our table never again was graced by such fresh eggs. With only five chickens it was inevitable that we gave them names. When the time came for Frederike or Ulrike or Suse to be declared ripe for our table, and that happened around Christmas, Easter, or on similar occasions, my father had the unpleasant task of chopping off Suse's head. He did this reluctantly, since to him it was almost like killing a member of the family. But it had to be done. The lesson I learned from all this is that in times of need one modifies standards or even adopts new standards to fit the situation.

Religion, politics, and school began to collide for me in our new Communist society. I was fourteen years old in 1950. Mine was the last year group that was allowed to be confirmed or to receive first com-munion without being pressured not to. I am a Protestant, so I was con-firmed. After that, youngsters were directed to take the *Jugendweihe*, the Communist substitute for confirmation and first communion. It became a less than popular act to also submit to religious rituals of coming of age. We had no religion in school anymore, which we had even under the browns. Instead, we had a so-called *Pastorstunde* when we went to our church and received instruction. Looking back I believe that those few hours with our pastor had a substantial influence over what I like to refer to as "my inner fitness." The teachers in school were all 120 percent reds. My father was exactly the opposite, very conservative, against Communism, and a Christian. In typical Protestant fashion he maintained that to communicate with my God I need no church, and, therefore, locking down the churches had little effect on our family.

In school my teacher would say one thing about a particular subject. My father would say something very different, and the most surprising to me, my pastor would say something different yet again. The result was that I and my classmates developed a deep sense of mistrust and suspicion of adults and what they told us. In addition, the newspapers wrote about things which we could check up on and discover to be untrue. We questioned everything. We believed nothing on face value. For example, in school we watched the Russian movies about the bat-tles for Stalingrad and Berlin. Long and boring movies, always in two parts. Watching the movies was mandatory. Before the actual movies they always showed a brief *Kulturfilm*. One of the subjects was on Cologne, a western city. They showed the old cathedral and right next to it the concrete bunker–like structure of the new opera house. Somehow, it just didn't fit, and we didn't believe what they showed us. They were lying to us again, we all agreed. It's clearly a photo montage. No one would build such an ugly opera house next to this famous cathedral. To my surprise in 1956 when I voted with my feet and went west, I saw that the opera house was in fact exactly the way we had seen it in that movie. This was an instance when they didn't lie, but that was surely the exception.

The school system in the Deutsche Demokratische Republik, the DDR, was organized so that we took our *Abitur* after twelve years, at age eighteen. My year group had missed a year of school in 1945 and therefore graduated at age nineteen. One year prior to the *Abitur* the decision was made about what we could study at the university. University admission was centrally controlled. One could express preferences, but the state ultimately decided if one was allowed to study and what it would be. I was given to understand that I would probably be allowed to attend the Karl-Marx Universität in Leipzig to study physics. About this time the KVP, the *Kasernierte Volkspolizei*, not actually a police force but a real military force equipped with tanks and MiG-15 jets, the predecessor of the *Nationale Volksarmee*, NVA, expressed their interest in me. Each year prior to the *Abitur* the senior class was assembled in the auditorium and addressed by officers of the KVP who presented opportunities available to those who chose to join. There was no pressure to join. A very small number of students decided to join the KVP.

In February 1956, nine months after the KVP presentation, the NVA was created. The announcement was made on the Black Channel, the speaker was Karl Eduard Schnitzler, a nightly program, mandatory listening for all good Communists. That night Schnitzler said, and I remember it clearly, "Never again a weapon in our hands, never again an army." The next morning, after this broadcast, the KVP became the NVA. The Russian-look-alike uniforms were discarded, and new Wehrmacht-like uniforms completed the transformation of the KVP into the NVA. None of us had an inkling of this. The following night, after the transformation of the police into an army, after his "no guns, no army" pronouncement, without missing a beat, Herr Schnitzler announced the proud reinstitution of Prussian military ideals in the new NVA. From the moment of the creation of the NVA there was a huge need for manpower, especially officers.

I began my *Abitur* examinations in April 1956. Two weeks later, NVA representatives appeared in my school. This time the senior class was not called into the auditorium to listen to a sales pitch; instead every individual met with the four NVA representatives—alone. The school principal and several instructors were also present. The question no longer was if I would want to join, rather it was when and in what capacity—army, air force, or navy. In a democracy I could have said, no thank you, I like to serve my country in a civilian capacity. That option was not open to me, because I was given to understand that there was no more honorable duty than serving in the armed forces of the DDR. I was upset. I responded to the pressure by saying, "I am really already earmarked to study physics in Leipzig."

Their reply was, "You can do that with us too."

Then I said to them, "It is rather early for me to make such a decision. Maybe I will not pass my *Abitur*." The principal and the instructors laughed at my comment. Obviously, graduating was not an issue. The principal then said to me, "Don't worry about that, my boy."

I was a good soccer player, so I couldn't claim a physical disability. I was at a loss as to what to do next. I didn't want to serve in their army. Out of options, I said to them, if I must serve, I prefer the air force. But maybe we could talk about that after I pass my *Abitur*. They whispered among themselves, giving me strange looks. When I left that room it was clear to me that I would never serve in that army. My only option was to leave the DDR. But I had to wait until I received my diploma or I would have nothing to fall back on once I was in the West. I knew that in the West they wouldn't just take my word for it that I had passed the *Abitur*.

For new graduates it was mandatory that first summer to help on a communal farm with the harvest before the diploma was presented, or to join brigades of youngsters which were cleaning up the rubble in the city of Dresden. I managed in a roundabout, clearly illegal manner to obtain my diploma and avoid the summer of forced labor. I chose to leave the DDR. I didn't tell my parents of my intentions. One morning

I told my mother that I was going on a bike trip with friends and packed my rucksack and left. I rode my bike to Leipzig and took a train to Berlin. Once in West Berlin I informed my parents where I was.

The following story is important to understand my actions and my family situation. My father continued to work at Leuna. He was a competent engineer who held many patents and was given lofty titles by his new red masters. He also was the East German representative on the International Committee for Measurement and Control Technology Standards, known as DIN standards committees. As a result of his technical eminence and committee membership he frequently traveled to the West and was able to reestablish old contacts. He had many confrontations with the system. Here is one of them as I remember it, which clearly indicated to me at the time that his time at Leuna was limited too.

Chemical factories such as Leuna manufactured their own sensing instrumentation—time, pressure, and temperature sensors necessary to control automatic chemical processes. All this fell under my father. For instance, his people built their own mercury-filled manometers. The man who built manometers, which required much experience and who was highly skilled at the task, was seventy-one years old. It was nothing unusual to employ seventy-year-old men then because many year groups had been severely decimated by the war. My father wanted to give him a raise. This required the approval of the labor union, which of course was controlled by the Communist Party. They said no. He is too old. My father said, according to the way he told it to me, "*Ach*, when I hear you saying that someone who is seventy-one years old is no longer capable to perform his job, that makes me uncomfortable." They didn't know what he was leading up to. "Do you gentlemen know how old our president, Wilhelm Piek, is?" There was stunned silence in the room. Piek was sixty-seven or something like that at the time. "Are you gentlemen telling me that our president is incapable of performing his job because of his age? Are you insisting that age is the only criterion that matters if a man should or should not receive a pay increase?" The man got his raise, but the party bosses never forgave my father. The pressure on the job became intense. I don't know what he would have done if I had not gone to the West.

In the Berlin refugee camp I was questioned by members of intelli-gence organizations from the *Bundesrepublik* and the United States. They wanted me to verify photos of Leuna. I shook my head. The only thing I said to them was, I have no comment. My parents are still over there and I have nothing to say. And I don't know you. Maybe you work for the other side too. I am not talking to you. They soon left, angry of course at my obstinacy and for implying that they might be double agents. I didn't turn in my DDR identity papers at the camp either; rather, I mailed them back to the town of Merseburg. They paid four hundred West marks for a personal identity pass. It was a lot of money in 1956. I decided I could do without it. I didn't want to do any-thing that could possibly endanger my parents.

The question then was, what next? I went to the Bayerhaus in Berlin to see the representatives of the Bayer Company, formerly a part of IG Farben, to which Leuna had belonged, and for whom my father once worked. My father had met with some of them after the war as a member of the DIN standards committee. I introduced myself and asked them if they could help me in some manner find a job. They listened and told me to return in three days, they first needed to do some checking on my claims. I returned in three days and was offered a training position in one of their plants in Leverkusen as a metalworker, sales or chemical specialist. I chose metalworker. Several days later they flew me out of Berlin to Leverkusen. My par-ents showed up in 1957, less than a year after I left the DDR. They chose the same route of escape I had taken, and a day after their arrival in Leverkusen my father started work as a department manager at the plant where I worked.

I completed my apprenticeship in three years, worked for another two years as a mechanic, and then joined the new Luftwaffe. My

Gymnasium class in Merseburg consisted of sixteen boys and seventeen girls. Of the boys, four went into the NVA. Two, including myself, chose the *Bundeswehr*. The *Bundeswehr* gave me the opportunity to continue my studies at the university, and I found that very attractive. In addition, I liked serving in a democratic society where individual choice was respected. My mother was initially opposed to my career choice, but eventually saw why I did it. She died at age seventy-two, a young woman. I believe that the war years and postwar years were especially hard on her. It started in 1944. Unknown to me at the time, she took the little fat we had—butter, margarine, lard, or whatever its source—and gave it to me and my father. She denied herself that which she thought her son needed to grow up properly and what her husband required in a job which frequently required him to work twenty-four-hour days. The first sign of trouble came in the early postwar years when she developed gallstones. There was no medicine available to consider an operation. She suffered incredible pain. I knew her not only as my mother, but also as a suffering woman. An operation in the early fifties helped to relieve her pain. She died in 1967. She was a tall, attractive woman who came from a long-lived family. In contrast, her life was, if not short, then very much shortened when compared to others in her family.

My two children and I have spoken often about those days during and after the war. Naturally you can't overdo it. But I thought there were some important lessons for life which I wanted to make available to them.

Wolf Stäglich is a graduate of the 18th Generalstabslehrgang der Luftwaffe at the Führungsakademie der Bundeswehr in Hamburg-Blankeneese. We were classmates. I remembered this tall, lanky Sachsen with the warm smile, the oldest German officer of our small class of thirty-three, including the four exchange officers from Italy, France, Great Britain, and the United States. I, a former German refugee, a major in the United States Air Force, was the American exchange officer in 1973 to 1975. We called Wolf "Oma" (grandma) because of his age. Why "Oma" and not

War from the Sky

"Opa" (grandpa)? Who knows. Wolf was different from his classmates in ways other than his nickname. He had a distinct Sachsen accent, marking him as a refugee from the DDR, the reds, the potential enemy. Neither his nickname nor his accent kept him from having a brilliant career in the new Luftwaffe. Wolf retired in 1998 in the rank of brigadier general and makes his home in the remoteness of the Hunsrück mountains.

Rita and Ingrid Nille

{Ages 6 and 10}

Arneburg, Saxony-Anhalt

The cost was very high, 55,573 aircrew. . . .Bomber Command's casual-
ties amounted to almost one-seventh of all British deaths in action by
land, sea and air from 1939 to 1945. The pitiful prospects of surviving a
tour of bomber operations were only matched in hazard on either side by
the German U-boat crews.

—Max Hastings, *Bomber Command*

We could see a plane burning brightly in the night sky, falling, coming
directly toward us. We were petrified with fear. We ran and ran, and the
burning plane came closer and closer. Oma and Mutti threw us children
against the hillside and covered us with their bodies. We knew we were
as good as dead. Suddenly the plane veered and fell into the Elbe River,
missing us by only a hundred yards.

—Rita Nille

Rita: Arneburg lies about eighty kilometers west of Berlin, on the
west bank of the Elbe River. In 1945 Arneburg was a small town of
around two thousand people which had experienced a population
explosion as a result of an influx of *Flüchtlinge* from the East and evac-
uees from the larger cities. Its population had swollen to around six
thousand. My sister, Ingrid, and I always referred to Arneburg as a *Dorf*.
Our *Bruder-Onkel*, Karl-Heinz Krüger—we referred to him as our
"brother-uncle" because he was only four years older than my sister,
Ingrid—tried to set us straight every time we said *Dorf*. "Arneburg is
not a *Dorf*," he would yell at us. "Arneburg is a *Stadt*." We continued

---

Previous page: Ingrid, Mike in combat fatigues, and Rita in Arneburg, 1945

to tease him by referring to Arneburg as a village, and he steadfastly maintained that it was a town.

The focal point of Arneburg was Saint George's Catholic church. We lived in a small house on Burgstrasse, down below the church. The house sat on a bluff overlooking the Elbe River. Ours was the only two-story house on the street which was to be of some importance when the Americans came and occupied the town. The streets of the nearly one-thousand-year-old town were of course narrow and paved with the customary cobblestones.

Our family consisted of my grandmother Dora Krüger, Oma Krüger to Ingrid and me; our little uncle-brother, Karl-Heinz Krüger, a late arrival of Oma's in 1931; my mother, Anita Krüger Nille, Mutti to us girls, born in 1914; my older sister, Ingrid, who was born in 1935; an old great-grandmother in her early eighties, Karoline Whilhelmina Krüger, and me, Rita. I was born in February 1939, six months before the outbreak of war. Oma was widowed in 1932, soon after Karl-Heinz was born; Gross-Oma Karoline died in February 1945. We were a family of women and children without the support of a man.

My father, Fritz Nille, was born in 1911 in Durlach in southern Germany. As a young man of nineteen, in 1930, he emigrated to the United States to make a better life for himself. He was not the first in his family to emigrate to the United States. His mother's sister Johanna and her husband had left Germany earlier to make their life in Amerika. On my mother's side we had an equal exodus for the land of *unbegrenzte Möglichkeiten*, unlimited opportunities. Uncle Wilhelm Krüger, my grandmother's brother, and his wife, Martha, had left in 1924 and lived in the state of New York. When they came on a visit in 1929 they convinced my uncle Franz, our mother's brother, to follow their example. Franz left for Amerika that same year and found work on Long Island.

One day in 1930 as Fritz Nille, our future father, was standing in an unemployment line in New York seeking work, he met Franz Krüger, my mother's brother. Franz showed Fritz a picture of his sister

Anita as they were standing in that unemployment line. Fritz liked what he saw and wrote to Anita. After several years of ever more arduous correspondence Fritz returned to Germany in 1933 and married Anita. After the wedding he returned to the United States and left his young bride behind. When Anita received her visa eight months later she followed Fritz to New York. They lived in the German section of Brooklyn, and my sister, Ingrid, was born in Brooklyn in December 1935.

After Ingrid's birth my mother became very homesick. She missed her mother and younger brother, Karl-Heinz. It didn't help that her husband was frequently unemployed and gone, looking for work. The United States was in an economic depression at the time, and although Fritz was a skilled tool and die maker, he couldn't find work in his trade. Work of any kind was hard to find. Fritz finally went to work in his brother-in-law's bakery in Brooklyn, where he worked the night shift. My mother needed company and became very homesick sitting alone in her little apartment in Brooklyn. She and my father decided when she was three months pregnant with me, in August 1938, that she should return with Ingrid to Germany. My father stayed behind to work off her boat fare and to earn enough money for himself to join her at a later date. By February 1939 my father had saved enough money to purchase a boat ticket back to Germany. Early one morning he went to the bank and withdrew his hard-earned savings to buy his ticket. As he stepped out of the bank he was robbed at gunpoint. With the loss of his money he had to start all over again. The robbery was an astounding twist of fate, Ingrid and I believe. It may have saved our father's life. Had he returned to Germany in 1939, with the outbreak of war that September, he would certainly have been drafted into the Wehrmacht and probably been killed like so many other German men of his generation.

There was an opportunity, however, for my mother to return to the United States before it was too late. The American consulate contacted her in 1939 and offered to help her return home to Brooklyn via

Switzerland. She turned down the offer, not really understanding the polit-ical situation at the time. From her perspective there was the new baby to consider. And what was the hurry anyway? If war came, and it probably wouldn't, most likely it wouldn't amount to much, or last very long. I think she thought along those lines. So we—Ingrid, I, and Mutti—ended up trapped by the war in Germany. My father lived in the United States, where he worked throughout the war years as a tool and die maker. He was not drafted because his skills were in high demand in the defense industry. He had become an American citizen in 1940. Of course we didn't know any of that, and throughout the war years our mother wondered if our father was in an American uniform fighting Germans.

We six women and children lived in our modest three-bedroom house. There was a small living room on the ground floor, the *gute Stube*, which was used only on special occasions. A kitchen and a cel-lar, which later served as our bomb shelter, were the only other rooms. We had no bathroom and used an outhouse like everybody else.

Neither Ingrid nor I knew exactly what war was. For us war was the sirens going off—day and night in the later war years. There was a lot of fear in the faces of the adults, and we reacted to that. Running to the bomb shelter became as normal to us children as getting out of bed in the morning when it got light. Mutti and Oma had to decide where we were to go—into our cellar, into a more elaborate shelter down the street, or to a bunker in the marketplace in front of the church. The bunker on the *Marktplatz* was just a bunch of logs covered with dirt. We sat in there on crude benches for hours at a time. To this day, when I hear a siren it is like a knife going through my heart. It triggers old memories of hurt and deep fear.

During the worst days late in the war we slept in our clothes with our shoes on. We had a small suitcase next to our bed, and when the siren went off we grabbed the suitcase and ran for the shelter. I was only five years old in 1944. My mother would grab me under her arm, Ingrid would take the suitcase, and they would run out of the house to the shelter. Because Arneburg was in the flight path to Berlin, both British and American planes flew directly over us day and night, nearly every day. The siren would go off, and pretty soon the droning of engines from hundreds of planes passing overhead would become louder and louder, vibrating everything in our house. At night the sky was lit up from the fighting above us. On one occasion the warning was late, and as we ran out of the house the planes were already overhead. We ran down toward the Elbe to seek shelter near the water and under the bluff on which our house stood. We could see a plane burning brightly in the night sky, falling, coming directly toward us. We were petrified with fear. We ran and ran, and the burning plane came closer and closer. Oma and Mutti threw us children against the hillside and covered us with their bodies. We knew we were as good as dead.

Suddenly the plane veered and fell into the Elbe River, missing us by only a hundred yards. Oma later said it was "the hand of God" that made the plane veer away from us at the last moment. The plane, burning brightly as it lay in the river, exploded. Phosphorous from its bombs spewed out all over. The explosion blew tiles off the roof of our house which sat on the bluff above us. The furniture was blown about, and most windows were broken. It was pretty messy, but we were thankful that we had been saved. A very small piece of phosphorous from the explosion hit Mutti on her ankle and left an ugly sore.

Until now Ingrid had sat quietly at the table while Rita had carried the conversation.

Ingrid: When we were in school, we had the choice to run home when the sirens went off or to stay, depending on how close the attacking planes were to us. I nearly always chose to run home. On more than one occasion planes dove down at us running children and tried to shoot us. I had a hard time believing they would try to kill schoolchildren. I was taught to hide under a tree, and on a sunny day not to leave a shadow. I would walk along the side of the houses trying to avoid being seen. It was very scary and upsetting.

Rita: When Ingrid came running down the cobblestone street that day when the *Tiefflieger* attacked her, she was screaming loudly as she ran toward us, and the plane was shooting at her. All of us screamed, and we were utterly horrified. Then it was over and we were alive, unhurt. We were the enemy at the time, we women and children. Later the school closed, because there was no heat and all the windows were shattered.

Ingrid: The word eventually got out that I was an American. It may have been a teacher who informed on me. Mutti and Oma were called to report to the town hall. They never told me what exactly transpired, but when they returned they tried to prepare me that I might have to leave. They said the government wanted to send me to America to be with my father. I think that was a story Mutti and Oma made up. They knew where I would be going if they came to get me. Although my mother had always kept the memory of my father alive for us girls, I didn't want to go to America and leave her and my family behind. I pleaded with her to let me stay and not to send me away. I don't know exactly how the matter was resolved. My grandmother knew the mayor of the town, and she spoke to him. Then nothing more happened.

My mother and Oma always tried to do some normal, fun things for us girls. We would go on hikes along the Elbe if the weather was nice, or into the nearby woods. But that too had another purpose—we picked berries in season, collected hazelnuts and mushrooms. We had a little wagon which we girls pulled behind us. We filled the wagon with dried branches for kindling and sacks of pinecones. Mushrooms were a staple of our diet. We knew every mushroom even at a young age. If we were uncertain we went to the *Pilzfrau* in Arneburg. She knew if a mushroom was good to eat. At harvest time Mutti asked the farmers for permission to glean from the empty fields whatever might have been left behind. That way we collected potatoes, carrots, and ears of wheat and rye. That was always a fun experience for us girls. We also picked camomile in the meadows which we dried for tea.

There was little family income with no men in the house. Mutti was an excellent seamstress though and sewed dresses and suits for the more wealthy residents of our town. There were some factories and larger businesses whose owners continued to have access to scarce goods throughout the war. Oma worked at a vegetable canning plant which allowed her to bring home some food occasionally. All during the war my mother sewed and that way made our living. She sewed all of our clothes as well as her own. When the war ended she took the Nazi *Hakenkreuzfahne* and made dresses out of it for Rita and me. The dresses were red with black-and-white trim. They looked very nice, and others soon came to her bringing their old Nazi flags, asking Mother to convert them into something for their children to wear. Mutti wasted nothing. When bedsheets got thin in the middle she made spring coats out of them for the two of us and embroidered them with blue yarn. They were really beautiful coats.

Our main staple was *Pellkartoffeln*, boiled potatoes, which we peeled at the table, and mushrooms and gravy. For many years I thought mushrooms were meat, because Mutti made the gravy with mushrooms. When we first came to the United States I told my cousins that the only meat we had in Germany was mushrooms. They broke out laughing. "What are you talking about?" I remember one of them saying to us. "Mushrooms aren't meat. Mushrooms are mushrooms." Rita and I actually argued with them, we were so sure that mushrooms were meat. We finally went to Mutti to settle the argument and that's when we learned that meat came from animals. That's how it was.

Rita: There was a time when the *Flüchtlinge*, the refugees from the East, came through our village. It was very sad to watch them. There were many knocks on our door asking for food. We had little. Mother had her hands full to feed us three—Ingrid, me, and Karl-Heinz. There is one incident that stands out for me. A refugee father came to our door, he looked very hungry. His three children were standing off to the side while he begged for food. I think they were from East Prussia. All we had left was part of a loaf of bread. My grandmother said to my mother, "If we give him this bread what will we do?"

Mutti replied, "I think we need to share it with them."

"Ja," Oma said nodding her head, "give him the bread. God will provide somehow." So they gave the man our last piece of bread. Just like Oma said, three hours later, there was another knock on the door. There stood one of our neighbors with a live chicken wrapped in her apron. "I want you to have this chicken," the neighbor woman said to my mother. "Will you sew this for me?" and she held up something that needed mending. We had food again. Oma was right.

Ingrid: Yes, I remember that woman very well. The woman had a small farm on which she kept chickens, geese, rabbits, and other animals. Every one of the animals was counted by a Nazi Party member—every chicken, every rabbit, every horse, every cow. It was for the military, she was told. She couldn't just kill a chicken and eat it. She kept a secret flock of small animals which she hid from the inspector, and that's how she paid my mother for the sewing.

Other *Flüchtlinge* came down the Elbe River on small boats and barges. We could see them from our street as they moved past, since our house overlooked the Elbe. I saw women and children on a boat hanging their clothes on a line to dry when the *Tiefflieger* came and attacked the boat. I remember the screams of the women and the children. My heart breaks whenever I think of that. War should be among men, not against women and children.

Ingrid's voice broke. She looked at her hands as old memories brought back emotions which had never faded in spite of the many years that had passed. Rita picked up the conversation to give Ingrid a chance to find her composure.

Rita: We children were indoctrinated by our mother not to speak to anybody. She told us to say the common greetings of the day, or *Heil Hitler* if that was required. But not to talk to strangers because that was dangerous. Especially not to mention that we had an American father. Ingrid and I were obedient little girls and we did what Mutti asked of us. We had one neighbor, one of the few men in the village. He was visually handicapped, walked with a cane and a seeing eye dog, and always wore his swastika armband. But we thought he saw more than he wanted us to believe. He reported whatever it was he saw and didn't like. Mutti told us, "Don't ever speak to him. If he says *Heil Hitler* to you, say *Heil Hitler* right back."

There was always a military awareness in our lives. Soldiers, planes, sirens, bunkers, *Flüchtlinge*—and with it came fear. We'd go on walks and come across undetonated bombs. It was impossible to get away from war. Mutti and Oma constantly warned Ingrid and me never, never to touch anything that looked strange or unfamiliar. It might be a bomb of some kind. One time Ingrid and I went up to the old castle ruin overlooking the village. I saw this box lying there. Ingrid of course said, "Mutti says you can't touch it." So we threw stones at the box, thinking if there was a bomb inside the box would explode. As children we didn't think that if the box exploded we could get hurt. "No, you can't touch it, Rita," Ingrid repeated over and over to me. Then she ran off and got Mutti. Mutti took a long stick and flipped the lid off the box after first throwing some rocks at it. The box contained three pairs of sandals. What a delight. We gave one pair to my girl-friend Annemarie and kept the other two pairs. It was a blessing to find them. That was a happy day, like finding gold. We had no idea how the box got there or why.

It was a joyful day when the Americans finally arrived on the thirteenth of April 1945. The Americans promptly took over our house because it had two stories and allowed them to observe German military positions on the east side of the Elbe. There was some fighting, and they told us to evacuate the area. We packed a suitcase, and Grandmother (our great-grandmother had died by now), Mutti, and we children slowly walked west. As we came through Goldbeck, a woman who saw our exhausted and stumbling group moving down the street took pity on us and took us in. She herself was poor, had five children, and ran a small kindergarten and farm to make ends meet. We stayed with her until early May. On the seventh of May we returned to Arneburg. The fighting was over. Our house was still standing.

Ingrid: The Americans were my people, me being an American. I am an American, I shouted at passing American soldiers. My father is in America. A jeep stopped, and the soldiers picked us girls up and loaded us into the jeep. Then they drove us to our house. Once the soldiers met Mutti they asked her to translate for them—German into English and vice versa. They were just wonderful to us kids. They gave us our first stick of chewing gum, our first candy bar. They took us for rides in their jeep. They were so kind. Very different from the English who came after the Americans left that June. The English soldiers were strict and didn't talk to anyone. If the Americans had the same rules as the English, then they ignored them and did what they felt like doing. One of the American soldiers, Mike, we got to know well. One day Mike said to my mother, "Why don't you write a letter to your husband and I will mail it for you through the APO." After several months the first letter arrived from our father. Mike was from Rhode Island, and he came and visited us on Long Island after we returned to the United States.

The English left in July 1945 and were followed by the Russians. The Russians, with their tanks, came down our narrow cobblestone street. The houses shook. Everything shook. We girls were frightened, so were the adults. But nothing happened. The Russians didn't bother us. We saw little of them. Karl-Heinz had found a job at the railroad station where he met a young Russian soldier his age, a teenager. The Russian was just a regular guy who was homesick for his family. He went ice skating with us the winter of 1945 to 1946, and spent time with us every week.

In 1946 we accompanied Mutti to the American consulate in Berlin to initiate the paperwork for our return to the United States. To get there we had to cross the Elbe over a rickety, bomb-damaged bridge. The train was overloaded, and when we crossed that bridge the train went at a snail's pace, maybe three-to-five miles an hour. It was very scary crossing that bridge. When we got to Berlin we had another shock. The city was nearly totally destroyed. There was rubble everywhere. I remember one building that was totally destroyed except for two walls. At the fifth-floor level, on a small remnant of floor, stood a baby crib. I always wondered about the baby. Did it survive? Who were the people who once lived in these buildings? What happened to them? It was all so tragic. At the consulate we entered yet another world. I remember all these beautiful American ladies with their makeup and nylon stockings with perfectly straight seams in back. We went back to Berlin several times before the paperwork was completed, approved, and we were given permission to leave for the United States.

We took the train to Bremerhaven, to a holding camp, awaiting arrival of our ship. After two weeks they sent us back home. The same thing happened the next time we traveled to Bremerhaven. We became despondent and thought we would never get on a ship. But the third time we traveled to Bremerhaven it was for real. We boarded the USNS *Ernie Pyle* on the seventh of January 1947 and arrived in New York on January 16 after a stormy crossing. Our father was at the pier waiting for us, as well as our great aunt, Tante Martha, and Uncle Franz, Mutti's brother. Rita and I were arguing who would be the first to greet our father. As it turned out, I was on the quiet, shy side, and when the time came I pushed Rita forward and she ran into our father's open arms. We had never known our father except from pictures. Mutti had kept a picture of him in our bedroom and nearly every night she spoke of him. He was very much a part of our lives because she made him real to us. She told us he loved us, that he was waiting for us, and that it wasn't his fault that we were separated.

Rita and I thought of America as a fairy tale land, a land where people had food and clothes and didn't have to go hungry. Uncle Franz drove us in his big American car to our new home on Long Island. Night was falling as we drove through New York. All those lights. It was dazzling and exciting to drive through a city of light. We had come from a land of darkness. Our father had bought a house, a nice Dutch Colonial with a gambrel roof. It was so pretty! When we walked in, another surprise was awaiting us. A Christmas tree. And under the tree were lots of presents wrapped in colorful paper. And there was a cake for each of us—one for Mutti, another for me, and yet another for Rita. After eight years of separation our parents were finally together again. If they had any problems they worked them out just fine. I am sure that in hindsight our mother regretted her decision to stay in Germany in 1939, but that was the past and couldn't be changed.

Our parents and schoolteachers worked with us to help us learn the language. In 1947 I entered the fifth grade as if I had never missed a day of school and had always gone to school in America. Rita and I learned quickly. Our parents encouraged us to speak English at home, and they gave us additional assignments to get us used to writing our new language. Then when other refugee children entered our school, Rita and I were asked to help make them comfortable and integrate them quickly. My parents often would have these children over for dinner and help their families get settled—finding a house and a job.

Rita: But children can at times be cruel to one another. Many times when someone found out we were German they would call us Nazis. One boy in particular who sat behind me in class kept calling me Nazi. I didn't even understand what it meant, but I knew it wasn't nice. He kept yanking my hair and calling me "you dirty Nazi." I finally had it and turned around and slapped his face. It absolutely stunned my teacher that her star pupil would do such a thing. I explained to her, and she made the boy apologize. When we were in the eighth grade this boy asked me for a date. I said, No thank you.

When I was in the sixth grade I had a girlfriend. She was my best friend. On her birthday she invited our whole class to her house, except me. She came to me and said, "Rita, I am sorry, but I can't have you come with the rest of the class. Maybe alone sometime." I didn't understand why she did that. I cried when I got home. Mutti told me that her family was Jewish and that was probably the reason why, and that it was very painful for them to invite someone who came from Germany. Later on her parents asked me over to their home, and they questioned me about the war years in Germany. Of course I had no knowledge of the awful things that had occurred. I was only six years old when the war ended. As I grew into a teenager I didn't tell people anymore that I was German because of the stigma I thought was attached to my heritage. I began to feel sad and guilty about what had happened as I learned more about what the Nazis had done.

Let me end our story by saying that if we had to live our lives over again, Ingrid and I probably wouldn't change anything. We feel that all of our experiences, struggles, and trials were for a purpose which created our character and molded and shaped us into who we are. We had wonderful examples in our mother and grandmother. They were women with a strong belief in God. They were not only courageous, but they were also resourceful, which you had to be to survive. They were compassionate and sharing. They actually believed that God would provide for them, and they lived accordingly. They taught Ingrid and me to look forward in life, not back. Everything in life you can use either as a stumbling block or a stepping stone. We used the experiences of our early life as stepping stones, which I hope has made us compassionate, caring, and giving people. Ingrid and I were born into a world of war, and I believe had we not tasted war we probably would not appreciate this time of peace in our lives as much as we do, and all the freedoms we enjoy in the United States. Once you've lived in a war-torn country, you tend to see everything with different eyes—the freedom, the opportunities and everything else we have and often take for granted. I am very thankful to be living here in my country—America.

Anita Nille died at age fifty-six of cancer, Ingrid and Rita sadly revealed. At the time of my interview in March 2000, Ingrid herself had just bested that dreadful disease and was bravely recovering from the ordeal. Their father, Fritz, died in 1987 of a stroke at age seventy-six. Both Ingrid and Rita settled in Riverside, California, where they continue to be active in the German-American community.

Christa
Glowalla

{Age 10}

Berlin

[T]he air raids on Berlin were an unforgettable sight, and I had constantly to remind myself of the cruel reality in order not to be completely
entranced by the scene; the illumination of the parachute flares, which
the Berliners called "Christmas trees," followed by flashes of explosions
which were caught by the clouds of smoke, the innumerable probing
searchlights, the excitement when a plane was caught and tried to escape
the cone of light, the brief flaming torch when it was hit. No doubt about
it, this apocalypse provided a magnificent spectacle.

—Albert Speer, *Inside the Third Reich*

I learned . . . that everything can be taken away from you in the flash of
a moment. You need to be very, very grateful for what you have this
moment, because that's all you have. You don't have yesterday anymore,
and you do not yet have and may never have tomorrow.

—Christa Glowalla

I was born on November 13, 1935, in Berlin-Neuköln, Erkstrasse
10. Life was a happy time for me, until the bombing raids started when
I was about seven. I remember them only in the sense that we children
were awakened in the middle of the night. Toward the end of the war
we slept with most of our clothes on because it was too difficult to get
dressed in the little time we had between the *Vorwarnung* and the
arrival of the bombers. I still recall the sound of the sirens, and to this
day I don't like that sound. Sitting in the cellar we could hear the airplanes passing overhead, then the whistling sound the bombs made

---

Previous page: Christa in Berlin, 1949

before they hit and exploded. All of us sat there holding our ears because we knew what would come next—loud explosions, the cellar would shake, dust would envelop all of us until it was hard to breathe without holding a shawl or a handkerchief before our mouths. Some cried. Most of us just sat there waiting, waiting for what we knew would have to come one day. It was all very frightening. The house next door, which sat on the corner of Erkstrasse and Donaustrasse, became a pile of rubble. Many of our neighbors were killed. When the *Entwarnung* finally came, a steady sound from the siren instead of the wailing sound which warned of an imminent air raid, we went back up to our apartments, curious to see what we would find. My area of Neuköln was bombed heavily. We lived on the third floor of a five-story apartment house. Many of the apartment houses around ours were leveled. Miraculously our house survived.

In early 1944 many of us children and our mothers were evacuated from Berlin to get us away from the ever more frequent and intensive bombing. We were sent to a village called Heiersdorf in Lower Silesia. We lived there for nearly a year until January 1945. Then we were notified that the Russians were coming. Mutti got us children together, and we fled with a farmer on one of his ox-drawn wagons. We children rode on the wagon. The adults walked alongside. We could hear guns firing behind us as we left Heiersdorf. Our *Treck* was going as fast as it could, but of course it was very slow. Oxen don't go very fast. All of us were deeply frightened, because we thought that we had left too late and would be overrun by the Red Army. It was bitter cold. The wagon had a metal strip running along the top edges of its sides. We children entertained ourselves by spitting on the cold metal edge of the wagon and watching our spittle freeze as soon as it hit. We created a little mountain chain which we called *Spuckgebirge*, spittel mountains.

We were heading to Berlin. Berlin seemed safe, even though it wasn't. Eventually we were overtaken by German troops. They loaded us onto their Panzers and took us for long stretches. It was the German soldiers who told us children for the first time that we had lost the war.

War from the Sky

When we got back to Berlin we found our house still standing. The apartment smelled musty, but it was fine and it was home and felt good, initially anyway. Little by little a sense of normalcy set in again among us children. We adapted again to our surroundings, to the ruins and the rubble and the frequent bombing raids.

We had always gone into the cellar of our apartment house during bombing raids and then gone back upstairs, but as the Russian army entered Berlin we stayed in the cellar permanently. The cellar was filled with women, children, and some old men. About twenty families in all. Outside a battle was raging, we could hear it. At first German soldiers occasionally came into our cellar, then Russians. I remember when the Russian soldiers came. They were determined to rape every woman and girl. But my Tante Sophie, my father's sister who also lived with us in our apartment house, had anticipated our fate. Her family came from Hindenburg in Upper Silesia, and she spoke fluent Polish. She had everyone in our cellar wrap scarves or bandages around their heads from under their chins across the ears and over the tops of their heads. We were all very thin and must have looked like a colony of lepers. So when the Russian soldiers came into the cellar and saw all the bandaged heads, Aunt Sophie stood up and shouted to them in Polish, "We had an outbreak of diphtheria. Please send medical help." The soldiers seemed to understand her and looked frightened. People don't realize it now, but these soldiers were very primitive and very different from the Russians we met later on. The soldiers posted two guards by our cellar entrance. When other soldiers appeared we could hear the guards shouting, "Nyet, nyet, nyet," and something about diphtheria. We knew then we were safe because of Aunt Sophie's lie. When we got out of the cellar weeks later, we were very, very hungry. I don't know what we ate while we were down there. I can't remember. But I do remember that I was always very, very hungry.

In the summer of 1945 the Americans finally came. I thought it was our salvation. We were finally safe and dared to leave the cellar and go back up in our apartments to live. When we entered our apartment we immediately noticed that it had been used, or I should say misused, by the Russians. They apparently did not know what upholstered furniture was for, because they had used it for a toilet. Earlier while the Russians were still there and we lived downstairs in the cellar, we children had gone upstairs now and then and seen them washing their potatoes in the toilets, not knowing what the toilets were for. We tried to tell them, but they did not understand. At this point they no longer threatened us, but we stayed in the cellar anyway because they lived upstairs in our apartments and there was no other place to go. They wanted to know from us children how things worked. One soldier came over to my little brother Peter with a radio in his hands. He held it to his ear and in broken German he said something like, "The little man in there is not working anymore." Peter looked at the Russian kind of dubiously and then said, "You have to plug it in." Peter took the radio from the soldier's hands and plugged it in. It played. The soldier was absolutely amazed over the brilliant child who could fix radios and make them talk and gave my brother a hug and some Russian money, which we had no use for.

One Russian soldier took a real liking to my little sister Susie. She must have communicated to him somehow that she was hungry. He pulled Susie on his lap and then pulled sardines out of a pocket of his uniform. He apparently had found sardines somewhere, opened the cans and stuffed them in his pockets. He pulled out a sardine and held it over Susie's head. She opened her mouth and he dropped the sardine into her mouth. As hungry as we were, the rest of us were sick to our stomachs watching Susie eat the sardines. Peter and I yelled at Susie, "No. No, Susie. Don't eat that." But she was too hungry. She ate every sardine the soldier offered her.

I had two brothers and two sisters. I was the oldest in 1945 at age ten. Although my name is Christa, they called me Titta. My brother Karl-Heinz was eight; Susie, whose real name was Maria, was seven; Peter was six; and my youngest sister, Else, was five. There was another sister which came after my father was released by the Americans. Her name was Ursula, but we called her *Bienchen*, little bee. She was the child of all of us.

War from the Sky

Slowly I began to comprehend that Germany had lost the war. We children thought it was a terrible thing. It was quite a shift in our thinking, because we had always been taught to be proud that we were Germans, that we were superior and special, and that eventually we would rule the world. And I believed what they told us in school. And suddenly we had to digest the fact that these proud people had lost the war, whatever that meant. Which didn't mean very much to a child of ten except that we had nothing to eat. I did ask many of the adults, What is going to happen now that we lost the war? How are we going to rule the world now? The one answer I remember was "I don't think we will." But I couldn't grasp the change right away, and I reassured some of my friends that we were the greatest and we would overcome everything and eventually rule the world. For the longest time I thought that way.

I checked out a book from the library to find out what weeds were edible. As I remember it my brothers and sisters and I then went to the park with a handbasket and with our book. There we picked the weeds the book told us could be used for food. Nettles to make spinach. We learned that *Sauerampher*, sorrel, was good for us too. To this day I like to eat a little *Sauerampher* when I see it growing in a meadow. They were difficult days. Food was always uppermost in our minds. I also recall that my mother visited the American soldiers to procure food. Just how she did that I don't know. But we always knew when she was gone that she would come back with some Hershey candy bars and other stuff. To this day I have a soft spot for Hershey bars. My mother kept us children fed, however she had to do it. We also went on what we called hamster trips. We'd go to farms outside Berlin and try to trade what we had for food—clocks, tablecloths, linens. With four children she had too many mouths to feed. It was hard for her.

My mother, Hildegard, was my everything. She was strong and ruled us children with a *Bügel*—meaning she spanked us with a wooden clothes hanger. She, like my father, taught us children, "If you want to be something, get an education." She had a tremendous sense of fun. I believe she had some French in her background, and was sparkly and loved life. Mutti was very pretty, a little brunette woman with big black eyes. Of course she had to be mother and father to us children, but didn't neglect to tell us that we had a father and kept pictures of him throughout our apartment. To us children our father was a picture. She also had a picture of Adolf Hitler hanging right next to Vati's. At Christmas she would decorate the pictures, Vatie's and Hitler's, with tinsel and a little sprig of pine, meaning that these were honored people in her life.

I thought at the time that this Hitler was a great man. As school-children we were often led to where Hitler gave his speeches. I remember listening to him speak, but of course I don't remember what he was talking about. It was always this funny little figure with a little mustache standing way up on a podium and speaking at the top of his voice. We children were like children everywhere and would bet how often he would raise his right arm in a salute. When he raised his right arm, then we raised ours. We were looking forward to him raising his arm, because we had to stand absolutely still and remain quiet while he was speaking. Raising our arms to salute broke the boredom and the monotony; it also allowed us to move and talk a little. We didn't know what it meant. It was just something we did because we were told to do it.

School started again. I must say that the instruction was excellent and the teachers were really wonderful. The schools and the libraries were the first institutions to reopen after the Americans arrived. I took an examination, and it was decided by the school authorities that I should continue in the *Oberschule* and go beyond the eighth grade. There I took two foreign languages, English and French. I just loved going to school and immersed myself totally in my schoolwork. The teachers were just wonderful in every subject, I thought. But our teachers also were practical and knew their students were hungry. So they taught us to tie a rope around our waists and to tighten it and put a big knot right over our stomachs. It helped our hunger. We didn't feel it anymore. The teachers did that themselves. I often think back to those men and women, and I have a great amount of affection for them because they understood us children. They understood that we couldn't learn if we had to deal with empty stomachs while listening to them.

My father's name is Roman. When he came home in late 1946 he said to me once, "I was well fed by the Americans when I was their prisoner." He was in the infantry in the war and fought in the West. "Now I am home with you and there is nothing to eat." I could tell he was heartbroken. I remember him sitting at the kitchen table with his head in his hands. I went up to him and put an arm around him and said, "What's the matter, Vati?" He replied, "You know, my little one, I lost the war. And now I've come home and I can't feed my children. I can't feed you." Slowly I began to understand what war had done to him. What I remember most about my father has to do with education. He would say to me when he came home on a short military leave, "I can't leave you any money, Titta. And money is something somebody can take away from you anyway. But I will give you education. As long as you go to school, any school, I will work and support you." And when he returned in 1946 he told me the same thing again. "Continue in school and I will work for you and make a home for you." So I realized very early how important education was.

In 1948 and 1949, after new money was introduced, things slowly got better. There was food again. Not much, but there was food for all of us. I remember the first thing that was available on the open market was salt herring. We bought lots and lots of herring. My mother learned to fix herring in many different ways. The whole apartment house smelled of herring. Today I never again want to eat another herring. I remember the Berlin airlift of 1948 and 1949 very well, because I lived close to Tempelhof. I could see the airplanes flying very low. I would point at them and say to my friends, there goes another bomber and he brings us food. Of course they made the same sounds the bombers made which had come before and carried bombs. We were very glad and developed an affection for Americans because of the simple fact that they brought us food. It is an affection which Berliners to this day have never quite lost for Americans. After the airlift ended and food was finally in plentiful supply, we ate lots of bread and potatoes. It felt good just to feel full again. In later years someone called me a bread eater. Of course I am a bread eater. I believe it is the key food, followed closely by potatoes. To this day I love bread and potatoes.

When Titta made that comment I interrupted our interview because I couldn't help laughing. Titta is a small, gracious woman, and although she may love bread and potatoes, her slim figure is the very opposite of what one might expect from a lover of bread and potatoes.

I lived on the third floor of what as a child I thought was a big apartment house. In 1948 I turned thirteen. I was very close to my cousin Felicitas who was a year older than I. She and I were like twin sisters. We would lean out the window in her living room—it once was a very acceptable pastime in Germany—*aus dem Fenster kucken.* It made us feel grown up. We'd put a pillow on the windowsill and then look at the outside world. There was a tobacco and cigarette shop near us, and as the oldest child I was frequently asked by my mother to go there and pick up her cigarette ration. In the window of that shop was a violin on display. I became fascinated by that violin. I asked the shopkeeper once if I could hold it. He let me. Then I decided I had to have the violin. Eventually my mother bought it for me and I learned to play the fiddle.

Felicitas and I would also write novels. A problem was that we didn't have much paper, so we learned to use the edges of newspapers. We would write our entire novel on the edges of newspapers, and when we finished we had this big event where she would read me her novel and I would read her my novel. Our families knew to leave us alone when we were reading our novels. Any slip of paper, any old book, anything at all would do to write our novels. What did we write? Love stories. At one time we invited my mother to listen to our novels. Then my father listened in, and he broke out laughing at what we had written. Felicitas and I were deeply insulted by his behavior. I had read some western novels in the library and patterned my story after the American West. I would have cowboys in my novel having shootouts over their ladies, and my father would get very practical and say, "You can't do this" because of this and that. He destroyed my fantasy world, so I didn't invite him to our readings again.

As a child I don't think you justify events in your mind in an orderly fashion. For instance, all the destruction around us. It was just so. That's all. I found it difficult to understand, but then I found many things difficult to understand, and I just trusted that my teachers and my parents knew what they were talking about. Like most German children of this time we really believed in our elders. School and education were uppermost in my mind. I think I was brainwashed enough as a German child that I thought it was wonderful that I could learn so much. I was very anxious to learn all I could, and I felt privileged to be able to attend a higher school. I remember I loved the library and used it frequently. It was a friend. There was a bookstore near where I lived, on Wildenbruch Strasse. I always went there and picked out books by Karl May. I remember my father asking me to also pick up books for him which were by a French author. They were dirty books. They normally didn't give those books to children, but they knew me. Then my cousin Felicitas and I would stop and read from the book. We thought it was hilarious. By our standards today those books were not very dirty at all.

When I turned sixteen years old I thought I had to help my family and earn money. For a brief time I worked for the Americans as an interpreter and as a secretary in a printer's shop. It was in Berlin where I met my future husband; he was in an army band, and we married in 1956. I was twenty.

I had taken ballet training since the age of fourteen and participated in several operas in the *Berliner Staatsoper*. When I came to the United States in 1956 I decided to continue with my dancing, and I opened a series of ballet schools. The first one I opened in Rochester, New York;

later one in Jacksonville, Florida, at the Jacksonville university. I formed a dance department there, and to my delight, that dance department still flourishes and today gives out degrees. I founded it. I didn't have a college degree, but I persuaded them to give me a chance. As a dancer you really don't have time to get a degree. But I learned in America you do everything differently. I started one young boy there, his name was William Forseith. I understand that today he is a famous choreographer and director of the Frankfurt Opera ballet.

How did my experiences as a young girl influence me? I believe I gained a tremendous discipline from all I learned and endured—the ballet, the poverty, the hunger, the bombings. Those things shape a young person for life. I think that I learned a difficult lesson very young: that you have to work hard to earn anything—to earn love, or to earn food, or to earn the roof over your head. I believe I am more grateful than the average person for what I have because of my past. And I am grateful that when I step out on my veranda that the airplane passing overhead is not going to drop bombs. That fearful feeling I don't think will ever leave me.

I learned another lesson—that everything can be taken away from you in the flash of a moment. You need to be very, very grateful for what you have this moment, because that's all you have. You don't have yesterday anymore, and you do not yet have and may never have tomorrow. So this moment right now is all you really have. And I have learned to be grateful for the moment I am living right now. Over three years ago I was a passenger in a car. A pickup truck driven by a young man drove into my side of the car. The car was demolished. I was badly injured and in a coma for a month. I am just getting back to a near normal life, and I am grateful that I am still alive, that I can think and write, walk and talk. We know intellectually that this can happen to any one of us at any time, but we never really think of it. It happened to me, and woke me up. I was living a good life. I thought I had earned it, that I deserved it. I had become very impatient. I wanted things now, and I wanted them my way. I relearned a lesson I thought I had learned a long time ago as a young girl in Berlin, a lesson which I apparently had forgotten—that life doesn't owe me anything.

I was only marginally aware during the war that there was a Jewish issue. I remember my mother and Felicitas telling me that the Jews started the war. My mother said, "*Die Juden haben den Krieg angezettelt.*" Well, a *Zettel* is a little piece of paper. And in my child's mind I tried to figure out what that meant. I visualized a piece of paper being put on everyone's front door on which a Jew had written *Der Krieg fängt an*, the war starts now. Something like when Martin Luther nailed his theses to the cathedral door in Wittenberg. For the longest time as a very young child I wondered why the Jews did that. I didn't know any Jews during the war. One handsome young man was pointed out to me by friends one time. "That is a Jew," they said. "He is awful." I remember thinking, What is awful about him? I didn't see anything awful. But I didn't question it. After the war, at age fourteen and fifteen, like most children of that time, I was a very serious child. I was always reading and thinking, and I began to understand on my own that what I had learned in school under the Nazis was all false teaching. Still, I am grateful for my background. Not for Hitler, but for my background.

I don't think I hate anything to this day. Hate is really a very strong term to use, but I come close to it when I hear people judge others without understanding. To me people of different races, ethnic backgrounds, and religions are just men and women, that's all. They were little girls and little boys once. We should at least try to see each person as just another person.

How did I feel about being a German as I got older and understood all that had happened during the war? I am sad over what happened. I felt ashamed of what Germans had done to the Jews, but I was never ashamed of being German. Whenever I met a Jewish person I felt apologetic and guilty. Then, if the Jewish person was nice to me, I would wonder afterward, why was he or she nice to me? Why didn't she just hate me for being German? Yes, I feel guilt. But I am drawn to Jewish people. I like them. As for politics? I have always remained distant from politics and stayed away from all political parties.

My mother, father, and siblings remained behind in Berlin after I came to the United States in 1956. Maria, the one we called Susie, went over to East Berlin and got caught there when the East Germans put up the wall in 1961. She couldn't return and had to make a life for herself in the East. Susie met a man, married, and had two sons. My other brothers and sister, along with my parents, remained in West Berlin. When my father died in 1992 at age eighty-two, my mother helped form a neighborhood theater group. At age eighty-four she became the group's star performer. The young director brought together young and old people. Once a month the group sat down and decided what they wanted to do for their next performance. Once they agreed on a topic they assigned roles to each other. There was only a very general script, no names were assigned. Everything evolved during the performance. Each performance was sold out and had a long waiting list. So, my mother remains very active and is happy with her life.

Christa no longer goes by her childhood name of Titta. She lives in the warm climate of southern California, where she works as a successful realtor, an occupation she shares with her husband, Gerry. However, in the course of the interview there again emerged that little girl of ten, Titta, who in 1945 tried so desperately to cope with her changing world and make some sense of it. Although Christa has lived most of her life in peace in the United States, has a family of her own, has tasted prosperity and pursued multiple careers as a dancer, teacher of dance, and realtor, her distant past is as real to her today as it was nearly sixty years ago.

Siegrid
Mayer

{Age 6}

Kaiserslautern, Rhineland-Palatinate

The critical point is that none of the Allied leaders resolutely opposed a renewal of area bombing in some form or other [in 1944], and this was more than enough of a mandate for Sir Arthur Harris. . . . As the German air defences crumbled and losses fell, Harris found himself with more than a thousand first-line aircraft daily available. . . .

—Max Hastings, *Bomber Command*

When we left the shelter that night, our street was burning, the houses aflame. The night was fire red. I remember the flames. I remember the fire.

—Siegrid Mayer

As a young child of five and six years of age in 1944 and 1945 I saw and heard many things which I didn't really understand at the time. Later I spoke of them with my family and learned more about what I had seen and heard. I'd like to talk about some of these things first because they represent the environment in which I grew up. The Nazis closed my grandfather's health clinic and took away his livelihood. He was a doctor of *Naturheilkunde*, healing people by using nature's remedies. To the Nazis, however, he was practicing witchcraft. I recall the sadness that entered our family when my grandfather no longer could heal people who had relied on him for years. My mother, Elfriede, and I lived with my maternal grandparents, Wilhelm and Helene Mayer, and so their life became my life.

Previous page: Siegrid, 1950

War from the Sky

I usually accompanied my grandmother, Oma, when she did her daily shopping. On one of those occasions I saw our priest being marched down the street with a sign around his neck which read *Ich bin eine Pfaffensau*, I am a papal pig. I later learned that he had the temerity to protest something, and as a result he was promptly arrested. My grandmother raised her hand as he was marched by us, shouting, "That is too much to do something like that to our priest." One of the escorting Nazis grabbed her by the arm and said, "We'll take you too." Luckily our neighbor stood next to us; he owned the shoe store. To keep the store open he had to join the party, and he wore the party emblem on his lapel. He stepped forward and said, "*Kamerad*, I'll take care of her. Let me take her with me," and the man let go of her arm. If our neighbor hadn't been there, I don't know what would have happened to Oma Mayer. That is how things were.

My paternal grandfather wasn't that lucky. He had a discussion one day with two Wehrmacht officers in a coffeehouse about the state of the war. Apparently he said something they didn't like. One of the officers rose and excused himself to go to the restroom. He returned with a Gestapo officer who arrested my grandfather. We heard nothing about his fate. Then one day my father, Erich, who was a soldier on the *Ostfront*, received a letter from the Gestapo informing him that his father, Friedrich Krüger, had committed suicide in his cell by hanging, and that they had taken the liberty of cremating the corpse. I want to tell you, an American, these things as a form of rehabilitation of my people, the ordinary Germans. We had no say in things, and when we did say something to protest, retribution was swift and cruel.

It was in January 1944 when the air raids began, and they never stopped until the war ended. I recall holding onto my mother, who was pregnant with my sister, and running down the street toward the bunker near the internal revenue service building in Kaiserslautern. We did this so many times, I lost count. The bunker was inside a mountain. It was once a *Felsenbrauerei*, a brewery which brewed its beer in the huge, cold mountain cavern which had been converted into an

82

air raid shelter, one of many such bunkers in Kaiserslautern. My sister, Doris, was born in February 1945. In the beginning when we went into the bunker I was allowed to take my doll. But then I couldn't bring my doll anymore because it was made of celluloid, a fire hazard. When I played outside I couldn't go any farther than our front door, because any minute the planes could come and we would have to run for the bunker. So I played mostly inside the house near my Oma and Mutti. Kindergarten was closed because of the lack of air raid shelters. I had no one else to play with. Christmas 1944 we spent in the bunker. I remember Mutti saying to me, "The Christ child will come and bless you, but I have nothing to give you." And I remember the adults singing Christmas carols in the bunker. Toward the end, we spent most of our time in the bunker—we slept and cooked our meals there.

Around that same Christmas in 1944, the house next door was hit by a firebomb during one of the many air raids. I remember when it happened, and later my grandmother told me the details. The woman who lived there had three children—a girl, a boy, and an infant. Her husband, before he was drafted into the Wehrmacht, had renovated the basement to serve as a shelter for his family, and told his wife to stay there and not go into the bunker. The woman obeyed her husband, even though my grandmother warned her frequently not to stay in the house during the bombing raids. "My husband told me our shelter is safe, and that's that. Don't bother me anymore," she finally told my grandmother. One time when we were surprised by attacking planes my mother and I ran into her basement shelter. The man had installed extra beams to support the ceiling. Her children cowered under a table by the chimney. When there appeared to be a pause in the bombing my mother grabbed me and we ran to the bunker. As we ran Mutti shouted to me, "If she gets hit she won't be able to get out. It's no good for us to stay there, Siegrid." When the phosphorous bomb hit their house it penetrated alongside the chimney all the way into their basement shelter, which instantly filled with noise and a cloud of dust and flying debris. The woman ran outside with the baby and then returned to save the boy and the girl. They were covered with phosphorous, horribly disfigured, and soon died. My grandmother wouldn't let me look at them, but I knew something horrible had happened. The woman suffered deep burns in her attempt to save her children, and when I saw her in later years, with her disfigured face and hands, I knew again the horrors of war.

We had another air raid warning, one of hundreds since that first raid in January 1944. It must have been in early March 1945 because my sister was already there. My mother didn't want to go to the shelter, but my grandmother insisted. Mutti ran as fast as she could, pushing the *Kinderwagen* with Doris in it with her left hand, tugging me under her right arm. She heard the *Tiefflieger* approaching. The plane turned toward us. My mother had me under her arm in such a way that I was face up and I could see the airplane coming toward us. It was so low, I could see the pilot with his oxygen mask covering his face. As we drew even with the entrance to the bunker, the plane appeared. Mutti turned sharply left and threw herself down the steps, baby carriage, me, and all. I was terrified. The bomb exploded no more than ten meters from us.

During a night attack our family went into the bunker as always. Mutti left the baby carriage outside and carried my sister. My grandparents followed. We went toward the back of the bunker. Toward the front of the bunker sat prisoners of war and the air raid warden. Then the nightmare of all nightmares happened, liquid phosphorous came running down the shelter stairs. "We are all going to burn to death," the adults around me screamed with fright. My grandmother remained calm. She said to my mother, "Elfriede, you climb up this escape tunnel"—there were several tunnels leading from the bunker to the outside—"then I hand you the baby, and then Siegrid. You get out. Don't worry about us." My mother began to climb into the escape tunnel when the air raid warden stepped toward the flaming stairs. At the bottom of the stairs was a large cast-iron sewer lid. With a crowbar the warden removed the lid, and the phosphorous ran into the sewer, helped along by some of the prisoners who channeled the phosphorous away from us. When we left the shelter that night, our street was burning, the houses aflame. The night was fire red. I remember the flames. I remember the fire.

The air raid warnings became less and less reliable. Too soon after the sirens went off the planes already arrived. On one occasion, at night, we couldn't make it to the bunker on time. We were across from a house ruin, and Mutti decided it was better to seek shelter in the ruin than stand on the open street. She backed into what she thought was an entrance to the ruin, pulling the *Kinderwagen* with one hand and holding me with the other. Then the wagon wouldn't move anymore, as if someone was holding it. She said to me, "Hold onto the wagon while I see what's the matter." It was pitch black. The bombs were falling around us. She couldn't find anything. Then the raid passed, and she pushed the carriage out of the ruin, and we went into the bunker. The next day, when Mutti and I walked past the ruin where we tried to seek shelter the night before, she decided to take a look and see why the baby carriage got stuck. She found that we had entered a bombed-out auto repair shop. Had she taken one more step backwards, she would have fallen into a mechanic's pit. My grandmother and I always believed it was an angel who protected us that night. We couldn't find anything that the carriage might have gotten tangled in. To this day, I still believe an angel saved my mother's life that night.

In March 1945 many of our streets were unusable because of hundreds of unexploded bombs lying about. Our house still stood—damaged, but not burned. My father's mother came by. She lived in a nearby village. She said, "Elfriede, come with me. I live in the forest and it is safer there than staying here in town." We then followed her through the forest, my mother pushing the *Kinderwagen* with Doris in it. Then the *Tiefflieger* came. They circled over the forest, and when they saw us trying to run across an open area they came down low and fired their guns at us—an old woman, my mother, a six-year-old girl, and a baby carriage. They played with us all the way until we came to an area where there were German antiaircraft guns. Then they left us alone. They could have killed us at any time if they had wanted to. When we got to the German guns the commander said to us that he thought it was his relief the *Tiefflieger* were after; but it was only two women and two children. My grandmother's house was directly in the forest, and from there we watched the raids against Kaiserslautern.

Rumors made the rounds that the Nazis wanted all Germans to commit suicide. We had relatives near Alzey, north of Kaiserslautern, and my grandmother insisted that my mother go there to give us children a chance at life. On the farm we lived with Polish and Russian prisoners of war who worked the land. At night all of us sat around a large table and ate together. Even there the *Tiefflieger* continued to harass us. I was in the field with one of the Polish men when the *Tiefflieger* came and attacked. He grabbed me and jumped to the ground, throwing his body across mine to shield me. The horses took off wildly, upending the wagon. The *Tiefflieger* chased us like rabbits whenever they had a chance.

In late March the Americans came. But first came the German soldiers. Ragged, hungry-looking men dressed in torn uniforms, some without shoes. I saw that many were crying. There were many wounded among them, but they had not enough bandages for all. I could see their open wounds as they lay on a wagon, or as their comrades carried them past us. My uncle took pity on the German soldiers and gave them two of his horses and a wagon for the wounded. There was so much blood, so many blood-soaked bandages. I remember these soldiers looking like pictures I've seen since of horror scenes in the Middle Ages, that's what they looked like to me as a six-year-old. A horrible sight.

After the German soldiers passed, there was quiet. The next day American soldiers surrounded our village. Then their tanks came. For me as a little girl the tanks looked very big, unreal and frightening. The lead tank stopped in front of our house and moved his gun turret from side to side. I recall screaming at my mother, Mutti, Mutti, Mutti, he is going to shoot, he is going to shoot. Then he stopped moving his turret, a lid opened on the turret, and there I saw my first black man. He came out of the tank wearing a helmet. I screamed to my mother, Mutti, Mutti, the devil is coming to get us. I thought it was the devil who had emerged from the tank. As I calmed down and looked at the American soldiers more closely, what struck me as a child was that they all looked so well fed. Their faces were full, not haggard like those of the German soldiers I had seen the day before, and their pants seemed to fit tightly around their buttocks.

The Americans stayed. The war was over for us. Mutti, Doris, and I returned to Kaiserslautern on foot. On the way we passed a huge German prisoner-of-war camp. I remember the stench of the camp. And I also remember the stench of a forest we walked through, filled with dead horses and dead German soldiers. My grandparents had survived, and we moved back in with them. That July the Americans left Kaiserslautern, and French Tunisian troops occupied the town. Hunger began. That autumn Mutti, Oma, and I went into the country to help the farmers harvest their crops, hoping that something would remain for us. I slept with Mutti. At night I heard women screaming. Mutti held me close and quieted me down until I fell asleep again. Nearly every night I heard women screaming. One evening a jeep with French soldiers, not Africans, pulled up in front of our farmhouse. A soldier grabbed the farmer and put a pistol to his head. Another grabbed me and Oma by the arms and tried to push us into another room. A third soldier led my mother away. Oma screamed at the soldier, "Let the child go." The soldier took out his pistol and pushed it into her chest. French military police appeared. A Polish boy, who had seen the soldiers come into the farm and who worked for the farmer we stayed with, had run to the French military police in the village and saved us.

After we returned to Kaiserslautern the lack of food remained our greatest problem. My mother and I would walk every week to outlying villages to beg for food. Or we would take a train into the country early in the morning and return in the evening. A young woman and a little girl looked sufficiently pitiful to the farmers, I guess, because they nearly always gave us something to eat. But getting the food home was not always a sure thing. Once we returned on the train filled with people like us who had been to the country to find food. A German and a French policeman stopped the train at a small station and got on the first car. These men grabbed the food from everyone and threw it out the windows, onto the adjacent tracks. But as soon as they got off and entered the next car the train engineer and the boiler man threw the food bundles back into our car. I recall how happy we all were when the train pulled out of the station and we still had our precious food.

I started school in the fall of 1945. There was only one school in town and seventy to eighty children in my class. We sat four to a bench. In the winter we had to bring a piece of coal or wood to class each day so they could heat the school at least a little bit. The good thing was that in school we children received a meal each day. Without that meal, I believe many of us would have starved to death. The food, usually a noodle soup, porridge, or rice boiled in milk, was provided every day by the American Quakers. On a holiday we received rolls with raisins in them. That was a great treat to us children.

After the new money was issued in June 1948 things got better. The Americans returned to Ramstein, and my mother got a job cleaning their tanks after they came back from the field covered with dirt. We received child support for me and my sister. We began to rebuild our house. The roof was gone, and the upper story had been destroyed. We lived in the lower story and in the basement. Three years after the war ended my father was finally released from a Russian prisoner-of-war camp. He had been severely wounded and still had shrapnel in his skull. He soon died from his wounds. I never knew my father. I never even saw a picture of him until he came home to die. I miss not having had a real father.

For me my maternal grandparents were my focus. Especially my grandmother Helene. She was my *Vorbild*, my role model. I wanted to be like her. I lived in her house and went shopping with Oma nearly every day. It was Oma who put me to bed at night, dressing me in two or three dresses to be ready to run for the bunker. Oma said to me more than once, "When the war is over, Siegrid, then you can go to sleep totally naked." That was my wish, not to have to sleep in all that clothing. It was she who worried about my safety and made sure that my mother went to the bunker with me and my little sister, Doris. Oma was for me the person I looked to as my mother. My natural mother I saw as a big sister. She was only seventeen years old when I was born in 1939. Most of our neighbors thought I was the youngest daughter of my grandparents. When someone asked me what my name was I would reply Siegrid Krüger Mayer. Krüger was my mother's married name; Mayer was my grandparents' name, my mother's maiden name. I wanted to have the name Mayer. So that's what I called myself even at such a young age.

To this day I have occasional nightmares of planes attacking me. Chasing me down the street. Following me into my house through the window. Trying to shoot me. I wake up soaked in sweat, deeply afraid. I know planes can't fly through a window, but in my dreams they do. When I walk in the forest and a plane from Ramstein Air Base flies overhead, I instinctively pull my head between my shoulders, trying to make myself smaller. During the Gulf War and the Kosovo War I didn't get much sleep. The planes flew over my house day and night. For me, it was a time of fear and trembling and nightmares. Planes and fire are the two things I always remember and fear. I can hardly get myself to light a candle, that's how afraid I am of fire. I live with these fears. I know for me they won't ever go totally away. I don't have children myself and the young people I have contact with have little interest in my past, in the life I lived as a young child. Germany is so different today. The young people seem to believe that we make up such stories when they hear them.

Siegrid lives with her sister, Doris, in Kaiserslautern in the house she inherited from her maternal grandparents, the house she was born in, the house where as a youngster she played at the front door so as to be able to flee quickly for shelter. Next door stands an old building with a gruesome history: the path of the phosphorous bomb is still discernible, coming down alongside the chimney and finding its way into the cellar where it exploded in all its horror. Phosphorous was one of the most terrible weapons employed against the civilian population in the war from the air.

Karl
Kremer

{Age 8}

Köln, Northrhine-Westfalia

But on the night of 30 May 1942, crews in the later waves crossed northern Germany, skirting the heavy flak around Mönchen-Gladbach, unable to accept the reality of the vast red glow in the sky ahead of them. Some crews thought that a great forest or heath must have caught fire, others that the Germans had created an enormous dummy fire to draw the bombers. Only as they drew near did they perceive the incredible truth, that this was the city of Cologne, apparently ablaze from end to end.

—Max Hastings, *Bomber Command*

After a while, I could tell the difference between bombs—if it was a fire-bomb or an explosive bomb, and if it was a dud.

—Karl Kremer

I was born in Köln-Ehrenfeld in 1937 into what I believe was a hard-working German family. My father worked at the Ford automobile factory in Köln. I understand that it was a good-paying and steady job, but that his hours were long. My mother made certain he had something to eat and drink before he went to work in the morning, long before we children got up. I have an older brother and sister, Hubert and Mathilde, and a younger brother, Willi. When my father came home in the evening we children were put to bed soon after *Abendessen* so the adults had a few moments to themselves before they too went to bed. I hardly ever saw my father. Then in 1943 he was drafted. This is somewhat of a paradox because he had a family of four

Previous page: Mathilde, Willi, Katharina, Hubert, and Karl, 1944

children and occupied a critical position at Ford; either condition should have exempted him from the draft. But as I learned later, there was something else going on. His supervisor, a woman, wanted to have a liaison with my father. When he didn't acquiesce to her wishes she used her contacts with the Nazi Party to have him drafted. He was sent to the *Ostfront* and seriously wounded. Even before he was fully recovered he was sent back to the *Ostfront* again, and soon thereafter he was reported missing. We never found out how he died. Years after the war my father was officially declared dead, and as a war widow my mother was entitled to a pension and child support. I have no memories of my father as a person. He went to work early and came home late, and then he was drafted and never returned to us. There is a void in my life that will never be filled.

My mother's name was Katharina. A pretty woman, I thought, pretty into old age. She was orphaned at age five. Her father died of lead poisoning. The children were distributed throughout the village and she, according to her, ended up with a witch. As soon as she could, she escaped and went to Köln and found a position as a maid in a Catholic cloister. Later she worked for families as a maid. She met my father through the Catholic church, and they opened a small grocery store in Köln. My parents tried to stay out of politics and just live their lives. With her four children, the Nazi Party wanted to present her with the *Mutterkreuz*, the mother cross. She refused to accept it. She also refused to accept child support, which was offered whenever one of us was born. She wanted none of that. They were watched, and customers of their store were queried about what they thought of the Kremers and their possible political leanings. My mother and father decided to sell their little store in early 1937 and emigrate to the United States. They thought they were getting close to getting their papers, but evidently the local authorities did everything to delay their departure. Then, it was too late.

We lived on the third floor of a five-story apartment house, and whenever there was an air raid alarm my mother had the daunting task of getting four children to the basement—quickly. She assigned my ten-year-old brother the task of getting my youngest brother downstairs. My mother grabbed our things, and I helped her. Of the four children, according to my mother, I had the least fear. I think I had no fear. I wasn't scared of the dark, which the basement often was when the bombs hit nearby. I wasn't scared of anything. As a result I could help her manage the situation and retrieve things which were forgotten in the rush to the basement. Downstairs in the basement we sat on benches in long rows. Old men, women, and children prayed, cried, cursed, reminisced, or sat quietly. The full spectrum of human emotions played itself out in the sometime long waits before the *Entwarnung* came.

Our apartment house was connected to the house to our left and right. The basement walls had been breached and pressure doors installed to preclude adjacent shelters from being affected by an explosion, and to provide an escape route if our entrance was no longer useable. After a while, I could tell the difference between bombs—if it was a firebomb or an explosive bomb, and if it was a dud. I could tell just from the sound where the bombs hit.

After my father was drafted in 1943 my mother decided to move with us four children into the Eifel mountains, where she was born. She wanted to escape the mounting bombing raids and constant air raid warnings in Köln. It was not a totally satisfactory arrangement. My mother and I, and one of my brothers, stayed with one farmer, while my sister and my older brother stayed with two different farmers. But at least we were in the same village. We saw each other every day, but we weren't together as a family. The farmers gave us shelter and food and in return we worked for them. It was a fair exchange, I thought, and I have mostly pleasant memories of my time in the Eifel. I learned after the wheat or rye was cut to gather it, tie the stalks into sheafs, and to lean them upright against one another so they would remain dry until collected. Later I helped to beat the wheat and rye on the hard floor of a barn with hand implements to separate the grain. It was the way people had done things for hundreds of years. It was as if I lived in the Middle Ages, but it was 1943 and 1944. I remember the festive atmosphere on the farm when a pig was slaughtered and processed into hams, bacon, sausages, meat, and lard.

I entered school in 1943, but that didn't last long. Once we moved to the Eifel that year mother never enrolled me in school. What I learned she taught me—writing, reading, addition, and subtraction. Formal school didn't begin for me until after the war. In the Eifel mountains we were not totally removed from the impact of war. By 1944 the Aar valley was bombed and I saw the effect of many bombs hitting simultaneously, a *Bombenteppich*. First the *Tiefflieger* came down the valley and attacked with their guns and cannons anything that moved. Then came the bombers dropping their many bombs. In the winter of 1944 to 1945 we children played with our sleds in the snow. German soldiers also transported their weapons on sleds. I must assume as an excuse for those who flew the airplanes and fired on us that they couldn't tell the difference between children and soldiers. The *Tiefflieger* came and attacked us—tatatatata, tatatatata went their guns. Fortunately no one was hit. They also fired at individual cows, but never at a herd of cows.

Around Easter 1945 I attended a communion at the farm where my older brother was staying. We all sat around a long table eating a rare serving of cake. Here came the bombers and unloaded their bombs on us. I still hear my brother calling out to me, "Hurry up, Karl, and come in here." I was trying to finish a last piece of cake. I ran into the house and threw myself under the table. "*Hinwerfen, hinwerfen*," the farmer screamed. A powerful shock wave from the explosions rocked the house, but none of us were hurt. In the seventies and eighties, when I could occasionally still hear the sound of old piston engine airplanes, their passing immediately brought back the memories of war, of machine guns and bombs. When I hear such sounds they still bring back the memories of sudden terror from the sky. Those feelings will never go away.

Ground combat I don't recall. I recall German troops moving east through our village, retreating. Then it was quiet except for the *Tiefflieger*. The ground war passed us by. I only experienced the war from the air, first in Köln, then in the Eifel. In May 1945 we returned to Köln. The war was over. Our apartment was still there, but everything in it had been stolen or destroyed. The windows were broken, the roof was damaged, the door broken down. We moved in and made it liveable. I vividly recall this phase of my life. We lived in Köln on the outer Kanalstrasse. Across the street from us was a Kaserne occupied by German officer prisoners and English guards. We learned what MP meant, military police. To us MPs had the power to regulate and decide all and everything. They were everywhere on their motorcycles or in jeeps. The English were cool toward us Germans: distant, not warm and friendly like the Americans supposedly were. I heard from friends that the Americans were generous and warm, especially to children. That was not the case with the English.

I watched the German officers in the *Kaserne* and noticed that these prisoners had more privileges than we had on the outside of the fence. I saw them reading newspapers, lounging in the sun, eating real meals. The German prisoners of war were released before winter set in. Then came Belgian troops. They were more sympathetic to us than the English. With them we could do a little black market trading. They were approachable and wanted contact with us. Young women began to go out with the Belgians, something the English soldiers didn't do at that time. I never met Americans, but my wife told me about her experiences when American forces occupied the region where she lived. Apparently black Americans especially were attracted to children and were kind and generous to her. One gave her an orange. A whole orange for herself. I never had a whole orange. I picked up orange peels dropped by English soldiers and took them home. My mother cleaned the peels, ground them up and added them as seasoning to pudding or anything else which would be enhanced by the taste of orange peel. We Germans lived off the garbage of the occupation forces. If I would have to characterize the American, Belgian, and English soldiers of 1945 I would say the Americans gave things; the Belgians traded; the English did neither. None of them took things away from us. If someone says it happened, then it probably did. But I never experienced it or heard of it myself.

We children accommodated our play to the new world around us. When our world changed, we tried to find a fit. House ruins were everywhere. We went through the ruins looking for food and clothing. What we found we took home. An abandoned antiaircraft battery was nearby. We played with the guns and the ammunition. Some of the guns turned in a circle, and we played carousel on them. The ammunition we took apart and then exploded the rods of gunpowder in the gun pits. At times this brought us in conflict with the English MPs. We laid telephone wire which was lying about in abundance and hooked up field telephones. Our play was with the residue of war, and we thought it was great fun.

As we returned to school our play assumed new forms. We played a game called Landa. Landa meant *Land abstecken*, to conquer and take possession of another's land. To lay down new borders. We found a piece of soft ground and assigned countries to each other with rivers and bridges. We took turns throwing sharpened sticks into what on the ground had been designated a bridge. If I hit a bridge three times with a stick, it was destroyed, and I could move on and bomb the interior and carve out sections of land to add to my own. I now know that we children played a game which reflected the political situation of Germany and of Europe.

How did we live? We had a small garden plot which we cultivated intensely. We worked for a potato farmer. The potatoes we collected the first and second time across the field were for the farmer. After that anything we found on that field was ours. We collected heads of wheat and rye which had fallen on the ground upon harvest. We ground the kernels into flour. We collected sugar beets. My mother cooked the green tops of the sugar beets into a spinach. We ate turnips. We ate anything at all. My older brother and my mother at times took the train into the Eifel. They took some of the little we had, bed linens or a tablecloth, and traded it to farmers for a little tallow or whatever they could talk the farmer out of. We collected apples off trees growing on the roadside or in a remote meadow. We constantly had our eyes open for food.

We had nearly no fats; instead, fish oil was occasionally provided in various forms—cod liver oil, which my mother administered to each of us by the spoonful every day, when it was available. At times it came mixed in a white emulsion which disguised its awful flavor. There were even little balls of cod liver oil. To this day I don't like the smell and taste of fish oil. Of course we received rations and had ration cards—not enough to keep a person alive. We received a ration of cigarettes, and since my mother didn't smoke, she traded the cigarettes for bread and meat. At night there was a curfew—we had to be inside by eight or nine. But if we wanted to get bread at the bakery the following morning we had to devise ways to get out there early, because the baker never had enough bread. Late at night my mother, my older brother, or I would sneak outside and lay in a ditch near the bakery. Others would join us, and that was the line for the next morning. When morning came we all got up out of the ditch and lined up in front of the bakery.

In school we received a bowl of broth every day. One day it would taste like Maggi, another like cocoa. There were various other flavors. But it was always a flavored, watery broth. There was never anything in it, like meat or vegetables.

We also needed to stay warm. To do that we children stole coal. But since we were Roman Catholic, stealing was a sin which required absolution. Our needs and the situation made it difficult for my mother. It wasn't easy for her to teach us one thing and then ask us to do something different. But help came unexpectedly from Cardinal Frings for the parishioners living in his archbishopric. He recognized the people's needs and gave a blanket absolution for stealing *if it was for the purpose of feeding and preserving self and family*, and only for immediate usage. His ruling did not permit large-scale stealing, nor permit obtaining large quantities of anything to last through the winter. But it provided sufficient elbow room for us children to go out and steal enough coal to heat our apartment, one day at a time. For those Catholics, such as my mother, who even in spite of hunger and cold had moral conflicts about taking anything, Cardinal Frings's humanistic ruling resolved the dilemma. Doing what we did then became known as *fringsen*. We went *fringsen*, not stealing.

In later years I studied sociology at the university. I found as a result of some research I did that there were two types of losers in that war—those who lost material possessions and those who also lost material possessions and lost members of their family, like I lost my father. I frequently found that as we children grew up we sought out as partners people who had experiences similar to our own. We looked unconsciously for men and women who had also lost members of their family, not only material possessions. I believe our experiences, even if unrecognized by ourselves, seemed to influence our choices in life. Both my younger brother and I married women who lost members of their family in the war.

My mother never remarried. For one thing, she was Roman Catholic, and she was a war widow. The position of a widow in German society then was different than what it is today. It was a position which bestowed a certain status on a woman—a woman without a man, like my mother. Devout Catholics viewed widowhood as nearly a holy position or state. Another man for such a woman was often unthinkable. It bordered on sacrilege. Her *Aufgabe*, her mission, was to raise her four children rather than fall in love with another man. Widowhood, especially a *Kriegswitwe*, a war widow, elicited a certain amount of sympathy and support from others who still had their husbands.

Karl Kremer resides with his wife in the old and picturesque Rhein River town of Remagen. From his window he can see the abutments of the

War from the Sky

Remagen bridge, which at one time in March 1945 was hotly contested by German and American forces. The bridge elicits no memories from either husband or wife; instead, they simply watch from their balcony as heavily laden riverboats move past, a reflection of Europe's current prosperity and calm. After much consideration and many delays, they allowed themselves to bring back memories they clearly would rather have kept buried.

Ina
Hesse

{Age 6}

Westerburg, Rhineland-Palatinate

The bombing of German cities cost the Germans much in production and more in the diversion of military resources to defense; but we must nevertheless state that no critical shortages in war commodities of any kind are traceable to it. To cause inconvenience and unhappiness to the enemy is a reasonable military aim in war, but in view of the promises made by Douhet and his followers, and in view also of the great military resources invested in it, the urban-area bombing of World War II must be set down unequivocally as a failure.

—Bernard Brodie, *Strategy in the Missile Age*

I was in the kitchen and Omi was serving *Schwarzwurzeln*, salsify, with a cream sauce, *Salzkartoffeln* and meat dumplings—I am certain of that because salsify was one of my favorite foods. I was holding out my plate for Omi to fill when the bomb exploded and the air pressure threw me against the steel door leading to the center shelter room.

—Ina Hesse

My father, Alfred, was in a *Nebelwerferabteilung*, a multiple rocket launcher unit, about fifty kilometers outside of Moscow in late 1941. He was killed that year. I was just two years old then and never knew him. My mother, Hertha, and I lived in Leipzig where I was born. My father's parents owned a delicatessen store in Leipzig. I was an only child. Mutti was twenty-eight years old. After my father's death she decided to return to Westerburg, her hometown. Her plan was to leave me with her parents, Anna and Ewald

Previous page: Ina, 1945

Seekatz, and continue her studies at the university in Frankfurt to become certified as a pharmacist, studies which were interrupted when she and my father married in 1937. Westerburg lies a few kilometers north of Limburg, a typical small town such as one finds all over the Rheinland, with a castle ruin on top of a hill and a church steeple below.

My grandparents' house sat at the bottom of a valley with a small stream flowing behind the house. The stream had a tendency to overflow its banks in springtime and flood our basement. Across from the stream the granite mountain rose steeply up to the castle. Several deep caves had been dug into the side of the mountain. One cave was used by the power company, which also had a dam across the stream further down; another cave was used by the local brewery. Into these caves we fled many times during air raids. I remember my grandparents carrying me into the brewery cave in a laundry basket. I must have been ill, or I would have walked as I did all the other times we hid in the caves. Most times we sought shelter in our basement. The house was built in 1890 and was of sturdy stone and brick construction with a grey plaster facade. The center room of the cellar had supportive stone arches, reinforced with additional timbers placed beneath the arches. We built a wooden floor several inches above the basement floor, because when the stream flooded some water always ran into our basement, and also it was easier on the feet. In early 1945, when the bombing became a near-daily occurrence, we moved into the cellar permanently. Until then Westerburg had been a safe and tranquil place for me to grow up in.

We had a bedroom adjacent to the centrally located cellar room which served as the air raid shelter. A steel door separated this room from the other cellar rooms. We also had a kitchen down there. We were totally self-contained in the cellar. The cellar became a family room in the truest sense of the word. Some of our neighbors who had no shelters in their houses also came to stay with us at times. Our cellar was probably the most secure place in the immediate neighborhood, other than the caves. At least twice I remember bombs falling and exploding nearby. On one occasion I was in the kitchen and Omi was serving *Schwarzwurzeln*, salsify, with a cream sauce, *Salzkartoffeln* and meat dumplings—I am certain of that because salsify was one of my favorite foods. I was holding out my plate for Omi to fill when the bomb exploded and the air pressure threw me against the steel door leading to the center shelter room. On another raid the electric power went out. It was pitch black in the basement, and we were trying to feel our way into the shelter. Mutti had returned from Frankfurt for a visit. Some of our neighbors were already in the shelter, and they were eating their dinner when the lights went out. Mutti was feeling around with her hands trying to find a chair to sit on. She grasped the back of a chair and carefully sat down into a plate of mashed potatoes someone had put there before the lights went out.

The air raids were usually directed against a railroad bridge about a mile down the road from us. Our house was the first house on the road from the bridge. The roof was badly damaged, and the windows were blown out. Structurally the house remained sound, and we could continue to live in it. Another frequent target for attacking aircraft was a nearby cemetery, or at least that's where they dropped their bombs. The real target, a munitions dump located near the cemetery, they missed. The cemetery and the surrounding woods were blanketed with bombs, and the craters are still there today. Omi and Mutti wouldn't let me outside to play because of the unpredictability of the air raids. When I could go outside it was only in the back of the house in the garden, and I was instructed not to stray far from the door to the cellar. Much of the time I spent inside the house. After the bombing attacks things usually were dusty and dirty. Mutti would give me a dust cloth and tell me to dust. That way she kept me busy and my mind off the world I was living in.

I remember when the Americans came in April 1945. I was nearly six then, and I stood with my grandfather at the gate to our yard watching their huge trucks pass by our house hour after hour. Grandfather had a wooden leg and held my hand. I don't know how he lost his leg. I wore white high-top shoes, I remember. I was not afraid of the Americans. On the contrary, I felt good. I felt relief. I don't know why. It was just so. The Americans stayed in Westerburg for a while. They were unobtrusive, and if I hadn't seen them come into town I wouldn't have known they were there. There was a labor camp with foreign workers outside of town. The Americans opened the camp, and the people could go wherever they wanted to. Our neighbor was a jeweler. Some men from the camp broke into his store, breaking down the door and the store windows. My mother, who spoke good English, ran to the American military police station while the robbery was still in progress. The Americans came immediately with a truck and arrested the robbers. As the Americans led them away one of the robbers yelled at us, "Ami not do anything to me. Tonight we'll come and cut your throats." We were so scared by this threat, we spent several nights with my aunt who lived in town. There was no police, no one to turn to for protection.

We were lucky living in the country. I don't ever remember being hungry. We had a big garden behind the house where we grew nearly everything we needed. Omi would make jam, jelly, juice, syrup, pickles, and put up vegetables. Whatever you can think of, Omi did it all. And to this day I remember how a lot of those things were done. How to make sauerkraut with a slicer, then put it into a crock. Omi would go into the cellar once a week to wash off the rock on top of the kraut and stomp the aging kraut properly. She did the same thing with the green beans. She would pick over the apples and make sure the apples and potatoes were stored separately, because they didn't like each other. The carrots she put into sand for the winter so they would last. When she made jelly she put a stool upside down and tied a cloth to its legs. Then she strained the fruit mash through the rag, the juice running into a bowl. From the juice she cooked jelly. I especially liked her red currant jelly. Of course I had to help with everything. I peeled the apples for applesauce, shelled beans, and cleaned and prepared vegetables to put up for winter. I didn't play much. I always worked. Although I didn't think of it as work.

There was a dairy within walking distance up the hill from us. We often went there, taking huge buckets to get thin buttermilk. Everything was big or huge to me then, I was still a small child. Omi would let the buckets sit on the back of the stove where the watery milk would curdle. Then she poured the bucket into a rag and hung the residue outside to let the remaining whey drain. What was left was cottage cheese. That way we got our protein. I still make cottage cheese that way to this day, but of course I don't hang it outside my door like Omi did. To get cooking oil we went into the woods in the fall with bed sheets and placed them under beech trees and shook their branches. The little beechnuts would fall on the sheets, and we then traded the nuts at a mill for oil.

Our family grew as time passed. My mother's brother Günther returned after his release from an English prisoner-of-war camp. Her sister Margot and her two sons, Ludwig and Hanno, frequently ate with us. And often we had some of our neighbors eating with us also who didn't have anything themselves. There was always a large group of people to feed every day, so Omi got very good at stretching whatever food she had with flour or water. Scrambled eggs, for instance, she would stretch by adding flour. She was the greatest gravy maker. Gravy could be stretched to infinity with water and a few herbs and spices. To this day I like anything with potatoes, noodles, dumplings, and gravy, our staple foods. The other thing we had a lot of was soup—bean soup, lentil soup, pea soup. Between the garden, the chickens, and the buttermilk, Omi got us through the war and the early years after the war. As a result of my childhood diet, since we had nearly no meat to eat, I never developed a real taste for meat. I could easily live without meat. For us a standard dinner was cream of wheat, porridge, or rice pudding.

Flour dumplings with applesauce and a little bit of browned butter was delicious, I thought. Potato dumplings made from raw potatoes were really good. Once Omi made potato dumplings with a rich cream sauce for my uncle. My uncle Günther was still being held in an English POW camp and somehow managed to obtain a temporary release to visit us. He had the cream sauce with his dumplings while the rest of us had applesauce. He got very sick because he wasn't used to having fat in his diet. Although I never did any cooking myself, I was always there to observe Omi and to help her prepare the meal. That's how I learned to cook.

When we were not cooking or preparing food, which was much of the time, we were doing laundry. We would do laundry every four weeks. It was a major undertaking. We changed our underwear once a week. The laundry was soaked the night before, then put into a big kettle and boiled. Only then was the laundry washed by hand on a washboard. If it was white stuff it would go outside on the lawn to bleach in the sun. I would have to go out with a watering can three or four times a day and sprinkle the sheets and the shirts. Then the white stuff would come back in and be rinsed, put through the hand wringer, and hung up outside to dry. We folded the linens and took them to the nearest *Mangel* where they would be pressed. Laundry day was a major operation and took a whole week from beginning to end. As for our own hygiene, we took a bath once a week. On the other days we just had a sponge bath in the evening. When my cousins were there we took our bath together. There was no question about it, because that was the only time the hot water heater was heated. We didn't have electric power for a long time and had to use the wood-fired water heater.

There was the black market where one could trade for nearly any-thing. Mutti traded her wedding dress for one hundred pounds of sugar. We needed the sugar to make jams and jellies. My aunt still had some blue denim work pants. My grandparents owned a dry goods store in town, and my aunt traded the pants to farmers for food, and then she traded the food for tar paper for our roof, which had been damaged in an air raid. We picked up coal that had fallen off passing coal trains, and collected horse manure off the street to fertilize our garden. Nothing that was dropped or grew went to waste. As for treats, there wasn't much. Omi made some sheet cakes occasionally—plum, apple, and *Streuselkuchen*. Once we had raisin bread. I still remember the raisin bread because it was something very special. I never really felt deprived, though. Maybe that was because we were all in the same boat. Nobody I knew lived better or worse than my family.

The Americans moved on, and we found ourselves on the very northern edge of the French zone of occupation. My mother, who had obtained her certification as a pharmacist early in 1945, just before the war ended, went to Marburg to find work. She often went back and forth by train from Westerburg to Marburg. Westerburg was French, Marburg was American. Occasionally I accompanied her. As a child I needed no pass. But Mutti had to obtain a special pass to travel between Westerburg and Marburg. At the zonal border the train stopped, and the French and American military police would check passes. Not every time was Mutti able to obtain a pass from the French authorities, so she traveled without, hiding in the lavatory. I was always very scared that my mother would be caught and thrown in jail.

The one major difference between the Americans and the French was that the French kept us at a subsistence level, just a tiny bit above starvation. Without our garden it would have been very difficult to survive. Food rations became very skimpy. The Americans were much more generous. One day the French came and looked at my aunt's apartment. My great-grandfather had just died and lay in the hall in a coffin awaiting burial. They took her furniture, her silver and china and carried all of it out over his casket. It didn't bother them at all, but it bothered me.

I started school in Westerburg in the fall of 1945, of course with slate and slate pencil. We had no books, and later when we started using paper we did not waste any. If I needed a new notebook I had to take a bunch of rags to the local bookstore to get a new one. The paper was of poor quality, and the ink always ran. Through all my school years I had only two or three schoolbooks. We took lots of notes.

I stayed in Marburg with my mother off and on. Then in 1948 I contracted tuberculosis. I had to move out of my grandparents' house, because I would have infected my cousins who also lived with Omi and Opi. I moved in with Mutti in Marburg for two years. I was admitted to a clinic, and when the weather was nice they sat me outside under a tree. Nobody was permitted to come near me. I had to have better food to get well. The only way to do that was the black market. Mutti traded whatever things she still had to the American soldiers in exchange for coffee and cigarettes. Then she traded the coffee and cigarettes to farmers for butter, milk, and eggs. Slowly I recovered and was allowed to return to school. In school we were served one free meal every day—soup, a *Brötchen,* and on one occasion a chocolate bar. I put my bar of chocolate in my desk and somebody stole it. I was very, very upset over that.

Mutti took a job with the Americans as a cook in Marburg. I had my first banana. She would bring home leftover foods—bread and cake and other things. My first banana came from that source. Then I got to taste something really wonderful. I thought it was sweetened condensed milk. We later learned that it was a liquid ice cream mix. It tasted good, though, and I ate too much of it and made myself ill. She also brought home cans of peanut butter and creamed corn, strange foods which I had never eaten before. I had no idea what peanut butter was.

Through this early part of my life my grandparents were my focus. Although I visited my mother often in Marburg and even stayed with her for the two years when I was ill, I always returned to my grandparents. Then Mutti moved to Mainz, near Frankfurt, where she went to work for Blendax. There she met a coworker with a similar professional background. They eventually married and moved to Wiesbaden. In the meantime I lived with Omi and Opi. I spent most of my time with my grandparents, who for all practical purposes assumed the role of parents for me. My world was my grandparents' house, and I didn't go anywhere without them. The butcher and the baker were nearby, but that was as far as I went. I was isolated, with no close girlfriends, and as a result I never really played the games children play. I spent most of my time around adults. They were loving adults, but they were not children. I know I missed something important in my childhood.

I had no exposure to the politics of the time. I was just too young to have picked up on anything even if it had been discussed in my pres-ence. After the war people were busy surviving and staying alive, reuniting their families, getting a roof over their heads, finding work and making a living. In history class the material of recent times was presented in a matter-of-fact manner—it happened, these are the dates, those were the places. That was it.

We lived a frugal life, and to this day I am influenced by the way I lived as a child. I know where my money goes and what I am spending it for. I am not comfortable with debt. I still like a full pantry. This is funny, because I can just go down to a Giant or any other grocery store and buy whatever I want. But I still feel more comfortable having a full pantry. For instance, I lived in Florida when Hurricane Camille threat-ened. What was the first thing I did? I let the bathtub run full of water. Why did I do that? I thought about it. It is something I saw my grand-parents do when I was a child. When we had the bombing raids they filled our tub with water in case the water lines were damaged. I have a hard time throwing things away in our world of plenty. I don't like to throw away food, nor give away clothes that aren't worn out. I got my first store-bought coat when I was sixteen years old. Until then I wore someone else's hand-me-downs, or something altered by my mother, who was a good seamstress.

As for my father, I did not consciously miss him. I didn't know him. He was a picture for me. I never had a real father. My grandfather and grandmother gave me the love I needed. My mother was gone much of the time, but when I needed her she too was there for me. Not until I got older did I perceive that my father's death really affected my mother, and that to this day she has never really gotten over losing him. She would not speak much to me about him. My father's birthday was on the second of March. After she remarried and I moved to Wiesbaden with them, on the second of March each year, she would serve a special desert my father had liked. She didn't tell my stepfather what she was doing. I tried often to learn more from her about my father, but she wouldn't open up to me. I guess I still miss the father I never knew.

I met my husband, Stanley, for the first time in 1959 in Wiesbaden at a Porsche Club meeting. He was there on military leave from England. My stepfather drove a Porsche as well, and I had accompanied my parents to that meeting. The following year Stanley was transferred to Wiesbaden. He participated in Porsche rallies, met my parents at those rallies, and they got to know each other well. At first I saw Stanley more as a friend of my parents. I continued to see him, we began to date, and in 1961, the year Stanley was transferred back to the United States, we married. I was twenty-two then. I accompanied him on various military assignments until his retirement from the air force, when we decided to settle in Baltimore, a city with a German heritage. My mother lives in a senior citizens' home in Mainz. In May 2001 she is eighty-eight years old.

Hans Herzmann

{Age 12}

Remagen, Rhineland-Palatinate

Advancing on the right of the Ninth Army, the First Army captured the ruins of Cologne on 7 March [1945] against stout resistance. On the same day elements of its 9th Armored Division, probing to the Rhine further south, found the Ludendorff Bridge at Remagen intact and immediately crossed to the east bank, developing a small bridgehead. Such a windfall had been hoped for but not expected. . . .The bridgehead provided a serious threat to the heart of Germany. . . .It became a springboard for the final offensive to come.

—General Marshall's Victory Report, War Department, Washington D.C., 1945

I watched the American tanks as they rolled down the winding road into Remagen. There was no shooting. That afternoon the Americans crossed the Remagen bridge and almost immediately began to build a pontoon bridge a few hundred feet downstream from the old railroad bridge they had just captured.

—Hans Herzmann

I was born in 1933 in the little Rhein River town of Remagen to Christine and Paul Herzmann. My family lived on Pintgasse, the narrow cobblestone street that runs from the old market square down to the river. The house belonged to my mother's parents, the Strangs, who had lived in Remagen for generations. Under the Nazis we had to fill out an *Ahnentafel*, a genealogical table. On my mother's side we were able to go as far back as the 1700s. The Herzmanns, my father's family, were newcomers and didn't settle in Remagen until 1910 when the telegraph came. My grandfather supervised the installation of the telegraph lines in this area and then stayed on with the post office, which owned the lines. My father also went to work for the post office driving a postal truck, delivering the mail to the outlying villages in the Eifel. Both of my uncles, my father's brothers, also went to work for the post office. Understandably, in later life, I wanted to do something different. My mother of course did not work, as it was customary then for German women, and stayed home taking care of us children.

Neither my parents nor my grandparents liked the National Socialists. They never spoke of the Nazis, at least not in front of me. At age ten, when I joined the *Jungvolk*, I was strongly influenced by my peers and older boys, much more so than by my parents. I loved the *Jungvolk* and the uniform. We camped out, sang songs around campfires and participated in competitive sports, including firing an air rifle. I was a very good shot with the rifle and won many awards. Very important to both boys and girls, I believe, was that we got to wear uniforms. The uniform had an incredible pull for us. I don't believe that I was a Nazi at that age, nor were most of my friends, but putting on the uniform made us feel like we belonged to something greater than us. I believe uniforms are dangerous for young children to wear. They do something to children which they are not prepared for and are too young to understand. The older boys and girls who led us and to whom we looked up were in the *Hitler Jugend*, and they undoubtedly had political training. But in the *Jungvolk* it was still mostly fun and games, and that's what attracted us. The uniform was the glue that bound us all together, *Jungvolk* and *Hitler Jugend*. Of course I didn't know that then.

At home I perceived that my parents were trying to bridle my exuberant enthusiasm for the *Jungvolk*. Not so fast, was the message I got from my mother and father. My father only joined the party in 1942 when he was threatened with the draft if he didn't join. He was exempt at that time because he had a family. Three months later he was drafted anyway. I also recall my grandfather saying to me in 1941, I was eight then, "Remember my boy, everyone in history who has attacked incense and garlic lost." Incense and garlic was his way of speaking about Christians and Jews. When he said that to me I didn't understand what he meant. However, I understood that he was trying to hold me back in my enthusiasm for the uniform. So on the one hand I really liked belonging to the *Jungvolk*, on the other I received constant caution signals from my parents and grandparents.

In school there was nearly no political influence exerted. The reason is simple. All of our teachers were old. The young ones had been drafted into the Wehrmacht. I can't remember any of my teachers in Remagen whom I would classify as having been National Socialists. After the summer of 1944 school quickly degenerated because of the frequent air raid warnings. Air raid warnings didn't really mean anything to us children other than that we were told to go home, giving us lots of time to play. When finally bombs were dropped on us, then we saw things quite differently. I remember in February 1945 when Dresden was bombed. The sky was black with four-engined bombers passing overhead. They were not flying as high as they usually did, and I could see them clearly. I said to my grandfather, Why aren't our guns shooting at them? My grandfather said to me, "Boy, just think of it. If every one of those airplanes dropped only one bomb, then this whole area would be flattened. Let them fly. The people at the guns know what they are doing."

After the war, when I was seventeen or eighteen, I asked my father, How could you have possibly voted for Hitler in 1933? How could your generation vote Hitler into power? He replied, "You'll never understand. We were hungry. Our children were hungry. Hitler promised work and bread." My parents of course didn't show their antipathy for the National Socialist party to the outside. Their circle of friends also included Germans of the Jewish faith. My mother and I frequently visited one good friend of hers who owned a grocery store in town. One day we met this friend of hers on the street. I noticed that the woman wore a yellow star on the lapel of her coat. My mother stopped to talk to her, but to her astonishment her friend waved her on saying, "Please

don't stop and talk to me. Your husband is a *Beamter*, a civil servant. It
is too dangerous. It may cost him his job." I didn't understand what she
was talking about, but didn't spend any time thinking about it either.
After the war I remembered this chance meeting. Then I knew what
the woman had tried to tell my mother.

The air raids in our area began sometime late in 1944. As the raids
came closer and closer to Remagen, my mother moved with us children to the Bergstrasse, the home of my paternal grandparents, on the
west side of town near the Apollinaris Kirche. There we stayed during
the day. My grandmother had persuaded my mother that it was safer for
us at her house during the day when most of the air raids occurred. At
night we came back to our own house on Pintgasse. On March 2, 1945,
my grandparents' house was destroyed by a single bomb. The house had
a cellar with four rooms. The ceiling and walls of the room which
served as our air raid shelter had been reinforced with sturdy beams.
The bomb crashed through the roof of the house and exploded in the
cellar room next to the shelter. Nine people were in the shelter—three
survived. My mother died, her sister, the twins, Christa and Rolf, who
were not quite two years old yet, my grandmother, and my father's sister. Two of my sisters survived, Hilde and Anneliese. Anneliese is a
year older than I, and Hilde was only seven then. An aunt, a sister of
my mother's, also survived. This aunt lived to be ninety years old, but
in the explosion she lost her hearing as well as one eye.

At the time of the attack I was at the Apollinaris Kirche, very close to
my grandparents' house. I was helping in the construction of an air raid
shelter. I didn't like going into a cellar. I was deeply afraid of being buried
alive. In late 1944, just before Christmas, a bomb buried two of my
cousins. It took twelve hours to free one of them, sixteen hours to free the
other. They were stuck between collapsed walls and beams. I crawled
down to bring them water to quench their thirst. After that experience
no one could get me into a cellar. I always found a way to be outside.

I saw the aircraft that dropped the bomb on the house. It was an
American double-rump P-38 Lightning. The P-38 was being pursued

by two German fighters, and I could imagine that the American pilot released the bomb as an emergency measure to escape his pursuers. When the bomb dropped and exploded I had of course no idea where it hit. I was standing near the Apollinaris Kirche when a neighbor woman came running up the narrow street, out of breath, looking for a priest to give the last sacrament to people who had just died in the air raid. Her face was streaked with dirt. She had helped trying to uncover the dead and the survivors. When she saw me she cried out, "Oh, my God, there is the boy." She thought I had died in the cellar along with the others. At that moment it became clear to me that the bomb had hit my grandparents' house. I ran down the road and helped claw through the rubble of the house looking for survivors. They first found Hilde and put her on a truck to take her to a hospital. I ran over and jumped on the running board of the truck, wanting to take a look at my sister. An SA man in full uniform, Brockel was his name, recognized me. He slapped me hard across the face. "Down with you," he shouted. He was a big man. I kicked at him. A German soldier involved in the rescue saw what was happening and took me away. He led me back to the Apollinaris Kirche, trying to calm me, telling me about tragedies in his own family. Once I got to the church I sat down. I didn't know what to do. My world had collapsed, and I felt totally helpless. One of the Franciscan monks came over and said, "You can stay with us, my boy. We'll take care of you."

The same day I heard that my older sister, Anneliese, had also survived. Only her hair had been singed off her head, other than that she had suffered no physical injuries. Hilde, my younger sister, survived only by a miracle. Hilde had sat on the lap of my father's sister when the bomb exploded, with her head on her aunt's shoulder. The aunt sat with her back toward the bomb blast and was killed instantly by bomb shrapnel. Hilde's head must have been slightly above her aunt's shoulder because on the exposed portion of her head she had five deep shrapnel wounds. She was unconscious when they found her. I retrieved Hilde three days later from the hospital at Rolands Eck and carried her on my back for several miles to the Apollinaris Kirche, where I bedded her down in the cell the monks provided for me. Anneliese was put up with relatives in Remagen. When Hilde awoke she didn't remember anything. She didn't know me, didn't know Anneliese, couldn't recall anything of the previous seven years of her life. She never regained her lost memory. The first day of her conscious life began in March 1945.

Only a few days later the Americans came. I remember the exact time when they arrived, around two o'clock on the afternoon of the seventh of March. I saw the last German soldiers fleeing before the Americans as they came past the Apollinaris Kirche. The soldiers' condition was dreadful. They came on foot or with horse and wagon. Their deplorable condition became even more obvious to me when I saw the well-fed, warmly clothed, and heavily armed American soldiers, rolling down the road toward town in tank after tank. Theirs was a real army. At exactly twelve o'clock an older German soldier came accompanied by two very young soldiers. They had crossed the Rhein on a motorboat, and brought the screw of the boat with them, which they hid near the church. They each carried a *Panzerfaust*. One of the Franciscan monks standing near me said to them, "Now, boys, let's not start a war around here."

The older sergeant said to the monks, "We still have many German soldiers which have to get across the Rhein and we know the American unit coming this way. We faced them in the Ardennes. All we'll do is kill the first vehicle that comes down the road above us, that'll give us two more hours to get our soldiers across." The three German soldiers then climbed toward the road above the church through a pine thicket. Soon I heard an explosion and within minutes the three of them came running back down the hillside. Then they calmly sat down with the monks and drank a bottle of sacramental wine. The sergeant told us that they damaged an armored scout vehicle as it slowly drove past them. They hit it in the rear. I later learned that no Americans were killed in that attack. One of the monks said to the three German soldiers calmly drinking their wine, "You must hurry and get out of here."

"No, no," replied the older *Feldwebel*, "just look overhead. They are doing exactly what we expected they would." We looked up and there was a light American plane scouting the area, trying to determine the scope of the German opposition. The wine finished, the three soldiers took their boat screw and nonchalantly walked down the hillside toward the Rhein. Two monks and I walked up the hill to the gravesite of the Counts of Fürstenberg. There we waited for the Americans to arrive. Eventually an American patrol came down the Apollinaris stairs. The stairs led up to a religious statue. We didn't hear the American soldiers coming until they were on the last three or four steps, almost upon us. They walked without making a sound. Father Kamillus whispered to me, "Be silent and don't move." The Americans looked at us, but continued past without stopping. It was two o'clock.

After the American patrol passed we walked back to the church. The Americans had secured the church, sent the monks to their cells, and the rest of us they put into the air raid shelter we had been working on. I sneaked out of the shelter and hid among the vines of an adjacent vineyard. From there I watched the American tanks as they rolled down the winding road into Remagen. There was no shooting. That afternoon the Americans crossed the Remagen bridge and almost immediately began to build a pontoon bridge a few hundred feet downstream from the old railroad bridge they had just captured. The Apollinaris Kirche sits on a hillside overlooking the town of Remagen and the Ludendorff Railroad Bridge. An American officer and three sharpshooters scanned the valley below with binoculars, watching the fleeing German troops. I heard the officer give commands to the sharpshooters. They knelt down and fired. Suddenly down below a German soldier fell down. I got up and walked over to the officer, grabbed him, and shook him. He turned around and slapped my face, hard. I was so shocked at his action, I fell down. Then I fled into the church.

After three days the Americans evicted all civilians from the Apollinaris Kirche, as they thought a German artillery spotter was using it and directing German artillery against the bridge below. I carried Hilde on my back to a small village, Nierendorf, about seven kilometers away. There we stayed on a farm. The farmer knew my father when he still drove the postal truck and delivered the mail. So he took good care of us. Once the battle moved past Remagen across the Rhein, I returned to Remagen and left Hilde and Anneliese with relatives. I moved into a rudimentary block house built from old railroad ties near the Apollinaris Kirche. There were American antiaircraft guns on the hillside and from those soldiers I got some food to live on. When the mayor of Remagen, a friend of our family, learned of my life, I was informed to report to his office with my two sisters to get some money. It was a ruse. When my sisters and I showed up at the designated place, there was an American soldier waiting for us with a jeep. The soldier drove us to an orphanage. The orphanage supervisor beat me, so one dark night I escaped. I was walking through the forest, trying to get to an uncle's house, when I walked right into an American antiaircraft position. This was in May 1945. Suddenly someone grabbed me from behind. I flailed my arms trying to get away, but the American soldier, who was huge and black, just held me up with one hand as if I were a bundle of rags. He dragged me into a tent where I was interrogated. When they learned where I wanted to go, two of the black soldiers put me in a jeep and drove me to my uncle's house. I stayed with my uncle for about a week. Then I decided to rescue my two sisters from that awful orphanage.

My plan was to row across the Rhein in a boat and take my sisters to a friend of my mother's in Runkel, a small town east of Remagen. I found a boat, but had no oars. In the morning I saw a young woman come running up the road toward my uncle's house. His was the only house there, so she had to be coming to see him. People normally didn't run like that. I said to my uncle, My father has returned.

"You are talking crazy, boy," my uncle said to me. But I jumped on a bicycle, and as fast as I could I rode toward the young woman. "Your father has returned," she shouted as I got close. I ditched my bike and ran into Remagen. When I got there, my father was shaving in a neighbor's house. Our house was all boarded up, because the windows and the doors were broken during the air raids. He had been released on the twenty-eighth of May 1945. Only three weeks after the war ended. He was wounded on the eighth of March, the day he was notified that his wife and two children had died in an air raid. He stayed with his unit in the Heidelberg area and then retreated with them into Czechoslovakia, where they surrendered to the Americans. His American camp commander had studied in Bonn and spoke perfect German. When he learned my father was from Remagen he called him into his office. They talked for a while, and then the American confessed to him that as a student he drank away his money in Remagen in the Hotel Fürstenberg. He said to my father, "I am going to release you to Bonn, in the English zone. Remagen is in the French zone. I can only release you to the English or American zone. When the train stops in Remagen, where it will stop to get water, get off. We are going to leave here shortly, and the Russians will take over this area. So get out as quickly as you can," which my father promptly did. We got Anneliese and Hilde out of the orphanage and moved back into our old house on Pintgasse.

One immediate problem arose between my father and me. He had to establish that he was running the show, not his twelve-year-old son. I was used to responsibility by then and resisted. While he was away in the war it was I who fed the rabbits. I killed them to put meat on our table. I took care of our five beehives, fed them sugar water, and later retrieved the honey. I had my own, self-imposed tasks in support of my family, and I wasn't ready to again become just an obedient little boy. So we had a lot of friction between us, and we never totally worked it out.

The Rheinhotel no longer exists, that's where the Americans lived and ate. The hotel was down on the river. In front of the hotel stood several waste barrels in which the soldiers dumped their leftovers after they finished eating. For a time we lived off those barrels. I retrieved the meat and washed it, once I got home, then we reheated the meat and ate it. Hilde, Anneliese, and I went down there nearly every day. We were hungry, and we knew the Americans had food. The garbage cans were always full of surprises—chicken bones with still lots of meat on them, and thick slices of white bread. Often the bread was soggy, but we ate it anyway. The soldiers sat on the hotel balconies smiling, their rifles near them, watching us eat. Hilde was a cute little girl and occasionally they gave her a few cigarettes, saying to her, "For Papa." Hilde got to know one of the soldiers quite well, his name was Jimmy, I believe. He gave her a four-leaf clover hand carved from ivory. He told her it would bring her luck, and Hilde wore it on a silver chain around her neck for many years. There were white and black American soldiers, but they were all American soldiers to us. We weren't afraid of them.

One time a group of soldiers stood on a balcony of the Rheinhotel and tried to have a little fun with us. They dangled chocolate bars before us, tied to strings. When we reached for the bars they quickly pulled them up, out of our reach, breaking into simultaneous loud laughter. They thought it was great fun watching us children scramble for their Hershey bars. I thought there had to be a way to get those chocolate bars. I walked around the corner of the house and then returned unobserved under the balcony and grabbed all the lines in my arms. That was the end of the game.

I remember a Major Miller. He was a tall, fine-looking man. When he ate at the Rheinhotel, he would always come outside with a bowl or two filled with food and let us take what we wanted. He also told us what we should take out of the garbage barrels and what not to take. We were always happy to see Major Miller. The hotel was an off-limits zone, but we neighborhood children went there anyway, and the Americans tolerated us. The American soldiers were kind and generous to us children as well as to the adults. There were some of course we learned to avoid. You could tell who they were by the way they looked at us, by the way they carried themselves. But most were nice, black and white. I wonder today how the soldiers saw us. I hope they didn't see us as little Nazis.

Nevertheless, the Americans had killed my mother. I loved her very much, and her death was a great loss to me. When the American troops first entered Remagen less than a week after her death, I wanted to hate somebody for what had happened. I knew my reaction was unreasonable, even as a twelve-year-old boy I knew that, because the soldiers had nothing to do with my mother's death. Yet my sorrow demanded that I had someone to blame. But within two weeks, I believe, not much longer than that, I saw the Americans as ordinary people. People just like us. And with that my hate disappeared. My mother's death became an accident of war for me, with no one to blame. That's how I dealt with my sorrow.

My father married again, but for me his new wife never became my mother. Every Christmas Eve I had to play Christmas songs on the piano before we opened our presents. When it came time to open the presents I went to my room and cried. I cried for my mother. I missed my mother. When I was seventeen my father came to me and said, "You can't do that to Nora anymore. If you can't deal with your behavior I am going to have to give you a beating." I said to him, "If you do, I'll fight back and you'll lose." I couldn't give up my mother for Nora. My mother's picture still hangs in my home. Her death was a terrible loss. Although I think I dealt with her death, I never got over it.

Later that year school started again. The Americans had gone by then, and there were no more garbage cans with food for us. We were served some food at school—a ladle of rice, or soup; we had to bring our own utensils. Sometimes we were given a thick slice of white bread, or a candy bar, or a cup of cocoa. That's how we hung on.

My father's new wife, Nora, worked on a nearby farm. Occasionally she brought home some potatoes, at other times some funny-looking bran, something I thought was fed to animals, not to humans. She baked the bran into bread. I recall when eating this bread having constantly to spit out hard shells. It was awful bread, but it was food. Nora counted off the slices for each of us—two for me, two for Anneliese, and one for little Hilde. I was always hungry, and at times little scrawny Hilde would take pity on me and give me her slice. Two or three times a week we children went out to nearby villages to beg for food. I put Hilde in a little handwagon and pulled her behind me. We never got much going from door to door. A few potatoes, sometimes an egg. In the fall we went into the forest and collected beechnuts. We took them to a miller who weighed them, and for each pound of nuts he gave us a small amount of beechnut oil. That was really special to us, because then we could fry our potatoes in oil rather than in *Katrainer* ersatz coffee.

It was a special occasion when they killed a pig on the farm where Nora worked. Not that she got any of the meat or lard, but she could take the water in which they had boiled the blood and liver sausage. Nora brought home as much of that broth as she could carry and we all thought it was very good and nourishing. Ration cards were issued, but the trick was finding a store that had something to sell. Nora sent the girls out to stand in lines as soon as they got home from school. We stood in lines even when we didn't know what it was they were selling. If there was a line, there was something we needed. We had nothing. It seemed to me that life went on like that for a long time. It was a few years after the war ended before it got better again, and we were no longer hungry.

How else did war influence my life? To this day I believe I need to have a well-stocked pantry. I just don't feel comfortable unless I have an ample supply of staples in my house. Also in my professional career as industrial manager I always took the safe course of action. I never took any risks if it wasn't necessary. Although as a child in 1944 and the immediate years thereafter I took many risks, once I got older I played it safe. I can't explain my behavior other than that it was war related. I retired at age sixty-three and moved back to Remagen. This is my home, and it is where I want to live.

I asked Hilde, who had lived in Remagen her entire life, how she thought war had affected her.

Oh, those days of course left their mark on me. I taught my children never to throw away bread. Now I work in the kitchen in a hospital. It's incredible for me to see what we serve our patients, how little they eat, and how much of that good food we throw away. I feel it is a sin, and it pains me to see all that food wasted. I remember Nora counting off the slices of bran bread for me and my brother and sister. Admittedly, my early youth was awful, I can see that today. It seems I was nearly always cold and wet and hungry. Although that life seems awful in retrospect, at the time I didn't perceive it as especially painful. I didn't know anything else. I had no memory of a better past, and also children see things differently. They tend to take the world the way they find it. When the bomb erased my memory I knew nothing better than what I saw and experienced in Remagen. That world of burned houses, a bridge lying in the Rhein River, people dying of hunger and disease, that world was normal for me. My older brother, Hans, and sister, Anneliese, of course had known better times and saw things a little differently. They suffered more than I did, I believe.

Part II

War on the Ground

The great migration stretched from Königsberg and the Samland, from the ferries at Pillau along the Frische Nehrung, to Danzig and on through Pomerania to the banks of the Oder River—two hundred fifty miles of snowbound roads, sands, and marshes. In endless procession the horse drawn wagons moved, at times three abreast. Beside them, men and women dragged along on foot.

—Juergen Thorwald, *Defeat in the East*

The uprooting of the Germans from the east comprised two phases, both tragic in their effect: the first was a panic flight from the Red Army; the second a deliberate expulsion of populations from regions of settlement where Germans had lived for generations, in some places for a thousand years. The flight of January 1945 was an episode of human suffering almost without parallel in the Second World War—outside the concentration camps. Terrified at the thought of what the Red Army would do to the first Germans it encountered on home territory, the population of East Prussia, already swollen by refugees from the areas of German settlement in Poland and the Baltic states . . . left home en masse and, in bitter winter weather, trekked to the Baltic coast.

—John Keegan, *The Second World War*

War on the Ground

The war on the ground began nearly simultaneously for those living in east and west Germany. In late 1944 British and American forces were arrayed along the western border of the Reich, first threatening, then slowly penetrating into the mountainous western regions of the Eifel. In October, Aachen, a city founded by Roman legionnaires, was the first to fall. The western Allies reached the Rhein River by March 1945, and in April the armies of the West and East made first contact at Torgau on the Elbe River.

In the East advanced elements of the Red Army were within a hundred miles of Berlin by January 1945. In contrast to the West, where most Germans remained in their towns and villages, frequently greeting American forces as liberators, Germans fearing rape and death fled the Red Army by the hundreds of thousands. Violent behavior by Allied troops against German civilians was rare. In the East, however, violence against civilians was the norm. Red Army atrocities in East Prussia were widely propagandized by the Nazis, who hoped to strengthen the staying power of German troops. Instead, the propaganda served to terrorize the civilian population and sent them fleeing west. By late 1944 the sight of *Flüchtlinge*, refugees, passing through German towns with their horses and wagons had become common. I recall seeing these wretched columns of *Flüchtlinge* passing through my hometown of Sagan in Niederschlesien, exhaustion showing in their faces, fear in their eyes so palpable it terrified me, a nine-year-old boy. I didn't know that by January 1945 I would be one of them.

In East Prussia and Pomerania the majority of fleeing Germans were cut off by Russian armored forces. The German *Kriegsmarine*, which until then had largely been known for the U-boat war it waged in the Atlantic, turned into a rescuer of epic proportion, conducting the largest seaborne evacuation ever undertaken. Nearly 2.5 million people, mostly refugees, were evacuated by the German navy from the eastern provinces. This feat was executed through mine- and submarine-infested waters and while under frequent attack from enemy aircraft. Although the evacuation was a huge success, the resultant losses were some of the greatest experienced in maritime history.

Nearly all of the Germans who fled the East and escaped the Red Army felt lucky, believing that fate had been kind to them. The rest hunkered down and awaited their fate, which for some was worse than anything they could have imagined and for others was uneventful. Among all the mayhem and brutality were acts of kindness by Russian soldiers, some of them quite extraordinary. The Russians were especially kind to children, often sharing the little food they had.

In the West the American GI made his more benign entrance. To observers American soldiers seemed to be mostly men who had done their duty and wanted to return home as soon as possible. They entertained themselves by freely sharing their rations with grateful German children—Hershey chocolate bars, chewing gum, oranges, and grapefruit.

The behavioral contrast between soldiers from the East and West as observed by children surely reflected the norms of their respective societies. These same people, children then and now in their sixties, surprisingly carry no hate, grudges, or hostility within themselves as a result of their experiences. They exhibit instead immense tolerance and a willingness to reach out to one-time adversaries to further understanding and reconciliation.

In contrast to the war from the sky, the war on the ground had one characteristic that was very different—it had a human face.

Annelies
Sorofka

{Age 12}

Landau, Lower Silesia (Poland)

With nearly two million Russian deserters and former POWs at large in Soviet-occupied Europe, it is no wonder that banditry . . . became a serious problem.

—Norman M. Naimark, *The Russians in Germany*

At night the bandits came. The bandits were Russian deserters, Poles and Czechs. They came to plunder and steal whatever we had left, and rape the girls and women. I recall the Czechs were the most brutal. They broke into houses, and if they found a woman they raped her continually, and if she resisted they beat, shot, or stabbed her.

—Annelies Sorofka

Annelies Sorofka lived within a few miles of Breslau, in a village just off the Autobahn leading from Breslau to Berlin. At night she could hear German bombers passing overhead; they dropped relief supplies to the Breslau garrison and bombed Soviet positions. She heard Russian planes going in the opposite direction trying to locate and bomb the German airfields. ("After a while I could tell apart the Russian from the German planes by the sound of their engines," she said.) Annelies was reluctant to give the interview, to revisit such a painful period of her life. As she spoke her eyes at times filled with tears, her voice became unsteady. None of her pain appeared to have been diminished by the passage of time.

I was born on October 9, 1933, the youngest of five children, three girls and two boys. My brother Walter, the oldest, was drafted into the

Wehrmacht early in the war. He participated in the Battle of France in 1940 and brought home seashells from the Bay of Biscay. In March 1943 Walter was killed near Kharkov; he was twenty-one years old. I still miss Walter, and his picture hangs in my study over my desk. In 1944 Werner went to live with an aunt and uncle who owned a grocery and clothing store in the town of Weidenwerder. They had no children and planned for Werner to eventually take over the store. Werner was killed by a drunk driver on his honeymoon soon after the war ended. My older sister Elsa also lived with my aunt and uncle in Weidenwerder. In 1945 she was doing her *Pflichtjahr* of housework with them, rather than with a family of strangers. In 1945 only my sister Luzie and I lived with our mother in Landau, a beautiful Catholic village southwest of Breslau. Landau's tree-lined main street was flanked by prosperous farms and neatly kept houses surrounded by carefully kept yards. We had our own village smithy and a creamery, a grocery store, and a dry goods store. Our church was surrounded by a large cemetery where my father, Ludwig, was put to rest in 1942 when he died of cancer. He had lost his left hand in an accident at the brickyard—the reason why he had not been drafted. A large, beautiful mansion stood at the east end of the village, surrounded by lush meadows where yellow buttercups bloomed in springtime, and camomile grew in abundance in the warm days of summer. For me Landau was a place of beauty and tranquility until 1945.

Since our village was Catholic, numerous small shrines showing Jesus on the cross or Maria holding the baby Jesus were located at road crossings, near the church, and at the entrances to the village. We children were taught by the nuns and the priest that when we passed an icon we should bow our heads and make the sign of the cross. I did that without fail. We also had to say *Heil Hitler*, that's what our schoolmaster taught us. We did that too. Even then I knew that the two didn't really go together, the worship of a man and the worship of God.

I thought my mother was beautiful in a country sort of way. Like me she was thin, which made her seem taller than the five foot, five inches she really was. She carried her brown hair in a bun as it was customary in our Christian environment, and of course she wore no makeup. She was born in Jacobsdorf in 1896, one of the many villages nearby where everyone including her father worked on the local *Gut*, a large estate. There were few other jobs available. Before my mother got married she held a job on an estate near Posen as a *Stubenmädchen*. She soon was promoted to be first *Stubenmädchen*, which meant that she supervised other servants. Working for nobility provided my mother with the opportunity to learn about the finer things in life—how to dress properly, set a table, eat properly with knife and fork, and many more things a simple village girl normally would never know about. As a result my mother's demeanor, dress, and language became refined. She was by nature a gentle person, a perpetual optimist, and a woman who viewed life as a gift from God. Ernestine, a name she went by for all of her life, was forty-nine years old in January 1945. She had already lost one child to war, and she was a widow.

In January 1945 the first *Flüchtlinge* from the East began passing through Landau, heading west. The weather was terrible. We took in a mother and her four children for a night. We felt sad the next morning when they left. I remember how I cried as they were leaving us. It was bitter cold outside, the road was icy and the snow was deep. Little did I realize that only two weeks later it would be our turn. Landau was situated near the Autobahn to Breslau. Neudorf, another village, lay two kilometers to our west, and Kanth, the nearest town, was three kilometers past Neudorf. At night, two weeks after the refugees came through Landau, we heard a tremendous noise coming from the Autobahn, like the loud rattle of chains. My mother went upstairs and looked out a back window and saw Russian tanks rolling down the Autobahn. Landau was filled with German soldiers, several of whom suggested we leave because they anticipated a battle.

It was still dark when the farmers started assembling with their wagons on our main street. My mother, my sister Luzie, and I joined up with the Kalms, our next-door neighbors, since we had no wagon of our own. We had already packed some things in case we should have to leave on short notice, but if there ever was an optimist it was my mother. She said to Luzie and me, "We don't need to take much, we'll be right back." Luzie had our photo albums in her hands. Mother said to her, "Leave them. We won't be gone for long. No need to take them. Nobody will touch anything in our house." So we ended up taking very little because of my mother's ever-optimistic outlook on life. We took a large wicker trunk full of assorted things and two bicycles, although we couldn't ride the bicycles because of the deep snow.

The only escape route open to our trek was to the south, toward the Czech border and a mountainous region, the *Zobten Gebirge*. We started early in the morning. It was still dark. The road was covered with snow and ice. The horses had difficulty finding footing on the icy road and frequently slipped, some fell. The road got progressively steeper. Our progress was excruciatingly slow and difficult. We could walk faster than the horses could pull the wagons. My mother, Luzie, and I walked next to our wagon. At times I just sat in the snow on the side of the road and watched as the poor horses struggled. It was heartbreaking to see the animals trying so hard, only to fall down and have the wagon slide down the hillside. The men had to constantly put something under the wheels, boards and blankets or whatever they could find, to get some traction. The farmers had taken as many of their horses as they could and they switched them out frequently. We did this day after day for an incredible three weeks into February. People put us up at night or let us rest on their farms. I don't know how we survived in the snow and the ice, but we did.

We finally ended up in a small mountain town, Falkenberg, near the Czech border. There we stayed. The horses were exhausted, and so were we. We didn't know where else to go. Mother, Luzie, and I stayed in a house occupied by an old lady and her middle-aged daughter. The house was high up on a steep mountainside. We drew our water from a hand pump in the yard. Life was very primitive. We survived mostly on flour soup—flour cooked in water. After staying in that remote mountain town for several weeks, a German military convoy passed through town heading west. The convoy was several kilometers long. We asked them where they were going. "To surrender to the Americans," they said. "The Russians are right behind us." Our trek leader thought we too should leave. So all of us from Landau got our few things together, got back on our wagons and followed the fleeing German army unit. It was evening by the time we left town, already dark.

About an hour out of town my mother said to Luzie, "Oh, I've forgotten to take the cake. I baked a little cake, and I should have taken it." Somehow she must have gotten some ingredients to bake a cake, and she had left it behind. Food was very precious. "I want to go back and get the cake," she insisted. Luzie and I protested loudly. No, you can't do that, Mama, we implored her. Not only was the mountain road icy, but as we came down from our house to join our wagon train, we had heard women screaming and crying in houses we passed. There was no law anymore and the many foreign workers who had been assigned to work the small mountain farms were taking revenge and raping and beating the women they once worked for. No, we don't need the cake, Mama, we pleaded. Stay with us. Don't go. "Yes, we do need the cake," she insisted. She turned around, the night was pitch black, and disappeared into the darkness. She got the cake. On the way back, walking in the dark, she came to a fork in the road which she didn't recall being there. She took one fork, hoping it was the right one. "I thought I would never see you girls again," she said when she finally caught up with us after midnight.

We never once rested. We walked all night until the following afternoon when we entered the little town of Braunau. I was so tired and worn down I wasn't sure anymore if what I was experiencing was real. I didn't know if I was dreaming or if I had already died. We stopped and I sat down in the snow in the ditch by the side of the road.

About the time the German convoy and we refugees entered Braunau from one side, the Russians entered Braunau from the other. The German soldiers were not combat troops. As the Russians came upon them they shot many of them, the remainder they took prisoner. The Russians went methodically through every car, truck, and wagon. One German soldier hid in one of our refugee wagons and stayed with us until we returned to Landau. I don't know what happened to him then. The Russians threw everything out of the German military vehicles onto the road. I was sitting exhausted in the ditch by the side of the road, watching the goings-on, not knowing where I was or understanding what was happening. I was so exhausted that I didn't know if what I saw was real or a dream, didn't know if I was alive or dead. I prayed to God to help me find out where I was. And then I thought I heard a voice, and it said to me, you have not died. You still live on this beautiful earth. I got up and was fine.

Luzie and I were very hungry, but even more thirsty after having nothing to drink for most of a day. We found a water faucet in a building across from where our wagon stood and finally were able to quench our thirst. We retrieved as much food as we could off the road. The Russian soldiers watched, but didn't bother us. We thought they would kill us like the German soldiers they had killed before my eyes, but instead they told us to go home. On the way back to Landau we saw what the war had done to our beautiful country. Most of the villages we passed through were destroyed by the fighting. We slept outside. I became so used to sleeping outside, I viewed the sky and the stars as I would the ceiling of a room.

The war-ravaged villages we passed through were depressing. Finally our trek came to the last village before Landau. It was evening, and the people decided to stay there and move on in the morning. I believe they feared to see what lay ahead and pushed it into the following day. Our wagons drove into the large yard of an estate with a beautiful manor house. It was the only building still standing in the village. We entered the house. It had been plundered. No furniture remained in any of the rooms. Blood was everywhere, on floors and walls. Gruesome to look at. With all the blood in the rooms, people still slept there. I guess in war everything is different.

You just sort of survive every day and try to stay alive. Nothing else really matters.

My mother didn't want us to stay in the bloody rooms. "You sleep on the wagon," she said to Luzie and me. The trek wagons were covered by tarps, and we were used to sleeping outside. The next morning when mother came to wake us—Luzie was gone. My mother was frantic. Everybody was frantic wondering what had happened to Luzie. Someone finally said, "I saw a girl walking down the road last night. It was a full moon, so I could see her, but I don't know if it was Luzie." My mother and some others ran down the road leading to Landau looking for Luzie. They found her sitting by the side of the road. "It was the moon," Luzie said, "that made me do it." I believe she was just tired and wanted to go home.

That morning, the twentieth of May 1945, our wagon train reassembled and set off for Landau. The closer we got to our village the more people craned their necks to see if the village was still standing. The first thing we saw was the church steeple, a joyful sight. As we got closer we saw that with the exception of some outlying barns the village did not seem to have been damaged extensively. However, when we got into the village and took a closer look at the houses, we found incomprehensible devastation, like the setting for a horror movie. I began to comprehend the meaning of war.

Our furniture had been smashed, much of it burned in front of the house. In the ashes my mother found the iron parts to our bread machine and the syrup press, the remains of picture frames and the seashells my brother Walter had brought home from the Bay of Biscay in 1940. The lower level of our house was filled with an assortment of trash and human waste. It was impossible to enter our basement or the cellar in any other house. The stairs were strewn with rubble and feces. Outside every house lay mounds of clothing and linens and kitchen utensils, manure and human waste mixed among it all. The Russians had made a field hospital out of our next-door neighbor's three-story house. The floor of every room was covered with bloody mattresses. Although our village had appeared whole when we first saw it, the interior of every house was a shambles.

We had noticed a putrid smell when we approached Landau. First we thought of dead soldiers. Then we discovered the true source of the stench—dead animals. Our animals. There was not one animal left alive in the entire village. Bloated cadavers lay in yards and gardens, in the street and on the sidewalk—dead horses, cows, pigs, sheep, cats, and dogs. They had been shot and left where they fell. Cow and pig heads, guts, udders, skins and bones from slaughtered animals used for meat by Russian soldiers lay on the road and in front of houses. Animal carcasses had been thrown into our community wells, contaminating the village's water supply. The first thing we did was bury the animals and clean the wells. Of course we didn't have electricity either. I found blocks of wax which soldiers used to clean artillery barrels. I made candles from the wax by melting it down, pouring the wax into a handmade form and putting a string down the middle when it began to harden. The village didn't get electricity again until February 1946.

My mother, Luzie, and I got busy cleaning our house. We went through the trash outside and retrieved beds, tables, and other furniture. A hammer applied here and there made them, if not pretty, useable. We had to think about our future and planted some potatoes and beets in the garden behind our house.

In all the ugliness surrounding us a surprisingly nice thing happened one day. My cat showed up, holding her tail high and meowing. I was delighted to see my cat again. After a while I could tell she wanted to tell me something. She kept on walking in circles toward our barn in back of the house. Then she climbed to the second floor. I put up a ladder and followed. There, in the straw, lay a litter of kittens. A week later I went back up to the barn loft to check on the kittens. I wanted to bring the kittens down and find a better place for them in our house. I had the kittens in my apron when I heard a noise behind me. I turned and I saw a Russian soldier coming up the ladder, pointing a pistol at me. The soldier had a submachine gun slung over the left shoulder and bandoliers of ammunition wrapped around his upper body. He looked fearsome. I thought, now I have to die. He kept talking as he approached me, waving his pistol back and forth. I continued to back away from him. I backed up until I couldn't go any further. Behind me was a small open window with a single iron bar across it. I grasped the iron bar in one hand, still holding the kittens in my apron, and prepared to jump from the second floor of the barn onto the concrete below. Then the soldier suddenly turned around and left. I watched him walk away until I could no longer see him before I came down the ladder. After that experience I was afraid every waking hour.

In the following weeks we had so little food people ate each other's cats and dogs. Not their own, but their neighbors'. One day my cat didn't come home. I knew what had happened to her, and it made me very sad. All the village cats vanished. There were no dogs. The once numerous village sparrows steadily dwindled in number until they also disappeared. Although we boiled our water for twenty minutes once the wells had been cleaned and the water began to flow again from our faucets, sickness came anyway. Typhus and cholera. People died. My father had worked for the mayor of our village until he died in 1942. As the single village employee he had done everything from picking up the ration cards in Breslau to digging graves. When he passed away my mother assumed his duties. There were only a few old men left in the village. The younger men had all been drafted, with the exception of a few farmers who had to take care of not only their own farms but also those of their neighbors who had been drafted.

The first three weeks after our return were quiet. Then the terror started. The Russians came usually during the day and took whatever they wanted. No one had a radio, watch, clock, or sewing machine anymore. Pianos and other large items of furniture were taken away on horse-drawn wagons. The Russians took our clothing, my sheepskin, and our blankets. One day three soldiers came and took Mother's only nice dress, the black dress she wore to my father's funeral. Then they searched and found our last piece of bread. We went hungry for days afterwards. Mother took Luzie and me by the hand and we went begging. A few weeks later a Russian unit came into the village, rounded us up, and marched everyone out into the fields to bring in the harvest that had been planted the previous fall. After we manually flailed the kernels from the wheat, rye, and oats, the soldiers drove off with the grain. Our reward for this hard labor was a bowl of potato soup. The meat disappeared from the soup after the first two days.

At night the bandits came. The bandits were Russian deserters, Poles and Czechs. They came to plunder and steal whatever we had left, and rape the girls and women. I recall the Czechs were the most brutal. They broke into houses, and if they found a woman they raped her continually, and if she resisted they beat, shot, or stabbed her. When we heard the bandits—they always fired their guns—my mother, Luzie, and I hurried outside. We had learned that staying in the house was the worst thing to do. In the house you had no place to hide or run. One night the Russians came and rounded up most of the village horses and many of the men too. All that remained in Landau were women and children and a few old men.

Just because the war was officially over, it wasn't over for us. Another kind of war was raging, and it was much worse than anything we could have imagined. I cannot even put into words the terror, the horror, and the fear I felt in that year until we finally left in 1946. I just don't have the words to describe what my family lived through, night after night, day after day.

The Kalms lived next door to us. Erich Kalm was taken away by the Russians when they came for the horses. Frau Kalm was terrified to be alone, and she had a little baby boy. My mother let Luzie stay with Frau Kalm to help her care for the baby. I continued to stay with my mother. One night the bandits came and went next door to the Maders' house. The mother, father, four daughters in their teens and early twenties, and two young children of one of the daughters lived in the house. One of the Mader girls escaped and came screaming past our house to warn us. "Frau Sorofka," she shouted, "they are coming, they are coming." She was in tears, terrified. My mother and I quickly ran into the street, away from the Mader house. Herr Sauer, another neighbor, was in the street already. He too had heard the Mader girl's screams and come outside. He was older, that's why he hadn't been drafted and the Russians hadn't taken him. Herr Sauer, Mother, I, and the one Mader girl stood on the sidewalk in the dark to watch for the bandits, listening to the screams of the Mader family as the women and girls were being raped.

Then Herr Sauer said to my mother, "Frau Sorofka, you better step back. They are going to shoot when they come out of the house." After they finished raping they always fired their guns indiscriminately down the street into the dark of the night. I stepped away from our little group. Then the shooting started. One bullet passed through my mother's shoulder, but when it happened she didn't know she had been shot. Another bullet hit the left arm of the young Mader girl standing next to my mother. The night was pitch black. No moon. All I could see were dim outlines. When we reached our door my mother said, "I feel weak, Annelies. I think I've been shot."

I said, Oh, no, no, no, Mama, that can't be true.

Mama said, "*Ja*. I think I am. I can feel the blood running down my body." Others had been hurt too. One of the Mader girls we heard screaming had been stabbed by her assailant seventeen times. After the bandits left, someone got one of the few remaining horses in the village, collected the wounded, loaded them on a wagon and drove them to Kanth. Kanth had a Polish hospital. At the hospital they bandaged people's wounds and provided some extra bandages, but refused to give them medicines or keep anyone for treatment because they were Germans.

When my mother got on the wagon I asked her, What am I supposed to do now, Mama? I am all alone. She said to me, "Go home and go to sleep." I thought my mother was dying and I would never see her again. At age eleven I thought if you were shot you had to die. I went home and went to bed. The next morning when I awoke, Mama lay next to me in the other bed.

Every day more people were shot. I had seen all this often enough to know what came next. Soon the bullet wound would get infected and pus would ooze from it. Then they died. To me, there was inevitable death at the end of a bullet no matter where it hit. I was elated to see my mother again, but I thought I knew her fate. She lay there sleeping, a bandage covering her wound. The Sauer girl who had been hit in the arm had a bandage wrapped around her wound too when I next saw her. Her wound healed and she didn't die, but her arm was forever useless. To my great surprise, her sister, who had been stabbed seventeen times as she struggled with the rapist, also survived.

My mother lay in bed getting sicker by the day. The pus came, and I was sure she was dying. I cannot describe the depth of my sadness watching my mother lie there, knowing she was dying. I wanted to do something, not just sit and watch her die. It was the time when the camomile was in bloom. Although I was afraid to go outside, I went to the meadows by the mansion and picked camomile flowers. I boiled the flowers and strained the tea through a cloth. I boiled the cloth first to disinfect it. Next I washed Mama's wound with the tea and covered it with the tea-soaked cloth. I washed her bandage with ashes because I had no soap, boiled it, and dried it again before repeating the process. I did this over and over again. It kept me from thinking too much. After awhile the pus disappeared, and I could see the hole the bullet had made. I was all alone. No one came by to check on us.

Annelies handed me a diary in which her mother, Ernestine Sorofka, had recorded their day-to-day suffering. "It is the first of January 1946. The night is quiet. Not a sound. No joyously tolling bells from church towers. We pray to our God to help us bear our burden in the coming year, to help us get from one day to the next. Since returning to our village last May I dug 15 graves. It is very cold again. We have no coal, only wood, which we laboriously carry from the forest to our house. And the forest is so far away. Life has become so difficult. Everything we need to stay alive we have to make ourselves. We grind flower from kernels of rye and bake our own bread, cook syrup from cattle beets, spinach from whatever greens we can find, and we press oil, the only fat we have, from rape seed. It is so hard to keep our clothes clean without soap. I use ashes from the kitchen stove. There is no other way. I got a small tree from the forest for Christmas and Luzie and Annelies decorated it with their own creations. Annelies made candles. Who would have thought that some day we would experience such awful times. Sunday—I visited my old father in near-by Jacobsdorf; Monday—I went into the forest for wood; Tuesday—I got sick from tonsillitis. Wednesday—Luzie cut her foot with the axe chopping wood. Thursday—Annelies came down sick."

Annelies continued.

I got very sick. I don't know what it was, maybe strep throat, or diphtheria or something like it. My mother thought I would die. I couldn't talk anymore, but my mind was clear. Herr Sauer came by to sit with my mother. I think it was a death watch. I understood every-thing they said. They were talking about me dying, and I was thinking, I can't die, I can still think and hear them. But I couldn't talk or open my mouth. I had big sores around my mouth, in my mouth and down my throat. One day the priest came. He gave me the last sacrament, came close and blessed me. I thought that was so precious for him to come close to me, because everybody else was afraid of catching what-ever I had. After several weeks I got well.

In March 1946 Frau Kalm received a letter from her husband. He was one of the men who had been taken away with our horses by the Russians in June of 1945. Now we had hope that others might be alive as well. Martha Kalm's joy was short lived. Her husband was shot and killed try-ing to escape the camp he was in. My mother dug the graves by hand for all who were killed by guns or died from disease. It was very hard work. People made caskets if they could, but most were buried without a casket. I always wanted to help her, but she wouldn't let me. "Children shouldn't do that," she said. I went to every funeral if she let me go. Sometimes she would say to me, "Don't come today. We don't have a casket." The ceme-tery was like a home to me, I went there that often.

There was no school for German children after the war, but until January 1945 we had school. Our teacher was a strict old man and believed in Hitler. One day he told Luzie's class to finish a sentence, and to use their imaginations in the completion of the assignment. Then everyone would read his or her sentence to the class out loud, and they would briefly discuss it. The sentence was: "It could be possible. . . ." Luzie wrote, "It could be possible that we lose the war." The teacher was livid when she read her sentence to the class. The children laughed loudly, then froze into silence when they saw their teacher's crimson face. He screamed at Luzie and called her a three-horned cow. The entire village heard that Luzie Sorofka had said that it was possible we could lose the war. Luzie had said what people thought in secret but couldn't say out loud.

The first Polish families arrived in Landau in July 1945. Many more followed. They moved into any house they chose, and whoever lived there had to move out. A Polish mayor was appointed. His wife spoke fair German. I thought she was a nice person. They had three cows and asked me to watch the cows for them. In the morning when I arrived they gave me a bowl of milk and dumpling soup. I watched their cows without food and drink for the rest of the day. My mother had nothing to eat. After several days I asked the Polish woman if I could eat my bowl of soup at home. They were puzzled by my request, but let me do it. Mama and I shared the soup. Then I went and watched the cows. I don't know for how many weeks I did this until one day a boy I knew came running by; he also was a cowherd. He yelled at me to take my cows home quickly. "The bandits took my cows," he shouted. I took my three cows and ran them as fast as I could back to the barn. After that the mayor no longer let his cows out of the barn, and I didn't have a job—and no soup in the morning.

I was a tall skinny child, and the other children called me *Oma* because I liked to help older people. I visited them and talked to them. An older woman came by one day and asked my mother if I could accompany her to Neudorf. She wanted to see if she could find flour to bake bread. When we came to the Autobahn overpass we saw Russian soldiers coming toward us with their submachine guns at the ready. One soldier came over and motioned for us to turn around and go back. We hadn't gone far when suddenly shooting broke out. We ran into a rye field and lay down on our stomachs, making ourselves as small as we could. Then the bridge over the Autobahn was blown up. I had no idea what was going on. After it was quiet for a long time we finally got up and walked back to Landau. It was just another day in my life.

Frau Hoppe was an older woman who had three sons. All three had been drafted during the war. None of them had come home yet. Her daughter-in-law had come to stay with her. She stayed behind when the Russians came and was raped many times. Eventually she had a Russian baby.

In March 1946 Ernestine Sorofka records in her diary, "It has been three years since my dear boy Walter was buried in Russian soil. How painful it is for me to bear. But it would be even more painful if my dear son had come home a cripple only to see what had happened to his beloved home. We are working again, but for nothing. The Russians are having us fill in two kilometers of trenches running through the fields outside our village."

Annelies continued.

In April 1946 cattle trains were being assembled in Kanth. People were being evacuated. The Polish mayor knew where the trains were going. He came by one day and said to my mother, "You should go on the train that is now in Kanth. It is going west." Once he had told us to avoid a particular train, because "it goes to Siberia," he said. People had no idea where the trains went. They just got on. We walked to Kanth where Polish militia herded us, with hundreds of other people from other villages, into an open field. We stayed there in the open for several days. Luckily it didn't rain. I don't remember how we survived, because no one fed us or gave us water.

The Maders, the family with the four girls, had somehow been able to hide a large number of silver coins. We saw that bundles were being searched by the Polish militia when people boarded the cattle cars, and anything of value was being taken away. Frau Mader distributed the coins among her family, and she gave some to my mother, hoping that at least some coins may be saved. My mother hid some coins on herself, put others into Luzie's and my hands. The guards searched our bundles, but didn't search our bodies, so we got the coins through. Once the train got under way I remember the absolute silence in the car. There was only the sound of the wind and the train. A baby died in our car. It saddened me to see another death. I had seen too many people die over the past year. Just before we left Landau a girlfriend of mine died. Edith. One week we were running around and playing, the next week she was dead from typhus.

While on the train we were told nothing. We didn't know when the train would stop, or, when it did, for how long it would stop. People wanted to relieve themselves, but we were scared to leave our car because we saw them leave people behind at the first stop. When we crossed the border into the British zone of occupation, our first stop was Uelzen. There we were put into a temporary camp. I remember the white powder they sprayed all over us to delouse us. We had no lice. We had stayed clean. We were put into a huge camp of Nissen huts. We slept on straw spread on the concrete floor of the hut. We were fed soup once a day and given a piece of bread which was to last for an entire week. I trained myself to take one bite of bread every morning. In this camp they separated the people from our village and sent us to different towns in the British occupation zone. My family ended up in a small Protestant village near Hannover, Wülferode. Luzie and I walked three kilometers twice a week to a German prisoner-of-war camp where they had a Catholic chapel. We did this for as long as we were there—rain, sunshine, snow and ice, nothing kept us from going to mass and communion. I finally went back to school. I got some clothing from the Red Cross. A pair of shoes and a coat. Still, I had next to nothing to wear. My mother and Luzie found jobs. My mother worked in a hotel. She brought soup home every evening. Luzie worked as a maid.

In 1948, with the new money, our world changed for the better. But shattered lives still had to be put back together again. Frau Hoppe's daughter-in-law who had the Russian baby was in our camp. She worried constantly about her Russian baby. "What will my husband say when he comes home?" she lamented to my mother. My mother in her never-ending optimism tried to lift her spirits. "Oh, it will be all right," she said. I really don't know how it all turned out, but her husband did come home. As for the silver coins? Years later we tried to return them, but the Maders wouldn't take them back.

In the years that followed I never spoke of those days of horror. Now my mother is dead. I wished I had talked to her, because there are so many questions I have to which I have no answers. But when I was younger I was not ready to talk. My children have heard bits and pieces of my story, but never all of it. I don't really feel like recalling those horrible days of my youth. I am just happy to be alive. I came away from it all with a deep sense of insecurity. What made me overcome my legacy of those days of horror was my deep belief in God. It gave me the strength I needed to move forward. After all, life is a gift from God. It is sacred. You can't just throw it away.

In the early fifties Annelies was a talented gymnast and dancer, performing with an entertainment troop throughout western Europe. A knee injury put an end to her dancing career. She met and married an American air force captain and accompanied him to the United States. After raising three daughters, Annelies opened a gymnastics center in the greater Washington, D. C., metropolitan area. Like others I interviewed, Annelies had been reluctant to meet with me, and only with the encouragement of one of her daughters did she finally relent. At times I saw her battle back tears in her expressive eyes: large, searching eyes, like those of a deer trapped in the headlights of an onrushing car. For Annelies the headlights are a war that came to her many years ago when she was a very young child. For her those lights have never been turned off.

One of her daughters wrote, "I find her childhood difficult to comprehend. Her experiences differ so greatly from anything I have ever seen or experienced. I have always found her stories from the war hard to believe." It is a comment I heard all too frequently expressed by children of German refugees.

Bernd
Heinrich

{Age 5}

Gut Borowki, Wartheland (Poland)

We moved at least 30 miles eastward of the line which originally had been set as the point where Allied and Russian forces would meet—and on Montgomery's orders, I clung to that "Wismar cushion," so that it could be used for negotiating purposes. We took it by force of arms, but we gave it up to the Russians later, as the diplomats and politicians came in to take over from the soldiers.

—General Matthew B. Ridgway, U.S. Army, *Soldier: The Memoirs of Matthew B. Ridgway*

An American lieutenant who had taken a liking to Ulla showed up one day. "Blondie," he said, "take your family and get out of here. Don't stop until you cross the canal." My parents harnessed Ulla's horses to an abandoned German army wagon, loaded the little we had onto the wagon, and moved out. At the bridge to the Elbe-Trave Kanal we were stopped by English sentries who wouldn't let us pass.

—Bernd Heinrich

I was born in 1940 on a large country estate by the name of Gut Borowki, pronounced Borofkee, about 120 miles due south of Danzig. The estate had been in my family for generations. Prior to the war that area of West Prussia had been Polish; and earlier yet, it was part of the German Reich under the kaiser. Today, it is Polish again. My mother, Hildegard, was of Polish heritage, while my father's heritage was German. During the war they kept my mother's ancestry quiet, because it didn't politically fit into the time. In late 1944 when the Red Army

---

Previous page: Bernd and his raven Jacob, 1950

reached East Prussia I was four years old. I had a younger sister, Marianne, born in 1941, and a very much older half-sister, Ursula, by a previous marriage of my father—we called her Ulla. Ulla was eighteen. My mother, Hildegard, a petite redhead, was born in 1921. In 1944 she was twenty-three years old; my father, Gerd, was forty-nine.

Farming did not particularly interest my father, and he employed a manager to run the estate. In World War I he served in the Uhlans, an elite cavalry unit. Then he transferred to the air arm. At first he flew reconnaissance over the western front, later bombers. He told me that Baron Manfred von Richthofen asked him to join his fighter squadron. "I told him," my father said to me, "that the life expectancy in a fighter squadron was just too low, and I declined his invitation." After World War I he devoted his life to the study of entomology, specifically the study of swift-flying insects, the *Ichneumoninae*. That was his life-consuming hobby, the only thing he never lost interest in. Although he never obtained a university degree, he became a well-known expert in his field, conducting his own expeditions to the highlands of Burma, Iran, and Africa. He also collected birds for numerous museums, including the British Museum and the Deutsche Museum, a sideline which helped him finance his insect studies and provided important contacts which proved invaluable in later years.

By 1943 my father was "encouraged" by the Nazis to enter the Luftwaffe, which he did in the rank of captain. He was assigned duties as an air base security officer at the small fighter base of Strebelsdorf, near Danzig. To insure that his unique and important insect collection would not be destroyed, he buried it. He soldered his precious collection in air-tight stainless steel containers, and with the help of my mother, Hildegard, skillfully buried the containers in a spruce thicket near our estate.

I have mental snapshots of the *Flucht*, our flight from the Red Army, but no comprehensive recollection of what happened in those early months of 1945. After all, I was not yet five years old in January 1945. Ulla, my half-sister, and my mother later filled in many of the details for me. The bottom line is, we made it. But so many *Flüchtlinge* didn't, that is the sad part. I keep thinking about them. It was mid-January 1945, I was told, when the sound of artillery could be heard at Borowki. The Russians were expected any day. My mother and father had worked out a plan. My mother was to come up to Strebelsdorf, the fighter base where my father was stationed, if she perceived we were in danger. If that failed, she was to head for Berlin, to stay with friends. On the twenty-third of January, when the sounds of battle were very close, my mother and Ulla loaded a wagon with food, clothes, and feed for the horses, bundled Marianne and me in heavy furs to protect us against the bitter cold, and drove off heading north. It was snowing heavily when they left the estate. The first several nights we stayed with friends. The sounds of battle came ever closer, and, according to my mother, we ended up being trapped. She did not know which direction to go in. A German Panzer unit bedding down for a night in the village where we stayed offered to take us along. They put Ulla, Marianne, me, and my mother in one of their medical Panzers. They had no wounded. We traveled with the German Panzer unit for many days. We went wherever they went. By the middle of February the soldiers we'd been traveling with put us on a military truck taking spare parts to Danzig. The truck took us all the way to the railroad station in Danzig, and, to my mother's great surprise, there were still trains running. We got on a train to Strebelsdorf and arrived late that night. There we learned that it was too late for us to get out over land. The Russians had cut the road between Danzig and points west. Our only alternative was to fly out.

By then my father had received a new assignment to an air base near Schwerin, east of Hamburg. At Strebelsdorf a Junkers-52 transport sat ready to evacuate women and children to Kolberg, from where they were to continue by ship to Hamburg. We boarded the plane along with others, only to sit there for hours. One of the plane's propellers had broken. We waited for a replacement propeller to be flown in on another Ju-52 bringing in supplies for the troops. The following day the propeller was replaced. Then the pilot announced that he didn't have enough fuel to reach a more distant air base, because Kolberg had been captured by the Russians. The quartermaster refused to give our pilot additional fuel. My father came up with a solution: a bottle of expensive brandy. He negotiated with the quartermaster for the additional fuel. When the pilot finally tried to run up the engines, the center engine failed to start. He flew us out on two engines, flying very low, shielded by the low-lying clouds from Russian ground fire. We landed at an air base to the west of Strebelsdorf, where we sat and waited while the bad engine on the tri-motor Ju-52 was being worked on. The following morning we reboarded the plane. Then the left engine failed.

In the meantime the runway of the air base where we had landed was being mined for destruction. The base people expected the Russians to arrive momentarily. All of us deplaned. The weather was brutally cold. My mother was getting ready to take Marianne and me and hide in the adjacent forest when the bad engine suddenly came to life. The pilot screamed, "Hurry, hurry, board the plane." German troops were ready to blow the runway when the ailing Ju-52 lifted off the ground. The flight was rough and bumpy. I remember feeling sick. Marianne happily played her mouth harmonica. We landed at an air base near Tütow, on the west side of the Oder River. Three days later we caught a freight train to Schwerin, where my father was to take command of an air base defense unit at a small Luftwaffe base. It was late February 1945.

The town and the air base at Schwerin were frequent targets of English and American planes. We were constantly running to the air raid shelter. My mother didn't think the shelter was safe, so we ran into the fields whenever there was an alarm. I believe it was on the thirtieth of April, the day Hitler committed suicide, or the day after, when my father sent us to Sulstorf, a nearby village. He had released all of his men at the air base, he later told me, and wanted to go into hiding himself. He did not want to become a prisoner of war. My father changed into civilian clothes, grabbed his bicycle, and pedaled to a prearranged hiding place near Sulstorf which Ulla and my mother had prepared for him. They had gathered pine branches and built a large brush pile at the edge of a forest clearing, making it look as if wood-cutters had left the pile of branches. Under the branches they hid several blankets for my father.

I believe it was on the second of May, late in the afternoon, when we heard vehicles moving into the village, sounding like tanks. Ulla sneaked a peek. In the street sat a tank with a large white star on its turret. She thought it was a Russian tank because of the star, and began to cry. Then someone shouted in English, "Come out, you bastards." We ran outside to greet the American soldiers. The war was over for us. The Americans handed out cigarettes to the women and Hershey candy bars to us children. Then they requisitioned our house. We had to find another place to stay. Mother found a hayloft in a cow barn and we slept there that night. At dusk she and Ulla walked to my father's hideout in the forest. He wasn't there. They left a note for him on the brush pile, telling him where we were. About midnight my father found us.

He told us that after he hid in the brush pile, a truck drove up and stopped in the clearing. SS soldiers got out of the truck and began changing into civilian clothes. They lit a fire, using branches from the pile of twigs my father was hiding under, and began to cook a meal. At the sound of approaching tanks they hurriedly left, leaving behind a crate of butter, potatoes, pots and pans, a typewriter, and a box of Iron Crosses.

Sulstorf soon turned into a huge prisoner-of-war and refugee camp. There was little food, even less water. The Americans shared none of theirs, not even the food they threw away. They put guards around their garbage dump to keep us away. Fortunately we had the food abandoned by the SS, and Ulla and my mother used the Iron Crosses to barter with the American soldiers for food. Ulla, who loved horses, found three abandoned German army horses and started riding them past the American camp site. Soon she was giving riding lessons to American soldiers. The GIs called Ulla "Blondie." An American lieutenant who had taken a liking to Ulla showed up one day. "Blondie," he said, "take your family and get out of here. Don't stop until you cross the canal." My parents harnessed Ulla's horses to an abandoned German army wagon, loaded the little we had onto the wagon, and moved out. At the bridge to the Elbe-Trave Kanal we were stopped by English sentries who wouldn't let us pass.

It turned out that two of the English soldiers guarding the bridge were Poles. My mother spoke to them in Polish, and they let us pass at night. We headed for Trittau, just east of Hamburg, where a prewar business acquaintance of my father's had a large estate. Once we arrived we found there was no room for us. The place was filled with refugees from the East. The estate bordered the *Hahnheide*, a nature preserve. We pulled our wagon into a cowshed for the night, at the edge of the *Hahnheide*. Exploring the forest we found a small window-less cabin belonging to the game warden. My parents located the war-den the next day in Trittau and gained his permission to live in the small forest cabin. The cabin was about twenty by twenty feet. It was to be our home for the next six years.

In the solitude of the *Hahnheide*, living off the land, I grew up. We were nearly always at the edge of starvation. It was a time when I was closest to my father, and I learned much from him about nature and biology. My father was familiar with woods and knew how to forage. We collected mushrooms and berries in season. Traded beechnuts and acorns to farmers for potatoes and beets. Farmers fed the acorns to their pigs; they pressed the oil out of the beechnuts and used the oil cake for feed. Fishing was the most fun. Not with a hook and a line, but with my bare hand. I caught brown trout by lying patiently on my stomach at the edge of a brook, very carefully reaching under an overhanging bank and catching the fish.

English soldiers occasionally hunted in the preserve. They were not good shots, and worse trackers. They would wound an animal and leave it to die. Circling ravens would show me where to find the dead animal. Occasionally we got a deer wounded by an English soldier. Once I found a wild boar in a thicket. The boar had long tusks. The birds had fed on

his innards, but his meat and fat was still good. We processed the boar
and lived off the meat for some time. Another time my sister, Marianne,
and I found a huge elk lying dead in a meadow. That night the whole
family dragged the carcass into a thicket where we cut it up. We hung
the meat in our chimney to keep it from spoiling. Large game, however, was infrequently available to us, so we trapped mice and shrews and
ate them. The skins we cured and stuffed, and later sold to museums.
We did the same with birds. One winter there came a time when we had
nothing at all to eat. We had eaten all of our dried mushrooms and
berries. I don't recall how we made it through that time.

   We sold our horses and the wagon early on to a farmer in Trittau for
sugar beets, potatoes, and milk. That food helped us through the first
summer and fall. My father also met a chemist, another refugee, and
the two set up a still at our remote cabin. Another refugee provided
several milk cans for the enterprise. In the dark of night my father and
his friends distilled alcohol from sugar beet mash. The resultant
schnapps he sold on the black market in Hamburg. It took all the
imagination we could muster and the help of each one of us to feed our
family of five.

   When I was nine years old I was totally at home in my forest environment. I had pet crows, jays, and pigeons—not in cages, but out in
the open. These birds would come to me when I called them, and I'd
feed them as they perched on my shoulders or arms. I raised Jacob, a
pet crow, from the time he was a fledgling. He was attached to me like
I was his parent. He followed me everywhere. We were different
species, but of the same world. Jacob was killed by a hawk. I missed
him. I collected insects too. I had a collection of beetles and another
of bird eggs. My pleasures were all derived from nature.

   Marianne and I went to school in a one-room schoolhouse in the
village of Hahnfelde. Like Hänsel and Gretel in the fairy tale, we
walked four kilometers each day through the forest to school, and four
kilometers back again. Marianne and I developed our own interests,
and only on rare occasions played together. At school I made one good

friend, Manfred. Manfred kept a pet owl. But Manfred's and my world did not truly meet. His world was in the village; mine was in the forest. I was a *Flüchtling*, a refugee. A lesser person. Manfred didn't come to visit me. In spite of all the hardship, I loved my life in the *Hahnheide*. I certainly didn't want to grow up and become an adult.

My father reestablished some old contacts to European museums, and we started collecting small mammals and birds for them. He would take me out with him into the forest. I would shoot birds with a sling-shot, and he and my mother, Hildegard, would prepare them. There were no reliable mail connections then, but my father had an acquaintance in the Netherlands who worked for the Bolls liquor company. He'd drive over to see us occasionally and take the stuffed birds with him. We got a little cash that way.

Before the war my father had written a two-thousand-page scholarly study dealing with the insects he collected over many years—the insects he buried near our estate in 1943 in their stainless steel containers. In 1947 he retrieved the manuscript from the Soviet zone of occupation, where it had been kept in safekeeping by a friend. He wrote Dr. Henry Townes, the leading ichneumonologist in the United States, and inquired what Dr. Townes thought of his study. Dr. Townes thought the study worthy of publication and sponsored our immigration to the United States. In April 1951 (I was eleven), we emigrated—my father, Gerd, my mother, Hildegard, my sister, Marianne, and I. Ulla had gotten married by then and stayed behind.

My father still had a prewar account with the American Museum of Natural History. Upon our arrival in New York a representative from the museum met us and presented my father with a check for three thousand dollars. That money allowed him to buy a farm in Maine. Marianne and I started school again in the fall of 1951, she in the fifth grade, I in the sixth. We both got good grades. My father, the entomologist and aristocrat who had never done physical work in his life, found himself making a living with his hands. He and Hildegard felled trees with a crosscut saw. The snow was deep, and they had to borrow a horse from a neighbor to bring the logs out of the forest. In that winter of 1951 to 1952 their labors earned them two hundred dollars. They knew they were not going to make it that way.

For me though, the old farm was a dream come true. For the first time in years I thought I had a home again. I played a lot in my new environment. In summer I searched for bird nests and watched bird behavior, in winter I packed a small rucksack and explored the ridges and swamps of my new world on snowshoes. I followed tracks in the snow. Built fires and roasted small morsels of meat. While I ate, in the solitude of the Maine woods, I dreamed about stories I had read by Jack London. Unfortunately my dream world ended all too soon. The following year my father got a job collecting birds and insects, something he was good at, and he and Hildegard set off on lengthy expeditions to Mexico and Africa. Marianne and I were placed in a school for indigent children in Hinckley, Maine, The Good-Will Farm and School. That experience was the most traumatic period of my life.

Marianne and I stayed at the school continuously for six years while our parents went around the world collecting birds and insects. At the school it was their policy that no one left for any reason, even if there was an opportunity for us to be with our parents. Either we were in, or we were out. Marianne and I were in. Deep down inside I never forgave my parents for tearing me away from our beautiful farm in Maine. I was totally in love with that place. They took it away from me without even a kind word to help me get over my loss.

The Good-Will Farm and School sat on a large tract of woods and fields and was largely self-sufficient. I spent a lot of my time in the woods, just as I had at *Hahnheide* and on our farm. My interest in nature deepened. Gordon Gould, better known as Lefty, was the postmaster at the school, and unwittingly became a father figure for me, partially because of who he was, partially because my own parents weren't there, and partially because of a particularly mean housemother. The housemother was a strict, religious person who among other things hated Germans. She called me "the little Hun," and didn't mean it as a compliment. She even tried to keep me from writing to my parents in German. I was in constant conflict with her. Lefty, on the other hand, was someone who listened to me. Not that I talked much, but he took the time to get to know me.

I was a mailboy, among many other things I did around the farm. Lefty, the postmaster, had fought with the 82nd Airborne Division in World War II and been badly wounded. He could barely walk. Whenever I brought the mail to him I lingered, and he'd tell me stories of the war. We formed a deep bond, and I stayed in touch with Lefty until he died. At the time I felt ashamed of being German. The constant hounding by my housemother deepened my feelings of guilt about my heritage. Lefty Gould, the wounded American war veteran, somehow put everything in perspective with the stories he told me about fighting Germans. And he always had a lot of good things to say.

He told me about the time he got shot up. Young German teenage soldiers picked him up and took him to a field hospital. The German doctor at the hospital told Lefty, "When you get back home your army doctors will tell you they will have to take that leg off. It is the cheapest thing to do. It will take a lot of work to keep that leg. You tell them that you want to keep your leg." It was exactly what happened when Lefty got home. The first thing the army doctor said to him was, "We'll have to take that leg off, Private Gould."

Lefty replied, "I don't want you to take my leg off."

"You'll have to die then," the doctor told him.

"Then I'll die," Lefty replied. He ended up being in the hospital for a year, but he saved his leg. I could tell I was not a Hun to Lefty Gould. There was no hate in his stories. To him I was just a boy from Germany. Lefty told me about a time in Belgium when they were dug in. They'd been there quite a while, shooting back and forth. One night when he was standing guard a German soldier held him up at gunpoint. He demanded his cigarettes, then he went back to his lines. Another time Americans were shooting at the German lines. A German held up a stick with a red flag on it, indicating that their shooting was bad and they hadn't hit anything. They did the same when the Germans fired. "We called it Maggie's drawers," Lefty said, when our German friend raised the flag. "When we finally attacked we made sure we avoided that section of the German line." That's the kind of stories I heard from Lefty Gould, and I began to feel better about myself.

I discovered that I was a good runner. In my senior year in high school we had ten meets, and I was first in nine of them. My principal suggested I go to the University of Maine because they had a great track team. I didn't have any dreams of going to college, my parents didn't have a penny to spare. But when the word "scholarship" was mentioned, I suddenly became excited. I went to the University of Maine to become a member of their track team and to study biology. But I never got a track scholarship. I ruptured a disc in my back in the weight room the first day I was there. I was totally laid up for a year. I lay on my back and studied. I passed my courses. How did I pay for school? I worked summers for a paper company in the north woods. I worked part time in the school cafeteria. I worked anytime I could. And I lived in World War II Quonset huts, which cost next to nothing.

After I graduated from the University of Maine I accompanied my parents on an expedition to Africa, a year in the jungle. It was exciting in ways, but not my kind of forest. When I returned it was 1964. I went to enlist in the airborne, to keep from being drafted. I was declared 4F because of my old back injury. One professor at the University of Maine who had befriended me suggested I get a Ph.D. and turn some of my experience in the forest into a thesis. So I went back for my master's degree at the University of Maine. The professor was impressed with my work and called his friend at UCLA. I was admitted to UCLA as a doctoral candidate, where I obtained a Ph.D. in zoology. In the process I discovered a new and unique method of how insects control their body temperature. I planned to come back to New England and settle on a farm. Instead, I ended up teaching and doing research at Berkeley. I stayed at Berkeley for ten years.

I feel fortunate that all of what could have been construed as negative in my early life actually acted to my benefit. There are many alternatives in life and minor decisions to make. In the long haul the little decisions add up and become important. You can use something to defeat yourself, or you can use it to make yourself stronger. Hurdles either beat you, or you jump over them. I guess I saw my life experiences as hurdles to jump over, as instructive lessons, and didn't let them go to waste. We are born what we are, but shaped by our environment. We adapt to circumstances. And often we don't have a concept of what will come of it, because we don't see far enough ahead. I see people with different depth of vision, vision which is shaped by different things in their environment. As I get older it is more and more difficult for me to say, this is right, or this is wrong.

My half-sister, Ulla, followed us a year later to the United States and settled in Chicago. As for the buried insect collection? My father eventually made a deal with the Polish government. In return for half of the collection, he revealed to them its location. The insects survived their thirty-plus years underground in perfect condition. My father died several years ago. My mother, Hildegard, settled here in New England.

Bernd Heinrich is a professor of zoology at the University of Vermont. He loves the New England woods and frequently leads his students on expeditions into the forest, summer and winter. He studies ravens, which he keeps in an enclosure next to his house; they remind him of Jakob, the bird which became his friend when he lived in the solitude of the Hahnheide. Bernd's home sits deep in the Vermont woods, near a small beaver pond, not far from Burlington. But then "far" is a relative concept in the woods of New England—when the snows descend in late autumn, burying all beneath a thick blanket of white, distance is measured in the stride of a pair of snowshoes. Bernd Heinrich's woods are quiet then, except for the occasional cries of the ravens.

Karl
Brach

{Age 11}

Domnau, East Prussia (Poland)

Reading the Soviet hate propaganda could lead one to believe that it was as important for the Soviets to humiliate the German population for what had been done to the Soviet Union as it was to defeat the German army. . . . Ilya Ehrenburg's chants of ritual hatred for the Germans were so often printed and repeated that they became national slogans.

—Norman M. Naimark, *The Russians in Germany*

We barricaded our doors, but they easily broke them down with the butts of their rifles and submachine guns. The only words they seemed to know in German were *"Frau, komm. Fünf minuten."* In the presence of my sister and me . . . my mother and grandmother were raped repeatedly.

—Karl Brach

I recall the end of the war quite vividly—first fleeing from East Prussia to Bromberg, then from Bromberg to Frankfurt-an-der-Oder, and finally to Jüterbog, south of Berlin. My father, Fritz, was in the Luftwaffe and since 1942 was commander of an aerial munitions depot in Domnau, East Prussia, a small town just south of Königsberg. In the First World War he was an ordnance officer in the kaiser's army. In 1936 he received a commission in the Luftwaffe as weapons and ground equipment officer, based on his World War I experience.

Until 1943 we lived in our apartment in Berlin, the same apartment in which I was born in 1934. The air raids began to pick up momentum in late 1942. The term *Fliegeralarm*, air raid warning, began to assume real meaning for us children. Sometimes on my way to and

---

Previous page: Fritz, Karl, and Margarete, 1937

from school the sirens would howl, and I would quickly run for the nearest air raid shelter. In every street there were signs posted pointing the way to the nearest shelter. At night we began to sleep fully dressed. When the sirens went off, all I had to do was put on my shoes, grab my coat and our emergency suitcase in which we kept our important documents, and go down to the basement. Once the all clear was given everyone exited the basement and filed first into the central courtyard to take a look. Each apartment house on our street was built around an inner courtyard. We were happy if all we saw were a few broken windows. In February 1943 our apartment was damaged, and in another raid that November it was totally destroyed. We then moved to Domnau to join my father in a house that had been assigned to him as commander of the munitions depot. Fortunately my father had the foresight to store some of our irreplaceable things, such as photo albums and old family silver, with friends and relatives. As a result, years after the war ended, we were able to reclaim many of these items.

In 1944 my father observed with growing concern the continuing retreat of the Wehrmacht on the *Ostfront*. He spoke about his fears to my mother at the dinner table, and I listened carefully. By December 1944 he insisted that my mother, Margarete, my younger sister, Barbara, and I move to a safer place. He didn't want us to be in Domnau and have to worry about our safety when the Russians arrived. He had orders to blow up the depot to keep it from falling into the hands of the Red Army. He sent us three and my ninety-year-old grandfather, Hugo Müller, my mother's father, by train to Bromberg to live with my mother's sister Gertrud Pfefferkorn. Bromberg lies halfway between Königsberg and Stettin. Both my mother and my father were born in Bromberg, where the Pfefferkorn family owned three furniture stores, and like my own family had lived there for generations. My aunt Gertrud employed a Polish cook, a woman who was for all practical purposes part of our family. By the time we arrived in Bromberg my aunt's husband had been drafted into the *Volkssturm* and only came home occasionally.

I fondly remember my grandfather Müller. He was an interesting and in many ways extraordinary man. My grandmother had died several years earlier. He was top-fit at age ninety, both mentally and physically, and that impressed me immensely. He walked seven kilometers every day to come and pick me up at school, and then of course he walked seven kilometers back again. He became a role model for me. I tried to emulate him in later life by also excelling in sports, but I never reached the level of athletic proficiency he was able to maintain into old age. The year before, at age eighty-nine, he had become the German master in senior gymnastics in a competition in Berlin.

On our long walks to and from school in Domnau we had plenty of time to talk. One interesting experience my grandfather shared with me on those walks was when he escorted the czar of Russia on a visit to Germany. My grandfather spoke fluent Polish, largely because of the population mix in the Bromberg area. As a result of his language skill he was selected by the *Reichsbahn*, for whom he worked, to accompany the czar as his escort and translator. The czar was so impressed with my grandfather's service that he personally presented him with a pair of gold cufflinks and a gold pocket watch. The cufflinks were decorated with rubies, diamonds, and other precious stones, and of course the imperial Russian eagle. My grandfather gave both the cufflinks and the watch to me. Unfortunately I no longer have the letter of appreciation which accompanied those gifts.

The winter of 1944 was very cold. The temperatures dipped to minus twenty-five degrees Celsius in our area. Nevertheless, we had a wonderful family Christmas in Bromberg. I remember all of us piling into a horse-drawn sled and driving through the snow-covered countryside. It was great fun. By January my father called my mother and told her that he was being transferred and that she should come back to Domnau to help him pack and close up the house. She dutifully got on a train and traveled to Domnau, leaving my sister and me in the care of my aunt Gertrud. I was pretty independent at age eleven, and my mother didn't have to worry about us. She stayed in Domnau for several days. While she was there my father's transfer was canceled, and he was directed to prepare the depot for destruction.

The very day Bromberg was being evacuated by the authorities, that day my mother boarded her train in Domnau to return to Bromberg. Busses with loudspeakers came down our street and announced that Bromberg was being evacuated and that all women and children were to board the busses immediately. They would take us to waiting trains at the *Bahnhof*. My aunt Gertrud said we had to go, that my mother would be all right and would figure out where to find us. My sister, who was seven at this time, and I said *auf Wiedersehen* to my grandfather and got on one of the busses with my aunt. All we could take along was our *Schulranzen*, our book bags. It was a hurried departure. My grandfather Müller refused to accompany us. He said to me and my sister, "This is my daughter's home and I am not leaving now. I am ninety years old. No one is going to harm an old man. They all know me around here. You children go ahead. I'll stay behind. I'll be all right." He was wrong. After the war we located our former cook and she told us that he was killed by Polish men who came to ransack the house. She pleaded for his life with them, but they wouldn't listen to her. To them he had exploited her and was a capitalist and for that he had to die. She built a simple pine box for ninety-year-old Hugo Müller, my grandfather, and buried him herself.

When we arrived at the *Bahnhof* in Bromberg, Red Cross workers, mostly women volunteers, cared for us children. They prepared notes and hung the notes around my sister's and my neck. The notes gave personal data about us, such as date of birth, home address, as well as our destination. Our destination was Frankfurt-an-der-Oder, not to be confused with the better-known Frankfurt on the Main River. My paternal grandmother, Marie Brach, lived in Frankfurt. Once the train arrived in Frankfurt, a Red Cross worker was to deliver us to Hindenburg Strasse, where my grandmother lived. My aunt intended to continue her journey to Berchtesgaden, where the Pfefferkorn family had a summer home.

The train from Bromberg bound for Frankfurt was the same train my mother had boarded in Domnau. When we got on the train, my mother got off. She didn't know about the evacuation, or that Barbara and I were getting on that very train. When she inquired what was going on she was told that Bromberg was being evacuated, and people urged her to stay on the train. She refused. "I have to get to my children" was her reply to people who tried to persuade her to change her mind. She made it to my aunt's house only to learn that, with the exception of her father and the cook, everyone else had left. She was crushed by this turn of events, but she was not a woman to give up easily.

It turned out that ours was the last train out of Bromberg. As a result it was crowded beyond comprehension. Still, the Red Cross women took good care of us children. They looked after us and cared for us until they had us safely delivered to my grandmother in Frankfurt. On the train we couldn't use the toilets because every centimeter of space was occupied. So they held us children outside the windows of the moving train to allow us to relieve ourselves. My aunt Gertrud had put me in charge of my sister when we got to the *Bahnhof* in Bromberg. She said to me, "You are already grown. You are eleven years old, Charlie. Take good care of your sister. Don't lose her." My sister was in a state of panic for the entire trip. She was visibly confused. She didn't really know what was happening, and she was fearful that she would never see our mother again. I had my hands full to keep her calmed down.

My mother in the meanwhile discovered that she had gotten off the last train out of Bromberg. Not knowing what to do next, she called my father on the phone in Domnau. "What am I to do?" she asked him, and told him that she had lost track of us. My father then called a Luftwaffe officer in Bromberg who was moving munitions by truck to Berlin and implored him to take my mother along. My mother dressed as warmly as she could and walked to where she was told the convoy was assembling. She then rode on an open truck for four days and four nights in the bitter winter cold as far as Berlin. The temperatures dipped as low as minus thirty degrees Celsius. After she arrived in Berlin she began to feel ill, and she learned over the following weeks that she had contracted pneumonia, a kidney infection, and various other exposure-related ailments. But she had no time to fret over her own condition. She needed to find her children, and nothing was going to keep her from doing that.

She went to the Alexandra Hotel, which was owned by her brother-in-law Herbert. Through him she learned that Barbara and I were with my grandmother in Frankfurt. It was only a short train ride from Berlin to Frankfurt, but in February 1945 the trip took an entire day. My uncle Herbert had promised my mother that when she returned from Frankfurt we could stay in the Alexandra Hotel. We did for several days. Then the hotel was severely damaged in a bombing raid, and we had to move and find another place. By then the Russian army was getting close to Frankfurt. My mother decided that we should get away from Berlin. She persuaded my grandmother in Frankfurt to join us, and then moved us to Jüterbog, a small garrison town south of Berlin where my father was stationed between 1936 and 1939. Mutti was very sick by this time.

Once we got to Jüterbog Mutti's plan was to visit a prominent family she and my father knew from their earlier stay there, and to ask them to put us up. Or at least have them help us find a place to stay. The man, a medical doctor, was a prominent Nazi. All four of his sons had attended the *National Socialistische Erziehungsanstalt*, NAPOLI, located in a renovated castle in Sonthofen, Bavaria. They were the people who were to provide the next generation of Nazi leadership. When we got to Jüterbog only the doctor's wife and daughter were living in their six-room apartment. She readily invited us to stay with her. My mother then asked her if she had given any thought to what might happen to her once the Russians came. "Don't you want to go somewhere else?" she asked her. "Once the Russians arrive they will surely kill you because you are known by everyone for what you are."

My mother was in possession of a *Flüchtlingsschein*, a refugee pass, which allowed her to obtain ration cards and train tickets. Amazingly, the trains kept running right to the very end. My mother bought tickets for the woman and her daughter, and they left a few days later. We stayed in the large, nicely furnished apartment. I buried all of the doctor's Nazi uniforms and paraphernalia in the backyard—the large colorized portrait of Adolf Hitler which hung in a prominent place in the living room, the graduation certificates of his sons from NAPOLI, a Luftwaffe sword and a hunting rifle. It's all probably still there. At that point in time we had no idea what had happened to my father or to my grandfather who stayed behind in Bromberg. Not until 1948 did we learn from the Red Cross that my father died in March 1945 in a field hospital on the *Kurische Nehrung*, the Courland Spit, north of Königsberg. He was probably waiting to be evacuated by the German navy, then was wounded and died.

Russian troops entered Jüterbog in April 1945. They were hardened combat troops. We Germans have a name for such men: *Frontschweine*, combat pigs. We barricaded our doors, but they easily broke them down with the butts of their rifles and submachine guns. The only words they seemed to know in German were "*Frau, komm. Fünf minuten.*" In the presence of my sister and me—we were very afraid, cowering in the large matrimonial bed in the main bedroom—my mother and grandmother were raped repeatedly. The soldiers entered the room, their genitals exposed, put down their submachine guns, and one relieved another who had just finished raping my mother or grandmother. I never forget the scene. I was terribly afraid, as was my sister. They often aimed their guns at us as if they were going to shoot, saying, "Ratatatat, ratatatat." This horror went on for several nights.

Just before the Russians arrived I was drafted, so to speak, into the *Jungvolk*, the youth auxiliary of the Hitler Youth. You didn't get into the Hitler Youth until you were fourteen years old. I had to report to a Hitler Youth leader, called a *Fähnleinführer*, and he taught us boys how to fire a .22 caliber rifle on a range in a house cellar. While the remaining German soldiers in the area traded their military uniforms for civilian clothes and deserted, we little boys were led by our Hitler Youth fanatic to attack the Russian army. He led us onto the roof of a house, and when Russian truck convoys came through town, we fired at the truck tires. The .22 rifle didn't make much noise. It just went pop, and didn't leave much of a mark when it hit a tire. The combat troops who had raped my mother and grandmother had moved on by then. These were supply troops we were shooting at. They had no idea why their tires were going flat. We kids thought it was fun. Our mothers thought we were insane. "If they find you they'll kill you all and burn down the houses," my mother warned me. I didn't listen to her.

By that time food was becoming scarce. So the next thing our Hitler Youth leader thought of was to take us at night to an abandoned German airfield. There in the hangars were canisters of emergency rations for air crews—chocolate, cigarettes, sugar tablets, and other high-energy foods. The hangars were guarded by Russian soldiers, but the soldiers usually were drunk. Our leader was so brazen as to take the submachine gun from the drunk guard, unload it, and then put it back in his arms. Then we removed the guard's boots, just in case he should awaken and try to follow us. He would have to do it barefooted. Once a guard woke from the noise we made in the hangar. He screamed, "*Stoi*," and aimed his gun at us. Of course the gun was useless, we had removed the magazine. Then he discovered he was barefooted. Afterward we laughed our heads off. We took everything from the hangars we could lay our hands on. The food, of course, but also the parachutes. The parachute silk we traded to farmers for bacon, ham, and sausages. We did this until there was no more left for us to take. We shared our take with needy families; we didn't just keep it for ourselves.

Once the Russian occupation troops and their staffs moved in and took the place of the front line combat troops, the raping abruptly stopped. These occupation troops were courteous and showed respect toward German women. The Russian officers looked like educated men to me. They were clean and well groomed, their uniforms neatly pressed and the boots shined to a high polish. As a child, I thought they always looked impeccable. Many of the Russian combat soldiers who committed the rapes, and of course those that followed, were generally kind to children, even generous at times, sharing the little they had. I remember one of them giving me a chocolate bar after raping my mother. They were different people coming from a very different world. I saw them wash potatoes in the toilet. Then, when they flushed and the potatoes disappeared, they took out their pistols and shot the toilets. In our housing area several toilets were ruined that way. The first soldiers who came through didn't use the toilets for anything. They didn't know what they were. They sat on the ledge of a bathtub and relieved themselves. The combat soldiers, many of whom were Asian, were incredibly primitive. Once the combat troops were replaced by occupation troops, many of whom spoke fluent German, the Russians, at least in the area where I lived, applied an American frontier style of justice to their own people. If they caught one of their own committing a rape, they often shot him on the spot.

A Russian captain, he was Jewish, and a first lieutenant and their batman were quartered in our apartment. They left us with two rooms. My mother was detailed to cook for them. They brought the food, she cooked. That was advantageous for us, because they were generous and readily shared their food with us. The captain eventually moved in with another woman in the apartment house. This was not an unusual practice. She had two children to feed, and the captain was her ticket. For the first time I also encountered open hate and disdain by Russians toward those who were of the Jewish faith, in this case the captain. The lieutenant spoke excellent German; the captain, to my surprise, didn't. I remember the lieutenant saying to my mother in the presence of the captain, "Hitler made one mistake. He didn't kill all of them." And then he ran his hand across his throat, staring at the captain. Until then I didn't know that they had problems like that in the Russian army.

By 1946 we were evicted. The officers brought their families to Germany from Russia, and they needed apartments. We took our suitcase and moved in with acquaintances. This was the fourth time we moved after losing most everything we owned—first from Berlin when our *Wohnung* was bombed, then from Domnau to Bromberg, Bromberg to Jüterbog, and then into a one-room attic apartment, a storage area in former times. There we lived for three years. Eventually we were able to obtain a two-room apartment in the same house, with a shared bath and kitchen privileges. There we lived until 1956. We kept the attic room because my mother thought I was getting too old to sleep in the same bed and the same room with my sister. My grandmother by then had returned to Frankfurt.

After our eviction, food more than ever became the most important priority in our lives. My mother did what she could. Rations were skimpy. The system was broken. I ran with a gang of boys, and we got rather good at stealing from the Russians. They transported their supplies on little horse-drawn Panje wagons to the various garrisons in the area. The wagons were covered with tarps. The smallest of us boys, and the one who could run the fastest, was selected to jump on the back of a wagon. Then he threw out everything he could grab—sausages, bread, whatever. The rest of us ran behind the wagon and picked up what he threw out. Then we met around the next corner or in an apartment house foyer and divided up our take and took off to the four winds. We were long gone before the Russian driver and his guard comprehended what was going on. At night we stole coal. We jumped on the coal cars standing on a siding. One would stand guard, the rest of us threw down the coal. We had to heat our rooms, cook our meals. We needed coal for our families to survive. In 1946 and 1947 we were always cold and hungry.

Russian soldiers showed up with brand-new bicycles. Factories in east Germany were working again. Our bicycles of course were ancient—paint peeling, tires in need of replacement. Most of the Russian soldiers didn't know how to ride a bike. We kids rode in circles around the Russians who were practicing on their factory-new bicycles. They spent more time on the ground than in the saddle. We of course showed off, riding around them in never-ending circles with our arms folded across our chests. We never expected what happened next. They waved us down and traded their new bicycles, which they believed didn't ride very well, for our unique, easy-to-ride bicycles. We handed over our bicycles and rode off, because we knew our old bikes wouldn't perform any better for them than the new ones did.

In May 1945, soon after the shooting stopped, I went back to school. I made my *Abitur* in 1954, at the age of twenty. I took seven years of Russian language instruction while in school and achieved a fair fluency. I was good in sports, especially volleyball, and I was a member of our school's volleyball team. As a result I was excused from participation in what I call *Parteiarbeit*, political indoctrination. I didn't have to join the *Freie Deutsche Jugend*, the FDJ, or the *Junge Pioniere*. Not until 1953, one year prior to the *Abitur*, did I finally join the FDJ because the pressure to join was getting too much. Teachers told me that if in the final exam I should by chance get a marginal grade, which was an implied threat, they wouldn't be able to help me unless I joined the FDJ. So I did.

I wasn't the child of a laborer or a farmer, but the child of a former Wehrmacht officer, and as a result I didn't have any privileges in the former Deutsche Demokratische Republik, the DDR. However, if you were good in sports, as I was, the system supported you in many ways no matter who you were. For instance, since I was good enough to be a member of a regional volleyball team, during tournaments I was excused from all schoolwork. When there was a major tournament in Potsdam I received a note from my trainer informing my teachers that I was to be relieved of all academic work for the days that the tournament was in progress. The school principal, the *Herr Direktor*, even came to my classroom and in front of my fellow students praised me and one other student for our achievements in sport.

They gave us the train fare to Potsdam. We took the money and instead rode our bicycles the sixty kilometers to Potsdam. There they put us up in a hotel, plus we got ten east mark a day in spending money.

When we had free time we took the S-Bahn to the Potsdamer Platz. There, in West Berlin, was a movie house where we from the East—we had to show our passes—were allowed to see western movies for only fifty pfennigs west currency. We traded our sixty east mark, our train trip money, into D-mark and used the money to go to the movie and buy spare parts for our bicycles. A lamp, a new dynamo, a tire, and inner tube. Things we couldn't get in the East.

As soon as we returned, our classmates questioned us about what was new in the West. "What's going on in the outside world?" they wanted to know. In our apartment house we had someone who kept watch over us and listened for what radio stations we were listening to. If he heard us listening to RIAS Berlin (Radio in the American Sector), for instance, he turned us in. It was the same in our class. Only two hours after our classmates had pumped us dry of whatever information we may have learned in West Berlin, there came our *Herr Direktor.* "It has come to my attention that you two went to the West and looked at western movies. I don't want you to ever do that again, or I will not let you participate in future volleyball games." I couldn't believe that we had a *Spitzel,* a spy, in our class who went to the principal to report us. It took a while until we found out who it was. Once we did, we excluded him when we wanted to talk among ourselves.

My volleyball team was frequently invited to play Russian army teams. We enjoyed playing them. They were enthusiastic volleyball players. For instance, if we played volleyball in the street, and a Russian came by, nearly always he would take off his pistol belt and hat, put them down and say, *"Dowoi, dowoi. Spielen."* We liked playing with them. It was also easy to communicate with them. Of course we learned Russian in school, but they also learned German quickly, even the lowest-ranking soldiers. It amazed me. Russians seemed to have a real knack for languages.

Because I was good in sports, just prior to my *Abitur,* I received weekly visits at home from representatives of the *Volkspolizei,* the people's police. They would say to me, "You are for peace, are you not?" Of course I am for peace, I replied.

"*Ja*, then you must do something to maintain peace. Don't you think so? Or do you see that differently?"

No, I would say, I agree.

"Then, why don't you join the *Volkspolizei*? We do something for peace. For instance, we protect the citizens of the Deutsche Demokratische Republik against the agents and subversives of the West."

I would like to continue to study at the university was one of my stock answers. There must be other ways for me to serve the DDR than joining the *Volkspolizei*. I would like to continue my studies at a university and become a sports officer in the *Volksarmee*, the people's army, I told them.

"You can do that with us too," they said.

I'll think about what you said, I told them. But first I have to make my *Abitur*.

The pressure to join continued to build. My friend, the other volleyball player, finally gave in and agreed to join the *Volkspolizei*. I told him he was crazy.

"I am not so dumb," he said to me. "I am going to fail my physical."

How are you going to do that? I asked him. You are one of the best in sports.

"Easy," he said to me. "I have studied color vision intensely, and I am now able to give the wrong answer consistently when I am shown a color chart. They won't take someone who is color blind." Indeed, he failed his physical as he told me he would. It took tricks like that to stay out of the system.

My uncle Herbert, the one who once owned the bombed-out Alexandra Hotel in Berlin, now lived in Bonn. In July 1954 he invited me to visit him as a reward for completing my *Abitur*. He sent me a round-trip ticket. In 1954 it was still possible to travel by train to the West, with an appropriate pass of course. By that time I had applied to the University of Leipzig and others to continue my studies in biology and sport. And since I was good in sports I thought I had a good chance to be accepted. But since I wasn't the son of a farmer or a worker, but instead in my file it read "son of former Wehrmacht officer," I wasn't accepted. My mother sent me the letters of rejection to Bonn with the accompanying advice, "Stay there. Don't come back. You don't have a chance over here." I took my mother's advice and stayed in Bonn. My uncle was generous, but he and his wife were still trying to get on their feet and had no resources to support me. He recommended that I report to a refugee camp and get processed as a political refugee from the East. I did that. After a few weeks I received my certification as political refugee, and I applied for a position with the *Bundesgrenzschutz*, the border police. In May 1955 I entered the *Grenzschutz* as an officer candidate. In 1956 I transferred to the new Luftwaffe.

My sister also was good in sports, and as a result she was ordered to report to the central sport school in Neubrandenburg. She was fifteen. She had no choice in the matter. They took her away from my mother, who had nothing to say about her daughter's whereabouts or schooling. My mother didn't accept that. She believed that she had a right to decide for her underage daughter where she went to school and where she was going to live. Nor did she like it when my sister came home from school and told her that she had learned how to throw a hand grenade, fire a rifle and a pistol. About that time the West Berlin Senate passed a law which said that Berliners who had lost an apartment or a house during the war could apply for a new apartment. My mother heard of this, so she went to West Berlin and applied. Although we now lived in the DDR, we had lost our apartment in 1942 in a bombing raid, and she felt as entitled as anyone else. After much bureaucratic haggling she did get a new apartment near the Tiergarten in Berlin. So, one day in 1956 she took my sister by the hand, again leaving everything behind, took a train to East Berlin, and then the S-Bahn to West Berlin. She just walked away from all her possessions for a fifth time. Nothing mattered to my mother other than the welfare of her two children.

How did I deal with the trauma of 1945, of my mother getting raped, and everything else that followed? I suppressed it. I didn't dwell on it. I couldn't deal with it. But I have no hate toward Russians for the things that happened back in 1945. To the contrary. I still audit courses at the university to keep up my Russian language skills. And for three years in a row my wife and I have hosted Russian children from Chernobyl, for two weeks at a time. I believe that the Russian soldiers frequently were not to blame for the acts they committed. Not only was the war brutal, but the Russian poet Ilya Ehrenburg encouraged the soldiers to be brutal. There was a poem he wrote which was wide-ly distributed which said, Soldier, when you enter Germany, rape the German women, burn and plunder. I don't remember exactly anymore how the poem was phrased, but this was the essence of it. With encour-agement like that, simple soldiers followed orders. And of course the Russians also saw how Germans treated the Poles in Warsaw, how Russian prisoners of war had been abused, and the concentration camps. No, I have no hate toward them. As for my own two sons, they are not interested in the past. When we occasionally talk about such things they look at me skeptically. "You exaggerate, Father," they say. "It couldn't possibly have been that bad."

Charlie Brach retired from the Luftwaffe as a lieutenant colonel and lives in Schleswig-Holstein right up against the Baltic Sea. He works part-time as a public relations officer for a prominent German nonprofit organization. And when he is not working he likes to savor the smell of salt water and the cries of the seagulls. Charlie is a free man, one of the few who is not tormented by his past.

Irmgard
Broweleit

{Age 7}

Königsberg, East Prussia (Russia)

The *Kriegsmarine*, mostly known for its conduct of the U-boat war in the Atlantic, in the waning days of World War II conducted one of the most amazing rescue operations of all time. In defiance of Nazi Party officials, the German navy undertook the seemingly impossible task of evacuating large numbers of refugees fleeing before the advancing Red Army. From ports and open beaches in the eastern Baltic nearly 2.5 million refugees and soldiers were evacuated across mine- and submarine-infested waters and under frequent air attack to ports in the west of Germany. The operation, which began as early as 1944, reached its climax in the final three months of the war and continued until the afternoon of May 11, 1945. In the operation 123 ships of all sizes were lost to enemy action. Nearly twenty thousand women, children, and men died at sea. The loss of three ships to Soviet submarines accounted for most of the dead: the *Wilhelm Gustloff* sank on January 30, 1945, with the loss of around five thousand persons; the hospital ship *Steuben* sank on February 10, 1945, with the loss of three thousand; and the *Goya* sank on April 16, 1945, with the loss of over six thousand. The loss of the *Goya* was the largest single-ship catastrophe ever recorded in maritime history.

—Extracted from Wolfgang Müller and Reinhard Kramer, *Gesunken Und Verschollen*

January was nearly over when my mother again heard there were ships leaving Pillau and other harbors, taking refugees west to safety. We walked to the harbor in Pillau looking for ships, any ship, but specifically for the *Wilhelm Gustloff*, a large ocean liner which was to have anchored nearby. When we arrived there were thousands and thousands of people trying to get on the *Gustloff*.

—Irmgard Broweleit

Previous page: Gertrud, Irmgard, brother Heinz, and August, 1942

Irmgard Broweleit

I was born in Königsberg on April 23, 1938, to Gertrud and August Broweleit. I have a brother, Heinz; he was born in 1935. I tried to talk him into coming on this interview, but he claimed he didn't remember much. Maybe he doesn't want to remember. My father was by trade an upholsterer. He served in the Luftwaffe. I recall he came home on military leave one time in 1942. I didn't see him again until he returned from a Russian prisoner-of-war camp in 1948. To me my father was a picture until I was ten years old.

My mother's mother, Berta Neumann (my grandmother), my mother's sister, Elizabeth Neumann (my aunt), and my eighteen-month-old cousin, Gerd, we lived together in Königsberg. In the spring of 1944, because of the bombing, we were evacuated to Blumenau, a small town a few kilometers west of Königsberg. In Blumenau I started school in the fall of 1944. School lasted two months for me, then all the schools were closed as the bombing became widespread. The sounds of battle came closer and closer every day. I could hear the artillery in the distance. Late in December my mother decided we had to try to get out of Blumenau before it was too late. She had heard of ships evacuating people from Pillau and Danzig. It was her plan to at least try to get us on one of those ships.

We set out on foot walking through the dense forest, in snow three feet deep. Thousands of others were doing the same thing. It was bitterly cold and the wind blew hard. I was dressed in the only two dresses I possessed. I wore long stockings, socks over my stockings, and my winter coat. Still, I was cold. I had no real winter boots. My mother, my brother, and I, my aunt with my one-year-old cousin Gerd, and my grandmother trudged onward toward Fischhausen, scarfs wrapped tightly around our heads and across our faces to keep out the bitter cold. Our goal was to get to the port of Pillau and load on the *Wilhelm Gustloff* for safety in the West. Those were our dreams. The *Wilhelm Gustloff* was a large ship, and my mother had heard that she was running back and forth between East Prussia and ports in the west of

Germany, taking nearly ten thousand refugees at a time. There was no way to escape over land any longer. The Nazi Party had refused to evacuate anyone from the Königsberg area, and the Russian army had finally cut us off.

My little cousin Gerd, bundled up warmly, rode on a small sled pulled by my aunt. On the way he fell off the sled into the deep snow on the side of the road, and no one noticed. When my grandmother turned around she thought something was missing. It was little Gerd. We all walked back looking for him. I found him lying by the side of the road buried in the deep snow, sleeping soundly. At that point my grandmother said, "It is no use to go on. We will all die in this bitter cold or get trampled to death." A terrorized mass of people was making its way down the road to the ports in the hope of catching the *Gustloff* or any other ship that was taking on refugees. We walked back to Blumenau, our feet wet and cold. It was lucky we did turn back. The Russians broke through German lines, and many of the refugees on that road with us were killed.

I recall one powerful emotion that possessed me at the time—fear of Russian soldiers. As a child I understood a lot more than grown-ups thought I did. They spoke freely around me as if I didn't exist. So I overheard that the Russians were taking the mothers away from the children. We would be separated. That fear of losing my mother stayed with me the entire time. She was all I had. I heard shooting all the time, and I saw many wounded German soldiers pass by our house. All of it sustained my fear of the Russians. Fear was the biggest emotion I felt. Hunger was the other thing that became a permanent part of me. My mother did without to feed me and my brother. Although we were hungry nearly all the time, my mother always prepared something warm for us two. Dandelion soup and salad when that was available. We melted snow for drinking water and for cooking.

The owners of the house we lived in, in Blumenau, had connections and got out safely before we had left on our failed walk to Fischhausen.

When we returned to the house we went through every cabinet and found some canned goods. It wasn't much, but it kept us from starving. Heinz and I played outside when it wasn't too cold. We made snow angels, had snowball fights, and just ran around like children do. We always headed for home when we heard shooting in the forest. My mother was usually outside by that time and met us halfway to scoop us up and get us into the house. If the shooting was really bad everyone went into the basement.

My mother, Heinz, and I were in the forest gathering wood one afternoon, not far from our house. I looked up and on the pine tree before me I saw the frozen, naked body of a young woman tied to the tree. Several dead civilians lay in the snow nearby. My mother came running over to me, covered my eyes and said, "You didn't see that." Years later, I was in my twenties, I remembered that incident and I asked my mother if it was real or if I had imagined it. "No, it was real," she said. "It was obvious to me that the young woman had been raped and then tied to the tree to let her freeze to death." That's how close the Russians were to us.

A young German soldier befriended us. He was nineteen years old. He had recently married and came to visit us every chance he got. I believe he just wanted to talk. He brought us army rations, since we had totally exhausted the food we found in the house. He came late one January day and said to my mother, "I can't protect you anymore. The Russians are on the other side of the forest. We are out of ammunition. God be with you. We are pulling back. Stay in the basement. I hope they are kind to you when they get here." He left. We did what the soldier told us to do and went into the basement. There were fifteen of us. Others had come and joined us, seeking refuge in the house we lived in. My mother didn't deny them. A huge explosion shattered the silence. It shook our house and rattled the windows, breaking some. A munitions depot just a few kilometers away, on the other side of the forest, had blown up. Smaller explosions continued for the remainder of the day. In the direction of the depot the sky was red.

I was afraid as never before. My mother was crying, as were other women. I felt all that fear in my surroundings. We sat and waited. The shooting outside became intense. The basement windows were shattered by stray bullets. Now it really got cold in the basement. Then there was silence. We sat quietly, waiting for our fears to turn into reality. It seemed like an eternity had passed when I heard heavy footsteps coming through the house. The basement door opened and someone shouted down the basement stairs, "*Hallo. Wer da?*" I recognized the young German soldier's voice. He came down the stairs when he realized it was just us and not Russian soldiers. We were overjoyed to see him, our savior. "We were able to push Ivan back a little," he said. "We captured some ammunition. I have a truck outside. Come quickly. You can't take anything."

We followed him outside, and all fifteen of us piled on his truck. There was a machine gun mounted on the truck bed, and we held onto it. The soldier drove through the night and took us to Fischhausen. On the way he stopped and picked up some more people until there was no place for anyone else to stand. I took my *Tornister*, my school bag. Mutti had removed my slate of which I was so proud, and had stuffed some clothes into the bag before we mounted the truck. That was all we had. At that point I was scared of the unknown, but no longer possessed by the deep fear I experienced sitting helplessly in the basement. All of us got off the truck in Fischhausen, and the adults broke into an abandoned house where we slept through the night and well into the day.

I woke with my aunt standing in the room shouting to my mother, "I found a huge Hitler picture hanging in the living room. If the Russians come and see that, they'll think we live here and worship him." My mother and my aunt took the picture down, removed it from the frame, and tore it into little pieces. Then they took the pieces out in the backyard and hid them in the snow. We went through the house to make sure there wasn't anything else that could get us into trouble should the Russians arrive unexpectedly. We stayed in that house for several days. There was some food in the house, and the Red Cross served soup to refugees. My mother took a large bowl and went to one of the Red Cross soup kitchens. She returned with a fish soup. It looked like water with a little egg yolk and some fish heads swimming in it. I recall a young teenager who was with us exclaiming several times, "Oh, *das schmeckt*. Oh, *das schmeckt*," she thought it tasted so good. I thought it tasted like warm dishwater, but she was hungrier than I and thought the watery fish soup was delicious.

January was nearly over when my mother again heard there were ships leaving from Pillau and other harbors, taking refugees west to safety. We walked to the Pillau harbor looking for ships, any ship, but specifically for the *Wilhelm Gustloff*, a large ocean liner which was to have anchored nearby. When we arrived, there were thousands and thousands of people trying to get on the *Gustloff*. In the jostling crowd we held hands to stay together. Finally it was our turn. My lit-tle cousin was passed from hand to hand, from one sailor to another, onto the ship. As a sailor lifted me up, someone screamed from above, "No more, we are full." The sailor put me down. My aunt screamed, "I want my baby back. Give me my baby back." A sailor found little Gerd for her and handed him down to us. Another sailor tried to console us. "There will be another ship tomorrow," he said. "We will save you."

We walked back to the house in Fischhausen, dejected over the missed opportunity. The next day we were lucky. We got on a fish trawler and with many others went below deck where we lay on a thin layer of straw, side by side—old men, young girls, children, women. I don't remember much about the trip. I remember getting off the boat in a place called Peenemünde, on the island of Rügen. When we land-ed in Peenemünde we heard that the *Wilhelm Gustloff* didn't make it. It had been torpedoed, and everyone on the ship had died. Looking back, I believe it simply wasn't our time to go. That is the only way I can explain the strange events which kept us from going on the first time, when the others were killed by Russian soldiers, and then later kept us off the *Wilhelm Gustloff*.

In Peenemünde my family was put up in a large seaplane hangar with many, many windows. Hundreds of us stayed in that hangar for a number of weeks. When the bombs came they shattered the windows, and the glass fell on us like hail. Sacks of straw on which we slept were all around us, one sack next to the other. I stayed close to my mother. My brother, Heinz, and I tried to pass the time by playing with a button. We made the button hop by pushing down on its edge with the tip of a finger and tried to see who could make it hop the farthest. But we never let Mutti out of our sight. The Red Cross fed us in Peenemünde as they had in Fischhausen. Soup. We had one bowl and we took turns eating with the one spoon we had, but we all got something in our stomachs. Fortunately we never went really hungry like many others did.

I remember when we were first resettled in 1944 from Königsberg to Blumenau. The day we left Königsberg my mother got a small bag of sugar on our ration cards. That bag of sugar had to last us six months. As soon as we arrived in Blumenau she hid the sugar from me and Heinz. I knew she had it, and I found it. I got a spoon from the kitchen, locked the door and began eating the sugar one spoonful at a time. My mother caught me in the act. I must have smacked my lips too loudly. She reprimanded me, but there was no other punishment. She was a disciplinarian, but with love. When we fled Blumenau on the army truck with the German soldier, she had to leave behind what remained of the bag of sugar. It bothered her until the day she died that she stopped me from eating that sugar. "If I had only known what lay ahead for us, I would have let you eat that whole bag of sugar," she said to me more than once in later years.

Fear for my life and fear of losing my Mutti, neither fear ever left me while I was in Peenemünde. Fear stayed with me day and night, awake or asleep. The vision of the naked woman strapped to the tree made my fears seem all too real. So many times we ran away from something. Always running. And what I remember clearly is a picture of my mother with me on one hand and my brother on the other. Running. Trying to stay together. We never took off our clothes. We had nothing else to wear anyway. We always had to be ready to leave on a moment's notice. We did the best we could to stay clean. Often there was no water available. My mother sent us outside to brush our teeth with snow. Heinz and I put snow on a finger and rubbed it hard across our gums. Quickly it became a game, and soon Heinz and I were giggling and laughing. It is the way of children to play no matter what or where.

As the authorities found places for refugees to stay they shipped them out. Eventually we were loaded on a train which took us from Peenemünde to Hamburg. There we were put on a truck which took us to a *Gasthaus* in Wohlenbeck. This turned out to be a refugee distribution point. My grandmother, aunt, and cousin Gerd stayed there in Wohlenbeck. A farmer took Mutti, Heinz, and me by horse and wagon to a small village, Hackemühle. We ended up with the largest farmer in the area. They were forced to take us, had nothing to say about it, and weren't happy about the situation. As *Flüchtlinge*, refugees from the East, we were unwanted, although we were Germans. I recall comments by the local villagers describing us as having lice and fleas, and asserting that we would bring disease. We were treated like "dirty foreigners." On top of all that, our farmer had to put us in his *gute Stube*, the good room, reserved only for special occasions. It didn't sit well with the farmer.

On the farm my mother worked from early morning to late at night. She did both household and field chores. We were city people, but we learned awfully quick. I remember her coming home late in the day after spending the entire day in the fields. She was so tired, she collapsed on our bed. Then the farmer's wife called her to do housework and to cook the evening meal. She dutifully got up and did as she was told. She did all the washing and ironing, walked behind the plow, and helped with the potato harvest. The farmer had us turn in our ration cards to him. In return he gave us potatoes and rutabaga. The family didn't like my brother at all, but they liked me. On my seventh birthday in April 1945 the farmer's wife gave me a *Butterglocke* as a present with a pound of real butter in it. It was a total surprise to all of us. I still have that porcelain butter dish decorated with pictures of cows. We didn't have our own kitchen, only our one room. We ate with the other servants at the same table.

Mutti made me a warm winter coat out of an old army blanket. I was proud of my new coat, and it was warm. But the coat was heavy across my shoulders. Our shoes were wooden soles with pieces of lamb leather across the top. When we walked to school the snow would cake under the soles, and we children tried to see who would have the highest clumps under his or her soles before they fell off. I had to wear my brother's outgrown long underwear, and she knitted scratchy wool stockings for us. I hated to wear those stockings, not to mention the underwear.

The war came to us again as it neared its end. I could hear shooting now and then. My aunt, my little cousin Gerd, and my grandmother were still quartered in Bohlenbeck, about eight kilometers from us. One day in April 1945 I baby-sat little Gerd while Mutti, my aunt, and my grandmother walked to Lamstedt to go shopping. Lamstedt was the nearest small town. While they were gone I heard gunfire and explosions. When they finally returned my mother told me that a bomb exploded outside the clothing store they were in, toppling over shelves and racks of clothes, but they were not hurt.

My grandmother and I went berry picking. We walked to a nearby sandpit with plenty of berry bushes growing near its edge. Suddenly *Tiefflieger* came upon us. I could hear the cannons firing and saw the explosions in the sand. The planes circled around an old woman dressed in black and a young girl, my grandmother and me, firing their guns. They could have killed us with ease, but they were only having fun with us. I saw the sand popping up where the bullets hit. We dropped our buckets filled with berries and tried to hide in the prickly bushes. Finally the planes flew away.

The war ended, and life went on as before. My mother worked so very hard for the little food we received for her labors. Although the farmer's wife was stingy, she was concerned about her reputation in the village and didn't want anyone to think that "her" *Flüchtlinge* didn't get enough to eat. She made sure that we never went hungry. In contrast, my aunt Elizabeth and my cousin Gerd barely stayed alive. At age two, Gerd was unable to walk because he was so weak. In 1946 my uncle

Paul, the husband of Elizabeth and Gerd's father, was released from a prisoner-of-war camp and located us through the Red Cross. My father, August, returned in the spring of 1948.

Mutti had thought our father was dead, since we had heard nothing from him since 1944. I was at my aunt and uncle's playing with Gerd the afternoon of my father's return. My grandmother Berta had died in 1946 soon after Paul returned. There was a knock on the door, and then I heard my aunt saying, "August! August!"—my father's name. I looked up, and there stood this disheveled-looking man dressed in rags. I didn't recognize him. It was my father. He scared me the way he looked. He still wore his old Luftwaffe uniform, ripped to shreds. Rags were wrapped around his feet for shoes. He weighed ninety pounds. He was not the father I remembered from the picture, the only father I knew. He came in and sat and had a cup of ersatz coffee. It was my job to take him home to Mutti. People looked at the ragged-looking stranger. I wanted to get him home as quickly as possible so he could take off those rags. I was ashamed of him. After he washed up, he sat down and ate everything we had. He ate all the food that was supposed to last us for a week. He didn't know that. In a few days he started to look puffy and bloated, like he was full of water. His metabolism was unable to adjust to our food. We took him to a doctor who prescribed medication and a stringent diet to bring him back to health. In a few weeks he adjusted, and the water left his body.

My father got a job working as an upholsterer, but then he was laid off and took a job with the police in Lamstedt. Once he felt the job was going to last for a while, he moved us to Lamstedt, into a cow barn. The cows were on one end of the barn; we lived on the other. There were four rooms on our end of the barn. A family lived in each room. We had the largest room of the four. It had a kitchen attached to it. There we lived for four years until 1952. Life normalized, although we still lived hand to mouth, one day at a time. We knew we could never return to Königsberg, our home. So when my father read in the paper that the American Lutheran Church was sponsoring people to immigrate to the

United States, he applied. "Why not?" he said to us at the dinner table. "We can never return to our homeland, and we are not really at home here in this barn. Why not try it?" My father had always had an adventurous streak in him, and my mother was the type to go along with nearly anything. My brother and I were not asked if we wanted to go to America. America to me was the land of plenty. I didn't really know anything useful about the country.

We had befriended another family in Lamstedt who were also from Ost Preussen. The two men went together to the American consulate in Hamburg to start the paperwork. Then there was more paperwork, and yet more paperwork. Eventually our applications were approved, and we reported to a camp near Bremen for physical examinations. We were there for two weeks, then had to return to Lamstedt to wait for our final departure notice. Once notified, we went to another camp near Bremen where we remained for six weeks until we and our friends were taken to Bremerhaven, where we embarked on the USNS *General C. H. Muir*, a passenger-carrying Liberty Ship. It was the twenty-first of February 1952. We had three suitcases with us containing all we owned.

My father and my brother, Heinz, were taken to one section of the ship, and my mother and I to another. Men and women bunked separately. The bunks in the bottom of the ship were stacked four high. I got the top bunk because I was the youngest. My mother was somewhere down below me. There were over a hundred women and young girls in the large hold. The conditions were terrible. Soon after the ship moved out, most became seasick. In the middle of every aisle sat several large garbage cans, and everyone who was sick, and that was nearly everybody, stood around the cans throwing up or just retching when they had nothing in their stomachs left to throw up. I thought they looked like a bunch of chickens in a farmyard, with their heads down over the cans as if they were pecking at something. The stench of vomit remained with us for the remainder of the ten-day voyage.

We ate in the mess hall. They had plenty of food for those of us who could eat. My mother ate one meal on that ship, her first. She never had another meal for the remainder of the voyage. I forced myself to eat. My stomach protested, but I didn't get sick. The Atlantic remained stormy for the duration of our voyage. I liked to get out on deck to smell the fresh salt air. One day I got lost. I stood before a steel door, opened it with difficulty, and found myself in the machine room face to face with a smiling black face. There was this incredible noise and heat, and the perspiring black face with the big smile and the white teeth—and I ran away as fast as I could. That was the first time I met a black man. I felt foolish later, remembering his white teeth and the big smile on his face. But at the time I was so startled and frightened I couldn't even scream. I was thirteen years old.

We landed in New York on the third of March 1952. As we came down the gangplank I felt bitter cold, cold like I had experienced in Ost Preussen when we fled the Russians. The Red Cross had set up a stand at the bottom of the plank, serving hot chocolate and coffee. I thought I was back in East Prussia in 1945. I felt the fear flash through my body, fear which I thought I had shed. But it wasn't Ost Preussen. We were in New York. In America. Our destination was Macon, Georgia. Our sponsor was to meet us in a waiting room by the dock. In Macon my father was to work in his learned trade as upholsterer. In the waiting room we were told that our sponsorship had been withdrawn and that there was nothing else. There we were with our three suitcases and no money in a strange land. My father insisted that there must be someone who would sponsor us. After much telephoning by the Lutheran representative he finally came up with a farmer in Syracuse, Nebraska. He was willing to take us if we were willing to work on the farm. My father said, "We are city folks, but we can learn."

We traveled for three days on a train. We changed trains in Kansas City and ended up in Nebraska City, Nebraska, where we were met by our sponsor and the Lutheran minister. The snow by the side of the road was three feet deep. Elmer, our sponsor, an old Swede, spoke little German. We spoke little English. Our new home turned out to be an abandoned old farmhouse which was leaning like the tower of Pisa.

It hadn't seen paint in over twenty years, had no lights, no running water, and had not been lived in for years. Most of the windows were boarded up with cardboard. In the kitchen stood a pot-bellied iron stove. Our spirits reached a new low. Elmer said to us in a mix of Swedish, German, and English, "Is this not nice? Have you ever seen anything so nice?"

My mother, who was still weak and ailing from the after effects of seasickness, began to cry. She whispered to my father, "Even in the cow barn we had electricity." He nodded his head, but there was nothing we could do. One of the stipulations of sponsorship was that we were to remain with our sponsor for one year and to work off the cost of travel, food, and housing. The farmer had paid for our trip from New York to Nebraska. My father worked on the farm from morning to night, six days a week. My brother, who was seventeen by then, was hired by a neighboring farmer at $2.50 a day. My father was supposed to get a regular salary; instead, every Saturday morning Elmer would say, "August, you need money?"

My father would say, "Yes, we need to buy groceries." Then Elmer would give him ten dollars for a week's wages. Elmer tried to recoup his travel expenses and the money he put out to buy overalls and rubber boots for my father as quickly as possible. As for myself, I lived with Elmer and his wife and their daughter. He had two houses. He and his wife lived in the new house, and his daughter and her two little children lived in the old house. I lived with the daughter. I had a beautiful room. In return I had to help clean the two houses, did all the ironing for the family and baby-sat. I worked every day when I wasn't in school. Occasionally Elmer would put a dollar bill on my bed. I attended school in a one-room schoolhouse. My transportation was a horse. One teacher taught ten children, first through seventh grade. This was the first assignment for the young woman teacher, and she didn't know what to do with me. She spoke no German. I spoke little English, so she gave me a lot of math to do. In seventh grade I was doing the math I had mastered in fourth grade in Germany. I whizzed through my assignments, leaving the teacher with a constant problem of how to occupy me. I tried to participate in the other subjects, but my English was inadequate. Donna, my teacher, and I muddled through. Just as I crawled into my jeans every day to ride to school, I dove into the American way to the best of my ability—and never looked back.

My brother saved every penny he made and after six months bought himself an old jalopy. On a Saturday afternoon Heinz showed up in his "new" car. About the same time my father came home and my mother said, "Let's go grocery shopping in Heinz's new car."

"We can't," my father replied.

"Why not?" my mother insisted, puzzled by his response.

"Elmer asked me again, August, you need money? And he did that once too often. I told him, No, Elmer. And he didn't give me any." The old Swede was tight with his money. So we couldn't go grocery shopping, but we had some food in the house. Elmer gave us a lot of liver from cattle he slaughtered. We had no refrigeration, but out in back behind the house there was a deep hole. Lowered into the hole by a winch, attached to a rope, was a cabinet with several shelves. In this cabinet we put our perishables such as butter and the liver. That was our refrigerator. A pound of coffee cost fifty cents. Ten dollars went a long way; still it wasn't much. If it weren't for the liver we couldn't have made it. I don't like liver to this day. That same day my father told Elmer we were leaving and going to the city.

"You are making a big mistake," Elmer cautioned my father. "You will starve to death in the city," he predicted.

My father replied, "Elmer, I can't do worse than I am doing now." We packed up, hopped in my brother's new old car and drove to Lincoln. It was September 1952. My father got a job with the gas company for $1.25 an hour. We moved into a two-room apartment on the third floor of a rooming house. My mother got a job working in the kitchen of a sorority house. I went to school, and my brother got a job with Western Electric. A year later we purchased our own home. A small, old, simple house. But it was ours. We stayed in touch with

Elmer. After a year Elmer came to visit. He couldn't get over how far we had come. He said to my father, "August, you did right. I was wrong." That's how we started life in America.

When I was eighteen and graduated from high school I hopped on a train to Milwaukee to visit our friends from Ost Preussen who had come over on the ship with us. They had two daughters my age. I fell in love with Milwaukee. Everything was German. I stayed for two weeks. When I returned to Lincoln I said to my parents, I'm moving. My father tried to stop me. But then he decided to check it out himself. He and my mother traveled to Milwaukee and stayed there with our friends. When they returned to Lincoln we all packed and moved to Milwaukee. That's where I met my husband. He got transferred to Tulsa, Oklahoma, and that is where I eventually raised my family. We struggled, of course, and I believe we made a good life for ourselves as anybody can in America, even today, if they are willing to work.

My mother lived for her children and her kitchen. She was loving and kind. Always put herself last. When I got older I would say to her, Mom, think of yourself. Whatever my father wanted, she went along with it. When she died he was a broken man. He couldn't face the world without her. My mother died from hepatitis C. She had chronic hepatitis which she picked up somewhere on our flight from the Russians. When her immune system became weaker as she aged the hepatitis surfaced and killed her.

How did it all affect me? On the one hand it made me a self-sufficient person. I think I could survive under nearly any circumstances. On the other hand, although my husband wants to visit Königsberg, now Kaliningrad, I don't. Just the thought of going there brings back the old fears. I can't go. I remember how lucky we were to escape to safety, and how hard it was for us. I have no wish to go back there. I have nothing but bad memories of that place, nothing but fear associated with East Prussia. Steve, my son, occasionally asks a question about that time as he gets older. But we seldom speak of those days.

Irmgard Broweleit

Never in its entirety as I have to you. I believe I am a stronger person because of my experiences. I could live with very little if I had to.

If you passed Irmgard on the street you would think that she looked just like any other middle-aged American woman. And if you asked her for directions you would hear the slight German accent, but only if you listened closely. Her eyes are full of laughter, belying the memory of hardship that lies at the bottom of her soul. She wasn't anxious to speak to me, but finally relented, and I believe that at the end of our interview she was glad to have shared her experiences with someone who was just like her, someone who understood what she was talking about and to whom she did not have to explain herself. Like others I interviewed before her, she carries no ill will toward anyone. However, the ghosts of the past never totally go away for Irmgard; like others, she has learned to live with them.

Arnold
Bieber

{Age 10}

Ortelsburg, East Prussia (Poland)

"Russian mentality is not based on common sense. It has nothing to do with common sense," the writer Tatyana Tolstaya told David Royle, one of our producers. "Our thinking is not orderly, logical. We do not have a linear consciousness. . . . In Western culture, European culture maybe, emotions are considered to be on a lower level than reason. But in Russia, no."

—Hedrick Smith, *The New Russians*

The young woman tried, but fell down again. Her mother quickly came to her assistance. That's when the officer pulled his pistol and shot the mother dead. Then he and his soldiers left. The Russians could be brutal, and they could be kind. I never knew what to expect from them.

—Arnold Bieber

I was born on August 28, 1935, in a little village in southern East Prussia named Farienen, not far from Ortelsburg. I was the oldest of three boys. My two brothers died in their infancies. My father, Otto, was a cartwright with his own business repairing broken farm wagons for local farmers. He was drafted into the Wehrmacht in 1939 and served in the Polish and French campaigns. After that he was released as a result of a petition signed by the local farmers who had no one to repair their farm implements.

There were few toys available in those days, and even if there were, we didn't have the money to buy such luxuries. My father made me trucks and trains from scraps of wood. He could make nearly anything out of

Previous page: Arnold, 1949

wood. He was talented in that way. He made my shoes too. When I grew out of my leather shoes, he cut off the tops and nailed wooden soles to the leather uppers. That's how we got by. My father, my mother, Auguste, and I lived comfortably during most of the war years, at least I thought so. For some reason Farienen didn't have electricity, although all other villages around us did. Everything electrical was operated by battery. We listened to the radio frequently, and I remember the speeches of Hitler and Goebbels. To this day I can clearly recall their strident voices and the thundering applause that would inevitably follow.

Our house, it was quite large, sat in the middle of the village. The local authorities requisitioned half of our house to house French prisoners of war, and later Italians, who worked on farms in the area. The prisoners were gone most of the day, but at night my father was supposed to guard them. We had to sleep too, so they were really on their own. I liked the French. They shared with me the candy and chocolate bars they received in their Red Cross packages, and at night they sang and played games. I spent a lot of time in their company. The Italians were hostile. They were Germany's allies at one time and then turned against us. The village people resented them. Russian prisoners were housed in a compound at the edge of our village. They were heavily guarded and worked in large groups in the fields. By late 1944 they were digging tank barriers along a defensive line being established nearby.

As a young boy I and my friends were envious of the Hitler Youths and the younger *Jungvolk*. They wore uniforms, marched and sang songs, camped in the woods, and did all sorts of interesting things. Our village life and the games we boys played seemed pretty boring compared to what we saw the older boys doing. We couldn't wait until we were old enough to be a part of them. In the meantime we followed them around the village, even into the woods when they went camping, to watch what they were doing. In mid-1945 I would have been ten, old enough to join the *Jungvolk*.

In school I had a very strict teacher when it came to following rituals. He taught every subject in my grade. When we children passed him on the street he expected us to raise the right hand and loudly shout *Heil Hitler*. If we didn't do it, or didn't shout loud enough, he would admonish us and shake his finger in our faces. If we saw him coming down the street soon enough, we ran away to avoid having to pass him.

By late 1944 I could hear the sounds of war in the distance. The boom of heavy guns became a constant background for my life. It made me feel uneasy, like there was some monster out there that any day could swallow us up. I became even more unsettled when my father was called into the *Volkssturm*, a militia of sorts of old men and young boys. He still had his rifle from his earlier days in the army, but they had no uniform for him. He trained in his work clothing. In December 1944 our area was alerted to prepare for evacuation. My father built several sturdy boxes in which he and my mother packed what they thought she and I would need, including bedding and dishes, pots, pans, and other kitchen utensils. The rest of our things my father buried in the basement and in the garden. A few days later he came and helped us onto the train. That was the last time I saw my father.

I thought the train ride was an adventure. I had ridden on a narrow gauge train before, but never on a *real* train taking me into an uncertain future. It was exciting, and I was not afraid. The following day Mother and I arrived in the small town of Flatow, in Pomerania. Flatow was about fifty kilometers west of Bromberg. We were assigned a room in a house occupied by a woman and her daughter. They were friendly to us and didn't mind sharing their house. Shortly before Christmas the woman and her daughter bade us *auf Wiedersehen*. They were visiting rel- atives in western Germany for the holidays, they said. They never returned. Mutti and I lived in the house for nearly a month. She enrolled me in school in January 1945. I attended classes for three weeks, and then the war put an end to it. I could again hear the sounds of war in the distance. The boom of the big guns. A number of antiaircraft guns were set up in a field next to our house. Their firing was frequent, and the sound was deafening. By the end of January the guns suddenly moved out. We were informed that same day that a train would leave the station at two in the afternoon for anyone who wanted to evacuate the area. Mutti and I put our few belongings on a sled we found in the house and headed for the train station. The snow was deep, three feet or more, and the streets were nearly impassable. After an hour we both were exhausted—she from pulling the sled, me from trying to keep it from toppling over. We turned around and went back to the house.

We had a second chance to leave Flatow. Soldiers of a German rear guard unit on the other side of town offered to take anyone on their trucks who wanted to accompany them. The snow was still too deep for us to get there. Mutti and I decided to stay put. The next day Russian planes bombed the center of town. The sounds of combat came closer and closer. When I looked out a window on the second floor the horizon was ablaze. Soon numerous buildings near us were hit by artillery and burning fiercely. That night my mother and I cowered in the kitchen near the wood stove. We didn't sleep. It was the thirtieth of January. The German soldiers were gone. I looked out the kitchen window, and I saw the burning inner city. Later we heard what sounded like machine gun and rifle fire. I was trying to be brave and not let my mother see how scared I really was. Mutti prayed a lot all night long.

In the morning we heard the sounds of trucks and tanks and the voices of soldiers. At mid-morning a group of five Russian soldiers suddenly broke down the front door and forced their way into the house. They searched the house for German soldiers, weapons, and ammunition. They rushed into the basement and searched it, looked into every room, under beds and into the pantry. They were thorough and professional combat soldiers it appeared to me, well equipped and well organized. When they found neither German soldiers nor weapons, they left. They didn't harm us, but Mutti didn't stop praying the entire time they were in the house. We didn't move very far from the warm stove in the kitchen where we had spent the night, sleeping on chairs with our clothes on, covered with a few extra blankets and cushions.

The next group of Russian soldiers arrived that afternoon. They went through cabinets, pulling out drawers looking for valuables. They

were interested in women, jewelry, and watches. Mutti and I were sitting at the kitchen table when they entered, shouting "*Uri, Uri,*"
pointing at their arms. Most already had several watches on their arms.
Mutti pulled her wedding band off her finger and gave it to them, and
then they too left. Although they didn't hurt us, it was nevertheless a
terrifying experience. I knew we were totally helpless and they could
do with us whatever they pleased. Did I fear rape at that time? I don't
believe so. I am not sure I knew what rape was. I feared the unknown.
What would happen to us? We had not been subjected to much propaganda, and it was only when we were evicted from this house and
forced to live with others when we heard about the rapes and beatings
by drunken gangs of Russian soldiers. My mother and other women did
their best to hide when they heard soldiers approaching.

The following day a Russian officer came into the house and in good
German told us to leave in five minutes. The house was needed for a
headquarters, he said. My mother and I grabbed some of our things,
and we put them on our sled. A Russian soldier escorted us to another
house down the street which was already occupied by several German
families, women and children of all ages, no men. We found some food
in the kitchen cupboards, but there wasn't enough for all of us. Soon
we were asked to move again. The house was requisitioned as a hospital. Over the next several weeks Mutti and I moved ten times. My
mother and I were certain the Russians only took over houses occupied
by Germans. If a house was empty, they seemed to leave it alone. By
the time we made the last move we only had the clothes on our backs.

Food became our number-one priority, warmth and housing was second. I roamed the streets with my friends looking for food. We
searched abandoned and burned houses and stores. We took anything
edible. At times we found flour and sugar, fruits and vegetables in glass
jars, dried-out bread. If it was edible, we took it. Nothing was too dry,
too old, too dirty. We knew if it was food it would help keep us alive
another day, no matter what its condition. There was a liquor distillery and bottling plant in Flatow. We boys climbed inside through a

broken window. Some large vats had been knocked over, their syrupy contents spilled across the floor. My feet stuck to the floor when I stepped into the syrup. I stuck a finger in the substance and tasted it. It was sweet. My three friends and I ran home and gathered up containers and ran back to the distillery. We climbed back in through the same broken window and began scraping the syrup off the floor, filling our containers. Suddenly I heard a noise. I looked up, and a Russian soldier stood over me pointing his submachine gun at us. He said something in Russian. We ran from the building and didn't stop running until we were out of gunshot range.

By late March 1945 it was nearly impossible to find anything to eat. Every house and store was cleaned out. There was no organized effort by the Russians to make food available to us. The streets were dangerous. Russian soldiers were usually always intoxicated, and they were always armed. I spoke a little *Mazurski*, a dialect spoken in our village by the older people, and I picked up a few Russian words, so I was able to explain to soldiers we ran into that we were hungry and looking for food. I recall being very hungry about this time. As I was walking along aimlessly one day near a Russian field hospital, I was stopped by a Russian doctor. In German he asked me if I was hungry. I replied, *Ja, ich habe hunger.* He said, *"Warte hier."*

I waited. I began to wonder what he was up to, what he might do to me. I nearly ran away. Then he reappeared with half a loaf of stale Russian army bread and gave it to me. *"Hier ist etwas für dich,"* he said. I was overjoyed. I gave the bread to my mother as if I were handing her a treasure. The bread lasted us for several days.

At night the Russian soldiers roamed the streets looking for women to rape. I could hear them coming, calling *"Frau, Frau,"* their tongues heavy with vodka. My mother and other women living in whatever house we were in at the time hid every night. We children would call out to the Russian soldiers, *Keine Frau hier. Alle Frauen sind weg.* They usually left. Fortunately I never saw them rape a woman, but I heard about their brutality from my friends who did. I noticed though when the soldiers came into our house at night looking for women to rape, once they saw us children they usually mellowed. I could tell in their faces that they remembered something. They had feelings for children. They weren't that old themselves, teenagers. Very young men.

My mother was petrified when the Russian soldiers came. She and other women hid under beds. The soldiers nearly always looked inside the closets, so that was not a good place to hide. I recall one situation when there were ten children in the room and three women. The women lay down on the bedboards. Then we children put the mattresses and featherbeds on top of the three women, one was my mother. Then we sat on the beds. The soldiers came, asking us where our mothers were. We said we didn't know. They looked in closets, touched the beds, but didn't dig in deeply, and they looked into the basement. Then they left. That's the closest my mother came to being raped.

None of us had access to news. We had no idea how the war was progressing. Sometime in the spring Russian soldiers said to me, "*Hitler kaput.*" I didn't know if I should believe them. I guessed the war was over, but I didn't know for sure. Then the Russians formed work brigades made up of German women and older children since the older men had all been shipped off to camps. The Russians dismantled workshops, factories, and railroad tracks. My mother was sickly, and they gave her a job as a cook in a hospital kitchen. That was a real blessing. Now we had enough to eat. By summer the women and children were taken into the fields and told to harvest whatever there was. There wasn't much. About that time Poles began to arrive and settle in Flatow, displaced from the eastern parts of Poland annexed by the Russians. The Poles opened several shops and schools. But only German children who were Catholic were allowed to attend school. I was Protestant.

In February 1946 my mother and I were told to report to a large building in town. In it were over a hundred women and children. We sat on the floor on our meager belongings. A Russian officer accompanied by several soldiers walked through the building, stopping occasionally, asking questions. He spoke good German. Many of them did. A young woman and her mother sat close to where my mother and I sat. The young woman was paralyzed. She couldn't stand or walk without assistance. She sat on a bundle of clothes. Her mother sat next to her. The officer stopped in front of the young woman and ordered, "*Steh auf. Steh auf.*"

The young woman made an attempt to rise, but she couldn't and collapsed on her bundle. The mother put an arm under her daughter's arms and tried to help her up. "*Nein,*" the Russian said to the woman sternly, "*ich will das sie alleine auf steht.*"

The young woman tried, but fell down again. Her mother quickly came to her assistance. That's when the officer pulled his pistol and shot the mother dead. Then he and his soldiers left. The Russians could be brutal, and they could be kind. I never knew what to expect from them.

Our group was loaded on trucks and driven to the Flatow train station. There we were loaded on freight cars; the doors were left open. The train departed without any of us knowing where we were going. It was bitterly cold, and we huddled together for warmth. Occasionally bandits, young punks, would jump aboard the slow-moving train and start throwing out suitcases or anything they could lay their hands on. No one resisted. The bandits never stayed long, because they had to recover whatever they had thrown out. The train kept moving. Now and then the train stopped, and escorting soldiers allowed us to get off to relieve ourselves next to the tracks. After two days and nights without food or drink we arrived in a camp in Stettin on the Baltic Sea. There we got our first food at a soup kitchen. The other thing I remember about Stettin is the delousing chamber. The women and girls were first told to disrobe in one room. They were then led into another room where their hair was liberally blasted with some sort of foul-smelling, white powdery chemical. The boys then went through the same process.

After the delousing procedure we were loaded on another freight train which eventually stopped in Eberswalde, close to Berlin. I had a fever and was gaunt from hunger. I soon recovered in a hospital. The food tasted so good, I recall, and the nurses were kind. I wished I could have stayed longer, but I had to make room for others as soon as the nurses saw that I was recovering. Another train ride and another camp, this time in the British zone of occupation, near Lübeck. Life was more organized here, but the soup was still devoid of meat. Our daily ration consisted of a cup of cabbage or rutabaga, some potatoes, salt, a slice of bread, and water. If we were lucky there was enough soup left over for seconds. Mutti and I and other refugees learned to make syrup from sugar beets. We made rutabaga sandwiches, which I thought tasted especially delicious. We children roamed the fields looking for bird eggs and young sea birds to supplement our diet.

My mother gave our name to the Red Cross to put on their lists of people looking for relatives. We found my grandparents, but my father's name never showed up on any list. The last letter we had from him was dated 18 February 1945. The *Feldpost* postmark read Festung Gotenhafen, just north of Danzig. He sent the letter to a cousin in Bochum, in the west of Germany, who sent the letter to us several years later. Nothing was ever found of my father. We think he probably died on a ship in the Baltic Sea as he was being evacuated.

After several weeks we were moved out of the refugee camp and given a room with a farmer on the west coast of Schleswig-Holstein, in the village of Poppenbull. Close to the water. A land of perpetual rain and wind. Mutti worked for the farmer in return for food. Our situation improved later in 1946 and early 1947 with a steady stream of CARE packages, as well as packages from various churches in America. In one of those packages, sent by a Mennonite family in Iowa, was a softball. I didn't know what to do with that ball. It was too small and hard to use as a soccer ball, and it wouldn't bounce. But I was sure that the people who sent the ball meant well. About that time we reestablished contact with an aunt in Chicago. Every month she sent a package of clothing which usually contained a pound of coffee beans in a foil package. She had opened the coffee bag, stuck a pack of cigarettes into it, and resealed it. My mother didn't smoke and we didn't use the coffee; instead, we traded the coffee and cigarettes on the black market for things we needed. One cigarette for one egg.

Looking back, I cannot recall how I felt during all that time. Occasionally of course I was scared, such as when the Russian soldier pointed his gun at me and at my friends in the liquor distillery. When the Russian soldiers first burst into our house searching for German soldiers and weapons, I was petrified. But most of the time I believe I just went from one day to the next, not worrying too much about what the future might bring. Children adjust to the way things are and don't worry too much about what might be. You adapt to the situation, and many times I saw my experiences as an adventure—not knowing their possible consequences.

It was different for my mother. She was always sickly, and that was one reason why I felt closer to my father. She spent much time in bed at home when my father was still there. My dad did much of the housework and the cooking too. However, during our time of stress, when my father was not around, my mother got better. Her health actually improved, and she managed amazingly well. The situation brought us closer together. We became a team with a common goal of staying alive. She looked after me, cared for me, and when we had food she would cook a fine meal. She became a good mother in those hard times. By 1948 my mother began to receive a small pension because my father was missing in action, and she also received support payments for me. It was the year of the new money and things started to look up for us. We still lived with a farmer, another one by that time, and my mother worked for him. We managed to keep our heads above water, as the saying goes.

Having missed most of the fourth and the fifth grades it was hard at first to get used to the discipline of school again. I had nearly forgotten how to read and write, but I learned fast and soon was back into the routine of learning. I went to a one-room schoolhouse which accommodated several grades. The teacher tried to do the best he could with the little he had. He couldn't use the old textbooks issued under the Nazis because they contained too much propaganda. There were no new textbooks. So we heard many stories, the same stories over and over again. History was ancient history. The Stone Age, Bronze Age, Iron Age. Noncontroversial periods. History instruction stopped with the nineteenth century. I could tell that history was a difficult subject for my teacher.

My aunt who lived in Chicago came to visit us for the first time in 1950. In 1955 her brother, my uncle, accompanied her on a visit. He talked to me about how much better life would be for me in the United States. I had a job, and I gave most of my salary to my mother for our household expenses. We were doing fine, I thought. I even thought I had a good life in Bad Wildungen, a small town which had never been bombed in the war. I eventually made up my mind to take my uncle's advice and emigrate to the United States. My mother stayed behind. My uncle sent me a ticket, and I flew on Lufthansa in October 1957 from Frankfurt to Chicago. It took twenty-five hours with all the stopovers. In Chicago I lived with my aunt. I started working as a sales-person in the toy department of a large department store. In July 1958 I was drafted into the U.S. Army. After two years I got out of the army and went to work for a company in Chicago, got transferred to Tulsa, Oklahoma, and finally to Philadelphia. When I retired, my wife and I returned to Tulsa.

Did my daughter show interest in my past? Not too much. Maybe that comes later in life. How did the experiences of my youth affect me? Well, I learned as a common person not to get involved in poli-tics. To this day I have an aversion to getting involved in politics, any part of politics. Of course I know the difference between the Nazi Party and the political parties in our country; still, there is something deep inside me that keeps me from joining or being active in a political party. The hardest part of it all was losing my father. I missed him very much when he left us in 1944, but I always thought he would come back some day. Having him taken from me at age nine left me with a void in my life which I never managed to fill. I still miss him. My mother never remarried and stayed in Germany.

Goetz
Oertel

{Age 10}

Stuhm, East Prussia (Poland)

We were all torn between wanting to weep and run away, and to scream
and run out to meet the danger. "No Bolshevik will ever tread on
German soil." But they were there by thousands, crushing it with frenzy
and jubilation—and there were eighteen of us to stop them: eighteen
young men ready to cling to any miraculous superstition to go on hoping
for a future as tormented as the present.

—Guy Sajer, *The Forgotten Soldier*

I remember Christmas 1944. The Russians weren't all that far away, but
my family hardly knew that. Neither did we know that the German lines
were weak and would not survive a serious attack. We lived in blissful
ignorance of our vulnerability. . . .To us, it was a given that Germany
would win the war, and that any Russian incursion into Germany would
only be temporary.

—Goetz Oertel

I was born on August 24, 1934, in the small town of Stuhm, south
of Marienburg, in East Prussia. My father, Egon, was the manager of
the local *Raifeisengenossenschaft*, a large flour mill and agricultural coop, with an output of ten tons of grain products per day. My younger
sister, Barbara, was born in 1938, and our brother, Burkhard, came
along in 1940. We lived with our father and mother in a large, comfortable house on the site of the flour mill, surrounded by storage
buildings, barns, and garages. We had a large vegetable garden, and
later on in the war also a chicken coop. The chickens provided eggs

---

Previous page: Goetz leading family members on their flight west from the Red Army, 1945

and meat, things which became increasingly more difficult to obtain as the war progressed. As the manager of the mill my father was allowed to keep a small car with a two-cycle engine, a DKW. It ran on a mixture of part gasoline and part light oil, or nearly any other low-quality combustible liquid. Depending on the quality of the fuel mixture, our car frequently trailed a thick cloud of smoke.

I entered school in September 1940, and until late 1944 my life was quiet and protected. The school wasn't far from my house, and I walked to it every day. When I was ten years old and about to enter the fifth grade there was some discussion by my parents to have me attend the Adolf Hitler Schule. What kept me out was that only out-of-town children were allowed to attend the school in our town. I would have had to go to such a school in Marienburg or Königsberg. My parents didn't consider those towns safe alternatives because of the ever-increasing danger of air raids. So I continued to go to school in Stuhm and transferred from the *Grundschule* to the *Hauptschule*, which would take me to the eighth grade. At the *Hauptschule* they offered English as a foreign language. Although I only received four months of English instruction before we fled the advancing Red Army, I acquired enough vocabulary to be able to make myself understood. In time, my English language skills would prove to be significant to my family's future.

In school we had all the usual subjects, including physical training, of course, because every German child was supposed to be strong. I wasn't. I had every childhood disease known to man and was a puny child. It didn't help either that our diet wasn't especially good. As part of our PT we started playing supervised games of capturing some objective; in other words, we played soldier. There were also flyers handed out to us which showed how to fire a *Panzerfaust* without hurting yourself or someone else.

I remember Christmas 1944. The Russians weren't all that far away, but my family hardly knew that. Neither did we know that the German lines were weak and would not survive a serious attack. We lived in blissful ignorance of our vulnerability. My father had some concerns, not very serious though, and relocated his precious collection of books to an acquaintance's house about sixty miles west of us, just across the Weichsel River. To us it was a given that Germany would win the war, and that any Russian incursion into Germany would only be temporary. It would have been very easy for my father to load our possessions on a railroad car used to ship flour from the mill to western Germany, and then have one of his many customers store them for him. I remember that option being discussed by my parents, but they rejected it as being defeatist and unnecessary. Their honest expectation was that the Russians would be stopped before they got to us.

I clearly remember the feeling I had at the time—one of invulnerability and superiority of being German. I didn't understand that feeling, but I clearly remember being taken in by it, feeling it as a child. There was a magnetism that radiated from these people when they spoke on the radio, Hitler and Goebbels particularly, which today is extremely difficult for anyone to understand. But it was real then. It captured even us children. Hitler, though, remained a distant figure to me, although I guess I must have somehow admired his ability to create images in people's minds. I recall the total war speech given by Goebbels in the *Sportpalast* in Berlin in 1943. Goebbels asked the audience if they wanted total war. They all roared, *Ja*. We want total war. I thought I had an idea of what war was, but total war? What was it? It bothered me at some level that I didn't understand. I put it aside. Maybe it was obvious to adults what total war was, but I didn't understand. With that I became suspicious of the system. The *Kohlenklau* campaign, on the other hand, an energy conservation program, I thought was intelligent and cleverly done.

Both of my parents came from East Prussia. My father was born in Gumbinnen and my mother in Ortelsburg. My mother, Margarethe, everyone called her Grete, studied music and attended a girls' finishing school in Berlin. My grandfather, who came off a farm as a young boy without a *Pfennig* to his name, started a small grocery store which he successfully built into a large business. He owned the local bank, but most importantly, he became the exclusive distributor for all alcoholic beverages in the county. A very lucrative trade which made him wealthy. He had a large family of eleven children, all but two being boys, many of whom later died in the war. My mother was the oldest. My grandfather on my father's side was a *Beamter*, a civil servant. His quite unusual title was *Kreisswiesenbaumeister*, county drainage engineer. His responsibility was to design drainage for low-lying agricultural areas, of which there were many in our part of East Prussia.

January was bitter cold. The nineteenth of January, that date is clearly etched into my mind, there was an alarm in Stuhm. The Russians had reached a small village by the name of Nemmersdorf, just south of Gumbinnen. There they apparently raped, killed, and burned, foreshadowing what was in store for the rest of us. The Nazis used this incident to build up the people's morale and fighting spirit, or so they thought. They made a big deal out of the thing, reporting the atrocities in great detail in newspapers and over the radio. Instead of building up the fighting spirit, it served to alarm all of us and told every German that the last thing they wanted to do was to be around when the Russians came. Suddenly it became an imperative for everyone to leave. This Nemmersdorf event was sort of a watershed; it changed the mood of nearly everyone. Very early the next morning my father drove my mother, us three children, and a friend and her young daughter in our old DKW to the town of Dirschau. Dirschau was on a major rail line between Berlin and Königsberg. He must have figured from there we would have a better chance of getting out. I recall the exhaust fumes of our DKW suddenly catching fire as we crossed the bridge across the Weichsel. My father managed to extinguish the fire before it caused significant damage.

We were the only people at the Dirschau train station when we arrived, two women and four children. My father returned to the mill. I remember how cold it was, somewhere around twenty degrees below zero Centigrade. We just stood around hoping some train would come by and take us away. After a while a German army officer approached.

He walked toward us across the railroad tracks. He asked my mother, "Where are you going?" Berlin, she replied. "All right. Follow me," he said. And with that he grabbed two of our small suitcases in his right hand and led off straight across the railroad tracks. That was exciting for me, because my parents had always warned me never to walk along or across railroad tracks. The officer took us to a military Red Cross train filled with wounded soldiers. One coach, the last car, had been added to the train to accommodate civilians. The officer led us into the empty, heated coach. The train sat on its isolated track for many hours. As time passed the officer brought more and more civilians, filling the coach far beyond its design capacity. People were not only standing body against body, but lying in the overhead suitcase bins. Every inch of space was occupied. Finally the train left, stopping many times en route.

Twelve hours later we arrived in Berlin. In Berlin we were met by Hitler Youths who took us to a huge concrete bunker where we were provided with blankets and assigned a place where we could lie down on the straw-covered floor. We were dirty and tired. But everything was nicely organized, and we were served hot soup and given information about when and where we could catch a train out of Berlin to Gransee. In Gransee, about fifty kilometers north of Berlin, friends of our family were expecting our arrival. That night there was no air raid on Berlin. The next morning we were escorted to our train and arrived in the afternoon in Gransee.

My father had not been drafted because as a young man he contracted tuberculosis. His lung capacity was severely reduced, making him unfit for military service. However, he was considered for the *Volkssturm*, the people's militia, and placed in the least able category. Categories one and two were older, but able-bodied men. Category three were young boys less than sixteen years old. And category four were the disabled, wounded, and infirm. That's the category my father fell into. After receiving permission to leave Stuhm from the *Volkssturm* organizers, my father drove off toward Gransee in the old DKW. En route he was stopped by German Panzer troops looking for gasoline for their tanks. They drained his tank, not realizing it contained a mixture of gasoline and other combustibles. The DKW wouldn't run because it was out of fuel, but the tank wouldn't run either because the curious fuel mixture from the DKW contaminated its engine. My father arrived in Gransee two weeks later.

Gransee was far enough away from Berlin not to be bombed, but close enough so I could see the bombers nearly every day as they bombed Berlin. In the newspaper they printed a map of Germany overlaid with a grid, which changed every week. On the radio they announced the progress of the bomber formations using these grid coordinates and a heading. I enjoyed listening to the radio announcer and locating the bombers on my grid map, trying to figure out which town was going to be bombed. That's how we children whiled away many of our hours.

In Gransee it suddenly dawned on me that I had lost my home, lost everything that had been dear to me. For the first time I realized that I would never be able to go back. That was a devastating moment for me. I cried for my loss, and also for my grandparents whom we had left behind in Ortelsburg. I didn't know what had become of them. I later learned from my grandmother that my grandfather was killed either by the Russians or by revenge-seeking Poles. She ended up as a servant in her own house. Someone denounced her as having been a Nazi, of belonging to the women's organization of the NSDAP, which was not only untrue but totally uncharacteristic of my grandmother. She was so openly anti-Nazi, my grandfather constantly had to restrain her from getting into trouble. She was convicted, served her term in jail and then walked to western Germany. Somehow that old woman walked across East Prussia, through Pomerania, crossed the Oder and the Elbe Rivers and showed up one day in Elmshorn, in Schleswig-Holstein, in a refugee camp. I never learned what she experienced on that long walk across Germany, a land ravaged by battles and at that time still without law.

Goetz Oertel

Soon after my father's arrival in Gransee a strange-looking contraption appeared at our front door. It was an old truck with a shaft attached to its front axle, pulled by two sturdy draft horses. The truck, no more than a wagon, was from our mill in Stuhm, driven by one of our workers to whom my father had given directions to Gransee. There he was, and we were all delighted to see him and the two horses. Now we had the means to go further west. After resting the horses for several days my parents decided to leave for Triptis, a small town in Thüringen, near the Bavarian border, where my mother had a girlfriend from her days at the finishing school in Berlin. Triptis was near the north-south Autobahn from Nürnberg to Leipzig, just north of Hof in Bavaria. We five trekked in our horse-drawn truck from Gransee to Triptis. It was February and bitterly cold.

I recall the great variety of receptions along the way as we passed from village to village, town to town. Some people callously told us to move on, saying, "We don't want you *Flüchtlinge* here," sharing nothing with us and our tired, hungry horses. Others took us into their houses and treated us as if we were family. Our horses were of special concern to us. Without them, or even one of them, we couldn't go anywhere. They worked hard all day pulling the overloaded truck. At night they needed food, water, and rest. After coming from as far as East Prussia, they had worn down their shoes and needed replacements. We finally found some iron and a willing blacksmith who shaped the iron into horseshoes to shod our horses. We stayed away from the Autobahn or major roads as much as possible because of the danger of *Tiefflieger*, and traveled instead mostly over small *Feld-* and *Waldwege*.

Triptis was a county seat with five to six thousand inhabitants. My mother's friend, who lived not far from the train station, although surprised at our arrival, cheerfully put us up. It turned out that the small train station was a frequent target for *Tiefflieger*. I remember one attack very well. I was playing in the yard when it happened. Their engines sounded different from what I had heard in the past. I soon found out why. They flew much lower than any planes I had seen before, and they were nearly upon me when I realized they were coming. I looked up and there they were. There were nine of them, twin-engine planes, flying in a V-formation like wild geese. They were nearly at treetop level. Then I heard another sound I hadn't heard before, that of dropping bombs. I dove headfirst under the table in the nearby laundry room. I heard several explosions down by the railway station. I ran outside, overcome by curiosity, and saw the first group of planes departing and a second group of equal size bearing down on me, flying the same curious V-formation. I dove back under the table in the laundry room. From my not-too-secure hiding place I suddenly noticed a foot-long bomb splinter lying nearby which had come down while I was gawking at the planes.

That air attack changed my family's life in two ways. First, my parents decided that Triptis was not a good place to be and we needed to move on. The second thing was more positive. A military supply train sitting in the nearby railyard had been one of the *Tiefflieger* targets. The train's cargo was strewn all over the area—bars of some sort of high-energy food similar to pemmican. Although my parents wouldn't let me out of the house, they gathered up enough of the pemmican bars to keep us fed for some time. We moved on a few kilometers south of Triptis to Leubsdorf, away from the train station, on the other side of the Autobahn. There marauding *Tiefflieger* were our greatest worry. They made travel by day on the Autobahn impossible. I recall walking home one day, approaching the Autobahn underpass, when I heard the *Tiefflieger*. As I ran for the cover of the underpass I saw the bullets throwing up dust only a few feet away from me. At the time I was very proud to have experienced such a thing, not old enough to really understand the possible consequences.

On April 15 the Americans came through our village. I ran outside to watch. As a ten-year-old I was impressed with how well ordered the Americans were. They looked to me like they were on maneuver, not in a war. The trucks and tanks rolled through the village in a seemingly endless column. Soldiers sat on tanks; later, infantry on foot followed. Not a shot was fired. All of us Germans were happy that for us the war was over. The Americans left a small garrison behind and kept on moving. All the soldiers were very well behaved. To me they looked like regular people, harmless. I heard my parents talking over dinner about how impressed they were with the impeccable behavior of the American troops. The small group of American soldiers remaining behind immediately implemented a curfew. We had to remain in our houses at all times, except from seven to eight in the morning and six to seven in the evening. After two days, when nothing happened, they lifted the curfew during daylight hours.

There were continuous troop movements on the Autobahn. The Autobahn was within a thousand feet of where we lived. We were instructed by the Americans not to go near the Autobahn, but to a little boy of ten there was nothing more interesting than watching soldiers and the endless columns of passing trucks and tanks. So I sneaked outside and took up a position by the side of the Autobahn, hiding in the forest. I quickly noticed that the soldiers were throwing a lot of stuff out of the trucks as they passed by me. The stuff turned out to be mostly K rations. In some cases all the soldiers took out of the ration were the cigarettes and then threw the rest away. In other cases they ate most of the food and left the cigarettes. I remember the cigarettes came in little boxes of four—Lucky Strike, Old Gold, and Chesterfield. All of the items were individually sealed in wax paper, so even after a heavy rain the cigarettes and the food would still be dry. Cigarettes were priceless to us.

I had my territory along the Autobahn which I patrolled regularly. Every day I came home loaded down with goodies. I never touched anything before I got home, even if I was very hungry. I waited until the food was divided by my mother among the five of us. I didn't want an unfair share for myself. I thought that would have been dishonest. I remember on one occasion four soldiers stopped their truck along the Autobahn, near where I was hiding. I watched them pull up wooden roadside markers, then build a fire with the markers. They got rations out of their truck and started to cook their meal. As they were cooking, one of the Americans noticed me in the forest, watching. He motioned for me to come over and join them. I got up and approached slowly, not sure what might await me. Three of the soldiers were black, one was white. I had never seen a black soldier before and was obviously curious, but I soon forgot about skin color. To me, they were just four American soldiers. They had the usual K rations, but also larger tin cans filled with various other foods. The black soldier who had initially called me over to join them opened one of the large tins, warmed it over the fire, and then insisted that I eat all of it. It turned out to be ham and eggs. The soldier was trying to be kind to me, not realizing that when your stomach isn't accustomed to having much food, let alone anything as rich and substantial as ham and eggs, it gets a bit difficult to get it all down. But the soldier insisted that I eat all of it, and indicated I would get some additional cans of food to take home with me for my family. I later figured out that some children probably never got to eat any of the things GIs gave them, so these soldiers wanted to make certain that I got to eat something before they gave me anything else. I was proud sharing a meal with those four soldiers, and even had a conversation with them using the little English I knew. They were amazed that a little German kid could speak any English at all.

I remained very interested in the Americans because they had jeeps, and guns, and food, and everything else I could think of that was exciting for a little boy. We children hung around them, hoping they'd say something to us. The village boys didn't understand what the Americans were saying when they spoke to us, but since I had some English in my last year of school in Stuhm, I understood enough of what one American soldier said to us that I answered him in English. The soldier was utterly amazed to find a German child speaking English, even if it was broken English spoken with a heavy German accent. Although I was going on eleven, I looked more like I was eight or nine. I was underweight and looked much younger than the other children. One soldier eventually asked where I came from, and I told him East Prussia. He kept pressing me for more information, and asked me why we ran away from home. I told him that I thought the Russians would execute my father if they got ahold of him, because we had Russian prisoners of war working at our flour mill. A day later the same American soldier talked to me again. This time he asked me to take him to my parents. I felt very important and led the way.

My mother spoke about as much English as I did. She spoke with the inquisitive American soldier. I only heard part of the conversation, but the essence of it was that the American encouraged my mother to move her family across the line from Thüringen to Bavaria, into the American zone of occupation—and that as soon as possible. To travel to Bavaria we needed a travel permit. The cost of the permit would be fifty fresh eggs, the soldier said. That was the price his first sergeant had set who had the authority to issue such a permit. My mother promised we would come up with the eggs. We tried frantically to round up fifty fresh eggs. It wasn't an easy task. My parents bought, bartered, traded their most valuable possessions, and we came up with fifty fresh eggs. The American soldier took the eggs and in return provided the permit. We packed up and left immediately. Just in time, it turned out. We stopped for a day in Bavaria after leaving Thüringen. When we set off for Stuttgart on the following day we could see Russian troops on the other side of the zonal border.

In Stuttgart we had some very distant relatives and hoped to be able to stay with them, at least for a while. I remember on our way to Stuttgart passing an American truck by the side of the road. As we approached I could see a GI in the back of the truck throwing an orange up in the air and catching it again. He did it over and over again. Passing time. My sister stared at the American and his orange. He must have noticed her, because suddenly he tossed the orange over to Barbara. As startled as my sister was, she caught the orange. That made my sister's day. She couldn't stop talking about the American soldier who shared an orange with her.

It began to rain. My pride and joy when we lived in Leubsdorf was a two-man tent I had found near the Autobahn, wrinkled and crusted with dirt. I cleaned the tent, repaired the tears and holes, made up tent stakes and poles, and put it up. It was my only toy. As we slowly traveled in our horse-drawn truck toward Stuttgart, my father insisted we put the tent over the truck's leaking tarp to keep the water out. I argued with him not to do that, because if an American saw the tent, he would recognize it as American and would probably take it from us. My father ignored me and put up the tent. Within minutes an American sergeant in a jeep stopped us, demanded to know where the tent came from, and promptly took it away from us.

When we arrived in Stuttgart our relatives took us in, but we had to feed ourselves. My father tried to get work at the local *Raifeisen* agricultural cooperative. He was well known within the organization as a manager. But there was so much unemployment, the locals weren't about to hire an East Prussian. His next attempt at eking out an existence for his family was to offer up our horses and makeshift wagon for hire. He wrote letters to the various counties around Stuttgart asking if they had a need for transportation. He received one reply from the town of Oehringen, about sixty kilometers north of Stuttgart. With a job offer in hand, the housing authority in Oehringen quartered us in the house of a local businessman. He was not too happy about his uninvited guests, but couldn't do anything about it. We had two rooms, both tiny; one room served as an improvised kitchen. We used wooden boxes for chairs and improvised a table and bunk beds. I don't remember how we handled bathing. The horses were stabled at the other end of town. Somehow we always found feed for the horses, I guess because we simply had to. My father hauled everything and anything. He was paid partially in near worthless *Reichsmark*, and part in kind—bread, eggs, and other essentials of life. After nine months of that, in 1946, my father had a severe relapse of his tuberculosis and entered a sanitorium.

My mother, sister, brother, and I continued to make a life for ourselves as best we could. We received a small social security payment each month which helped, although the payment didn't buy much except when accompanied by ration cards. I found an old rusty bicycle in the attic of the house we lived in. I received permission to restore the bicycle, working many hours with emery paper and a little paint. It was a lady's bike, but no matter, it worked. The bike tremendously increased my mobility, and I was now able to help my mother support our little family. I took most of the money she received, a rucksack, and a couple of two-liter milk cans, and rode on my bicycle from village to village, farmer to farmer, begging food. One farmer would sell me a half liter of milk, another some goose eggs, another a little butter. Not every farmer would sell me something, but after a while I knew who would and who wouldn't.

My little brother and sister didn't get involved in begging for food, but they helped in other ways. In the autumn we went into the forest and collected beechnuts. We found a mill which pressed the oil from the nuts. The miller kept part of the oil as his payment. We got highly efficient at collecting beechnuts. We scooped the nuts up by the handful and sifted most of the debris from what we collected until we had a pile of half nuts and half debris. That mixture of nuts and debris we put into burlap sacks which we then hauled home on a little handwagon. In the evening we dumped the mix on a blanket laid out on the floor, and all four of us would pick the nuts from the remaining debris. As we became more efficient at collecting nuts, the miller began keeping a greater and greater percentage of the oil. We still ended up with a considerable amount of oil which we used for ourselves, and the rest we traded on the black market. In season the whole family collected wild berries of various kinds—raspberries, blackberries, blueberries, and mushrooms. My parents received a ration of cigarettes each month, a pack a person. We traded the cigarettes for food on the black market. The cigarette turned into quasi currency. The value of an egg, a pound of butter, or any other article of food was expressed in numbers of cigarettes.

I entered school in Stuttgart in September 1945. I was fortunate and missed only eight months of school on our flight from the East.

By 1948, with the currency reform, shops suddenly filled with goods again. Our standard of living didn't improve much, because all we had was my father's small social security payment. When he was released from the sanatorium that year he decided to follow an old hobby to make a living—genealogy. He somehow managed to hook up with the Church of Latter-Day Saints, who asked him to do genealogical research. They paid well. My father's problem was getting around to the outlying villages. Public transportation was time consuming. We bought a new bicycle for me, and I did much of the research for him in the more remote areas. When I wasn't going to school I found myself bicycling all over southern Germany to remote villages doing genealogical research for American clients.

I attended the *Oberschule* in Oehringen until 1950. Since that school only went to the tenth grade, I had to transfer to the *Gymnasium* in Heilbronn, a town about twenty kilometers west of Oehringen. I took the train every day. In 1953 I made my *Abitur* and graduated. I was nineteen years old. I wanted to study electrical engineering and made arrangements to go to Stuttgart to do a six-month *Praktikum*, a requirement before entering school to test a student's aptitude. My father encouraged me to see a career counselor, because I kept on saying that maybe I wanted to study physics because it was what personally interested me. After looking at my school records the counselor told me my grades weren't good enough to study physics. That's all I needed to hear. On the spot I decided to study physics. I went to Kiel in November 1953 and entered the university. In 1956 I passed a comprehensive examination. That same year my thesis advisor was recruited by the University of Maryland. I had a choice to make, either follow my advisor or find another one. I spoke to him about it. He said, "You can follow me to the University of Maryland, and I'll make sure you get an assistantship. However, that's contingent on you getting a Fulbright travel grant." I applied and was fortunate enough to get a Fulbright grant. In September 1957 I found myself on the *Italia*, an aging and rusting ocean liner, heading for New York.

Goetz Oertel

As a foreign student in the United States, the one-time enemy country of Hitler's Germany, I was immediately impressed that people accepted me as if it was the most natural thing in the world. Only twelve years had passed since the war ended, and no one took offense at my presence. I found none of the resentment and discrimination I found on occasion in Germany as a *Flüchtling*. That open acceptance, combined with the loss of my roots in East Prussia, made it rather easy, even natural, for me to eventually become a citizen of the United States. In October I traveled to New York to meet with some students I met on the *Italia*. Only a couple of weeks earlier the Soviets had launched Sputnik I. We went to church that Sunday, and there was a man by the name of Norman Vincent Peale preaching a sermon about Sputnik and the dangers it represented to this country. I went away from that church service believing that Sputnik was a traumatic experience for the United States. That sermon helped me choose my area of concentration, the diagnosis of high-temperature plasmas, plasmaspectroscopy.

In 1963 I completed my Ph.D. in physics at the University of Maryland and was granted a formal degree in 1964. Even before I graduated, NASA, the National Aeronautics and Space Administration, asked me to come and consult for them at Langley, near Norfolk, Virginia. Those trips were valuable for me not only because I got to participate in a completely different work environment, but also because it augmented my pay very nicely. They paid me a huge consulting fee of fifty dollars a day, big money for a two-hundred-dollar-a-month graduate assistant. I liked working with the NASA people, and eventually they offered me a position. I told them I wouldn't be able to accept the offer, because after I graduated my visa expired and I must return to Germany for at least two years. The NASA person said to me, "Don't be so sure." He made me a formal job offer and told me that he would take care of the visa. NASA did just that. They got a waiver, and I got my visa allowing me to stay and work in the United States. I met my future wife, Brigitte, while studying at the University of Maryland. She was a German exchange student, like myself. She also was given a green card allowing her to work in the United States.

I worked on various NASA projects over the years both as a scientist and project manager. Later I accepted a position in the Department of Energy, ending up managing the Savannah River Defense Waste Disposal Plant. Nuclear waste. After ten years in the energy business, in 1986 I accepted the position of president of the Association of Universities for Research in Astronomy (AURA). I stayed at AURA for thirteen years, and now do independent consulting. For a refugee boy I have to pinch myself at times to make sure that everything is real.

What did I take away from my experiences in my early youth? I am conscious of costs on the margin of life. The small things which over time add up to become big things. Politically I am independent. As for my mother, she strongly influenced me in terms of setting an example, by doing rather than lecturing. Her work ethic comes to mind, making do with what you have and using the resources available to you. She was completely devoted to her family and loved to cook. She was a superb cook. Not just mother's cooking, but exquisite cooking. She enjoyed life, I believe—loved the beach, lie in the sun, drink good coffee, and smoke cigarettes. All very German activities for her generation. She was also a sensitive person, easily offended by a casual remark, nervous as are many heavy smokers and coffee drinkers. She died of cancer of the stomach. She missed the two great wishes of her life. First, not to have to worry about money and the future—*auf einen grünen Zweig zu leben*—to live on a green twig, as the German saying goes. Her second wish was to have grandchildren. My children were born after her death. Surprisingly, my father, with his severely damaged lungs, outlived my mother.

Goetz and Brigitte have prospered. Life in their country of choice has been good to them. Both of their children, Carsten and Ines, long ago left the parental homestead in the greater Washington metro area and are building their own lives. To Carsten and Ines, Germany is a vacation destination, not a place of hardship as it was for Goetz and Brigitte.

Fred
Rother

{Age 12}

Weisstein, Upper Silesia (Poland)

On my trip to Upper Silesia [February 1945] we decided that the railroad installations which would be needed in the future for distributing coal to southeast Germany were not to be destroyed. We visited a mine near Ribnyk. Although the mine was in the immediate vicinity of the front, the Soviet troops were allowing work to continue there. The enemy, too, seemed to be respecting our policy of nondestruction.

—Albert Speer, *Inside the Third Reich*

In 1945 I heard the rumble of artillery, but that was as close as the war came to Weisstein. I don't think I ever understood what was really going on throughout the war. The propaganda proclaimed up to the very end that Germany was going to win the war. Then all of a sudden the war was over. The day before the Russians occupied our town, I hung a *Hakenkreuzfahne* out our window. I had no real sense for the situation.

—Fred Rother

February 7, 1933, I am told, was a dreary, snowy day in the coal-mining town of Weisstein, nestled snugly up against the snow-covered forest, the Hochwald, at the foot of the Riesengebirge. My parents named me Fritz Friedemann, because my father liked playing the music of Wilhelm Friedemann Bach on his violin—the oldest son of the famous Johann Sebastian Bach. Since my middle name was underlined on my birth certificate, that was clearly the name my parents wanted me to go by. But everyone called me Fritz.

Previous page: Fred, Martha, Paul, and sister Marianne, 1947

Weisstein was a modest town sixty kilometers south-southwest of Breslau, the provincial capital of Silesia, and within a few miles of the Czechoslovak border. An ancient castle ruin looked down upon the town and upon our street, lined with functional, three-story apartment blocks. One building looked like another—once-white stucco walls had turned dirty grey from the sooty grime emitted by countless chimneys. These were "modern" buildings built in 1931 and 1932, modern in the sense that each three-room apartment—kitchen, living room, and one bedroom—had cold running water in the kitchen and its own toilet. Just a toilet, not a bathtub or a wash basin.

My family lived its life in the kitchen, the only room heated in winter. The living room, also called the *Gute Stube*, was normally used only for special occasions such as birthday celebrations, Christmas, and similar days calling for a festive atmosphere. The *Gute Stube*, in contrast to the unheated bedroom, had a floor-to-ceiling *Kachelofen*, which of course was coal fired but only rarely put to use.

With each six-family apartment house came a small backyard with two sandboxes for the children, an area where the women hung their laundry, and a wooden scaffold over which small rugs could be hung and beaten. There were several concrete ash bins behind each house, because everyone heated and cooked with coal. The basement stretched for the length of two apartment buildings. In this dual basement each family had a small fenced-off storage area. And on one end of the basement was the common laundry room which served the twelve families of the two apartment houses. In addition there were two community bathrooms, without toilets, side by side so they could draw hot water from the single boiler which served the laundry room as well. Faucets projected directly from the boiler so one could run the hot water into the concrete tubs. Each family was assigned a laundry and bath day. On the assigned day you made your own fire, heated the water, cooked, rinsed, and scrubbed the laundry, by hand of course, and finally, if there was enough hot water left you scrubbed the kids. All very hard work for the women.

My father, Paul, whom we children called Vatel, worked in a coal mine. He enjoyed music and played the violin, clarinet, and saxophone. He drove a little underground shuttle train that delivered the newly mined coal to the shaft leading to the surface. Vatel had two brothers, Otto and Walter; both were killed in Russia during the war. He also had two sisters, Martha and Gertrud. We called my mother Muttel. She had two sisters, Hedwig and Elizabeth. Hedwig and her husband, Fritz, emigrated to the United States in the late twenties and settled in Tonawanda, in western New York State, where they operated a small diner. Elizabeth soon joined Hedwig and Fritz in Tonawanda.

My mother was a housewife first, and, I recall, an excellent cook. In January 1937 my sister, Marianne, was born. I vividly remember the occasion for two reasons. First, because I got to ride in an automobile, a taxi, to the clinic to see my mother and my newborn sister. Riding in a car was really exciting. Not until years later did I again get to ride in a car. The second reason was that my sister was born in a hospital rather than at home and delivered by a midwife. I was born at home and, as it was customary, delivered by a midwife. I knew where the nearest midwife lived. I often walked past her apartment building. She lived on the third floor of a five-story building. A bell chain hung from her window, down the wall to just above the sidewalk where adults but not children could reach the handle. When childbirth was imminent the expecting father would run to the midwife's apartment and pull the chain. She would then lean out the window and ascertain the facts, and if warranted make her way to her patient, accompanied by the father.

Even after the war started, life for me was carefree and quite normal. At first we felt virtually no economic impact on our simple working-class lifestyle. Then, very slowly, the war began to encroach on our way of life. We were urged to contribute blankets and warm clothing for our freezing soldiers on the Russian front. Some food was rationed, and radio announcements warned us not to listen to foreign broadcasts. A clever cartoon character called *Kohlenklau*, the coal thief, appeared on kiosks and public buildings. A smaller version of these posters was pasted near every light switch in the stairways of our apartment buildings, and the *Kohlenklau* also appeared on little cards which we children collected. The coal thief was a shifty-eyed, shady-looking character, clad in black with a sack of stolen coal over his shoulder. He and his helpers sneaked through the Reich stealing coal sorely needed for the war effort. "Stop the *Kohlenklau*" was the message, turn off your lights when not in use, save electricity. I recall that one of the *Kohlenklau's* helpers was an old, shifty-eyed woman. Naturally she was clad in black. Her name was Miese. Since my English teacher looked somewhat like Miese, we children promptly referred to her behind her back as the *alte Miese*.

In 1943, at age ten, I was obligated to join the *Jungvolk*, the preparatory youth organization for the Hitler Youth which every boy joined at age fourteen. Those were the only two youth organizations allowed in Germany. There were equivalent counterparts for girls. In the *Jungvolk* I wore a Boy Scout–like uniform, went hiking, did a lot of marching, and sang patriotic war songs. I was designated lead singer. I had to first sing a few bars of the song as we were marching along before everyone chimed in—for me it was great fun.

By 1944 I occasionally saw fleets of American bombers pass overhead, but the Weisstein area was never bombed. In 1945 I heard the rumble of artillery, but that was as close as the war came to Weisstein. I don't think I ever understood what was really going on throughout the war. The propaganda proclaimed up to the very end that Germany was going to win the war. Then all of a sudden the war was over. The day before the Russians occupied our town I hung a *Hakenkreuzfahne* out our window. I had no real sense for the situation. I don't recall why I did that. Maybe it was because I heard Hitler had died. As soon as the neighbors saw what I had done they rushed over to alert my mother, who quickly took down the offending flag. I really got a talking to. Everyone else put white flags out of their windows, and I did that stupid thing.

I don't recall being afraid. One day Russian soldiers occupied our town. There was no shooting. Women were hiding because they had heard what the Russian soldiers did to women. We didn't have good hiding places. A Russian soldier knocked on our door late one evening, and I foolishly ran to the door and opened it. Fortunately he was so drunk I was able to slam the door in his face and keep him out. The adults spoke of neighbor women who had been raped, but it didn't happen to my mother. Surprisingly, throughout the period water continued to flow from our faucet, and electricity was never interrupted.

Although May of 1945 was warm and sunny, fields lay fallow. And those that had been planted remained untended. Stores, factories, mines, and schools were closed, and as a result the quest for food suddenly became our prime family objective. In the fall of 1944 we had purchased several hundred pounds of potatoes which we stored in our cool cellar. We had also purchased cabbage and put up several crocks of sauerkraut, and we had received our annual allotment of coal. By the spring of 1945 that modest stockpile of food and fuel was dwindling fast. We could not plant our little garden for lack of seeds. Although several of our fruit trees bloomed profusely, their apples and pears would not be available until later in the year, if they weren't stolen first.

My father had not been drafted into the Wehrmacht because working in a coal mine was considered war-essential work. That June he was back in the mine working, but the money he made bought nothing. After spending a full day in the coal mine he and I would head for the countryside to beg, steal, or barter for the food we needed to stay alive. My mother and sister would set off separately from us and do the same. We were down to only a few potatoes and a little sauerkraut. One day my mother with my little sister in tow went into town to see if anything was for sale in the one store that had reopened. One had to keep on trying. As she and my sister passed a warehouse, a Russian soldier with his submachine gun at the ready ordered her to follow him. They were frightened, but followed the soldier. They joined a group of other women similarly conscripted at the back of the warehouse. Several Russian army trucks stood there. The women were ordered to unload the trucks, loaded with four-pound loaves of freshly baked, mouth-watering sourdough rye bread. My sister was eight years old and worked alongside my mother. They worked for hours without a break, no food or water. At the end of the day when the trucks had all been unloaded, my sister and my mother were each given one loaf of bread. The reward was unexpected and made the ordeal seem worthwhile. The two four-pound loaves of bread fed our family of four for many days.

On another occasion my father and I walked farther than usual into the countryside. We knew the farmers near the town wouldn't even answer a knock on the door anymore. I, a skinny twelve-year-old, hoping to evoke sympathy from the farmers, did the begging for whatever food they might be able to spare. That day no one had anything they wanted to part with. Exhausted, my father and I finally sat down by a small stream to rest and cool our feet in the flowing water. While we were dangling our feet in the water we noticed a large trout caught in a shallow pool. That night we had fish for dinner.

When the fields were empty and the farmers no longer cared to share anything with us, my father and I decided to go to a flour mill within walking distance of town. We knew the miller was under strict orders not to sell, barter, or give away any grain or flour on penalty of death. But maybe there was something anyway, we thought. As expected, the miller shook his head when we asked him for a little flour. But he asked us if we wouldn't mind sweeping the place. "The floor is a mess," he said, with a wink of an eye. "I have no helper and no time to do it myself." We gladly grabbed brooms made of twigs tied to a stick and swept the mill floors clean. We filled our rucksacks with the sweepings. At home we separated the grain from the dirt.

Early one foggy morning as we prepared to leave on our daily scrounging expedition, I looked out the window and thought I saw an apparition. A lone cow was slowly walking down our street. I had no idea where the cow came from. There were no farms or pastures nearby, yet a cow appeared out of the morning mist. I alerted my father. He and a few other men who quickly responded to his call of *Fleisch, Fleisch*, drove the hapless cow through our building's front door into the backyard. There they killed the cow, skinned it, and cut it up.

Before the day was over there was no evidence that a cow had ever been killed there.

By constantly scrounging and with a little bit of luck we made it from one day to the next. Food was all we ever thought of. Our total energy was devoted to its acquisition. In a distant village my father and I came across a number of men standing over the carcass of a dead horse, run down by a Russian army truck. The men stood there talking, not knowing what to do. My father always carried a knife along. He offered his services to the men for a share of the meat. For the next several weeks we ate horse meat.

As the days passed, scrounging and luck were no longer enough. It was time to barter our valuables for the food we needed. My parents' wedding rings went first. Each ring bought five eggs. A crystal vase fetched a piece of bacon. My parents traded away most of the few cherished possessions they had. The story made the rounds that the farmers had Persian rugs decorating their barns. My best friend's mother one noon invited me to eat supper with them. It was a rare act of kindness, and I thanked my friend's mother profusely for the invitation even before we sat down at the table to eat. She served meat, serving me an equal share, which I thought was most unusual. I noticed that she peeled the potatoes she served, throwing out the peels. After we finished eating I asked her for the potato peels. I took them home and my mother served them to us as pancakes. Later I learned the meat I had eaten was dog meat.

That summer my sister and I headed into the nearby fields to see what we could find. It was fun. She and I enjoyed our outings together. She liked to take along her doll carriage. Along the edge of a field we discovered mulberry trees with their bows bending under the load of their mealy-tasting berries. I intended to have my sister fill her doll carriage with mulberries when I discovered a carefully hidden pile of sugar beets. We filled her carriage with beets instead, covered them with her doll blanket and lay her doll on top of it all. In several more trips we retrieved the remaining beets. The following weeks my family spent making sugar from those beets. I recall the kitchen dripping with humidity while we turned the beets into mash and extracted a few precious pounds of brown sugar. We ate the leftover mash. I can taste that horrible stuff to this day. The sugar was worth its weight in gold, and with it we were able to acquire other foods to supplement our diet.

Besides working in the coal mine my father moonlighted as a musician. He played the violin, clarinet, and saxophone in a small combo. The combo played at victory parties held by Russians, and later for Poles who began to move into our area. The party goers usually rewarded the musicians with drinks. My father collected his drinks in a flask he always carried with him in his violin case and brought the liquor home. He would later trade the mixed liquor for food on the black market. At one such event a drunken Russian nearly shot him for not drinking a toast. Someone who spoke Russian explained just in time my father's reason for abstinence, and the Russian finally put away his pistol.

Toward the end of 1945 my mother's parents, who lived across the river in Altwasser, were evicted to make room for a Polish family. They moved in with us. My grandmother died soon after the move. Then it was our turn for eviction. The relocation order was handed out and posted throughout town and read:

Special Order

For German citizens of Weisstein, Bad Salzbrunn, including the Sandberg area. It is hereby ordered that:

1. The relocation of the German population will commence on July 14, 1946, between 6 and 9 in the morning.
2. The German population will be relocated to areas west of the river Neisse.
3. Each German will be allowed to carry no more than 40 pounds of baggage.
4. Transportation by means of wagons, horses, oxen, cows, etc., is not permitted.
5. All inventory, living or inanimate, in undamaged condition, hereby

becomes the property of the Polish government.
6. The relocation process must be completed by July 14, 10 o'clock in the morning.
7. Resistance will result in severe penalties and will be broken with firearms.
8. Weapons will also be used to avert sabotage and plundering.
9. All persons will assemble at the train station in groups of four.
10. Those German nationals who have been exempted from this process must remain on their premises with their families between the hours of 5 in the morning and 2 in the afternoon.
11. All premises in the town must remain unlocked, with the key in the lock on the outside of the front door.

Regional Commander
Zinkowski
Lieutenant Colonel

A Polish official came to our apartment and informed us we had to vacate the premises within twenty minutes. In anticipation of our eviction we had packed several suitcases. We joined a long column of neighbors and headed for the train station. All the way to the station we worried that my father would have to stay behind because he worked in the mines. At the station we were searched, and everything of value was taken. In our case the inspector took my mother's treasured linens and my small stamp collection. Our names were recorded, and then we were assigned to a freight car. We hid my father far in the back of the boxcar in case the Polish officials came looking for him. Every boxcar was filled to capacity, with barely room for anyone to sit on the floor. There were no provisions for toilets, food, or water. Just before the train left the station my aunt Martha, my father's sister who lived nearby, found us and brought us a little food. We breathed a sigh of relief when the train jerked into motion. We had no idea where we would end up.

The train rumbled slowly on patched-up tracks through the countryside, day and night. The weather was warm and dry throughout the trip. We older kids sat at the open doors, dangling our feet over the edge, enjoying it all, not totally understanding what we had lost. Occasionally the train stopped in the open countryside for no apparent reason. Then, without announcement, it would suddenly start up again. If at these random stops houses were nearby, designated people would jump out of our car and run to the nearest house begging for food and water. In every case the kind people did the best they could for us in a short time. We also used those stops to relieve ourselves in ditches and nearby woods. On one such stop my grandfather, my father and I ran into the woods to relieve ourselves. Before we finished, the train started to move again. My father and I grabbed my grandfather and got him back into the boxcar. Then I barely made it in. My father didn't. He grabbed a handrail on the last car of the train and eventually, with the help of others, was able to get back on.

In the middle of the night the train stopped in the Soviet occupation zone of Germany. Russian officers came aboard each car and looked us over. They saw mostly old people, women and children, and refused to accept us. The train then continued west, to the English zone of occupation. At the border, it was still night; the train stopped. We all got out of the cars and were herded into a building. Males and females were separated. We had to undress and stand naked while given a rudimentary physical examination, followed by a thorough dusting with a white powder to kill any lice we may have had. Then back on the train. After another day of travel we were off-loaded at the bombed-out former Luftwaffe air base of Delmenhorst, just west of the city of Bremen. We were hungry, somewhat skinnier, thirsty, exhausted, and absolutely filthy. The shattered buildings on the air base served as our shelter for several weeks until local German authorities were able to place every expelled family with someone.

Prior to being assigned a permanent place, a group of thirty people, including my family, was relocated to a gymnasium in the village of Adelheide. Straw mattresses were laid out on the floor to serve as beds. Within a few days each family was assigned to a farm in or near Adelheide. The residents of Adelheide were none too happy to have to accept total strangers into their homes. In extreme cases people were treated brutally by their hosts and exploited. A single eight-by-twelve-foot room, adjacent to horses and cows, served as our home for the next three years.

Our small room was furnished with a one-burner wood stove, a small table, four chairs, a very small cabinet, and five straw mattresses. The stovepipe was routed through our only window. The outside wall of our room was concrete, and in winter the humidity in the room would condense on the concrete wall and freeze into a thin layer of ice. Occasionally a mouse would try to nest in our straw mattresses. After all, we lived on the barn side of the house and shared a common floor with the horses, cows, and whatever other creatures found shelter in the warmth of the barn during the cold winter months. The only toilet in the house was located next to the pigpen, which was attached to the barn where we lived. The outhouse got very cold in winter; it was not a place to linger. During the day we piled our mattresses in a corner of the room to gain a little space to move around.

Marianne and I attended the village school, a one-room schoolhouse. In the following year, 1947, I transferred to the middle school in Delmenhorst, where I began to take English lessons as part of my curriculum. My parents helped around the farm, and in turn the farmer shared food with us. Occasionally we received a package from our relatives in the United States supplementing our sparse diet, packages filled with luxuries such as canned ham, coffee, chocolate, and cigarettes, all items we could trade on the black market for other things we needed. Marianne and I were happily surprised when a free lunch was served at school every day. We had to bring our own bowl and spoon. My mother fashioned bowls for Marianne and me from tin cans by punching two holes near the top edge of the can and then threading a wire through the holes for a handle. Usually we received a milky, sweet-tasting soup, or another rather tasty soup, I never figured out what it was. We children called this soup *U-boat Suppe*. It was served with a slice of corn bread. We didn't like the corn bread, but we ate it anyway. It filled our stomachs. During mushroom season our whole family ventured into the nearby heath to search for wild mushrooms. Since my father had always been an avid mushroom hunter, it didn't take us long to find the places where the best mushrooms grew. Often we returned home with a basket filled with mushrooms, and Mother would then prepare a veritable feast for us on our one-burner stove.

At age fifteen I was to be confirmed in the nearby village of Ganderkese. I had nothing to wear for such an important occasion in my life, so my mother wrote her sister Hedwig in Tonawanda and asked her if she could send me a suit. Soon a package arrived containing a brown tweed winter suit. The local village children wore their best black Sunday suits. I looked very different in my brown tweed suit among all the black suits. Although I was grateful to have a suit at all to wear, I felt self-conscious throughout the ceremony.

My father joined a small combo. There was no work to be found anywhere. The group traveled to nearby villages and played at dances and folk festivals. They were paid in food, at times even with live chickens. Once a week we were allowed to take a shower in a public bath in Delmenhorst, a place where we could also wash the few clothes we owned. The future looked bleak, and my mother and father decided early on to apply for immigration to the United States. Our relatives sent encouragement. Quotas, however, were very low and restrictive. In 1947 only parents of children living in the United States who were U.S. citizens were allowed to enter. My grandfather applied, was granted a visa, but died within a year after arriving in Tonawanda. By 1949 the quotas were expanded to include immediate family of U.S. citizens; we qualified. In late November 1949 my mother, father, Marianne, and I boarded a train in Delmenhorst bound for Amsterdam. From Amsterdam we traveled to Liverpool on a ferry, where we embarked in third-class accommodations on the *Queen Elizabeth*.

The trip across the Atlantic took five days. The sea was fairly gentle most of the way. I figured out that if I stayed on deck and kept my eyes on the horizon I didn't get seasick. I did that much of the time in order not to miss all that great food that was being served three times a day. Imagine that, three big meals a day! On December 7, 1949, we passed the Statue of Liberty in New York harbor. Several hundred of us immigrants crowded the ship's railing to stare at the statue and our new homeland. My introduction to American life was memorable, I thought. Raucous New York automobile traffic, giant buildings, my first ride on an airplane from New York to Buffalo, my uncle's big car, wide-open spaces, and towns and villages with no bombed-out buildings. And I could drink all the apple juice I cared to drink. At age sixteen, only once before in my life had I tasted apple juice. Only once before had I ridden in a car. And never before had I flown on an airplane.

We jumped straight into the American way of life. My father found a job with a dry cleaner. My mother went to work in an ice cream cone factory. Marianne and I entered school barely four weeks after our arrival in Buffalo. I thought I wouldn't have any problems in school since I had taken three years of English in Germany. That proved to be a false assumption. I was placed in a junior high school class commensurate with my age, and to my horror discovered that I couldn't understand a word my teachers said in class. It took about three months of listening to radio shows such as *The Lone Ranger* until the rhythm of the language fell into place. I still recall the day when I understood everything being said. It took a little longer for me to emulate the American accent. A year later I was the second-best speller in my high school class. My parents attended English language for foreigners classes for several years. They were in their forties at the time, and learning a new language was difficult for them. We continued to speak German at home.

Six months after graduating from high school I was drafted into the U.S. Army. At Fort Dix, New Jersey, I went through four months of basic infantry training. There I met another German immigrant from Augsburg, his name was Fritz, just like mine. We became good friends.

He met my sister, Marianne, when we went home on leave in Buffalo, and in 1956 the two married. Because of my German language skill I was assigned to a military intelligence unit and put to work translating East German documents about their military and political systems. The work was tedious, and after three months on the job I applied for a transfer to Germany. Soon I found myself on a ship bound for Japan to become a teletype technician. Three months later I was living in a tent in Korea maintaining and repairing teletype machines. After two years I was discharged from the army and returned to Buffalo.

In Buffalo I was offered a job as a ticket agent with American Airlines in Cincinnati, Ohio. I took the job. A year later a position opened in Buffalo as a reservation agent, and I transferred back there to be nearer my family. Eventually I took advantage of a job opportunity at the Ford plant in Cologne, Germany. While there I met my wife, Irene, and within a short time I returned to work for American Airlines, working in the data processing end of things. We ended up in Tulsa, Oklahoma, where we chose to remain after my retirement in 1998.

With the concurrence of my parents I changed my first name from Fritz to Fred when I became a naturalized citizen in 1952. I retained my middle name, Friedemann, as a concession to my parents. Only my closest family continues to call me by that name. In spite of years of hardship, the war and its aftermath probably affected me less than others who were more exposed to violence than I was. However, I still turn off the lights when I leave a room, just as I learned to do from that energy-saving program called *Kohlenklau*.

Dieter
Hahn

{Age 7}

Posen, Wartheland (Poland)

The shooting might have stopped in May 1945, but I had never really felt that the war ended for us Germans. During the three years after the war, our suffering continued unabated. In many respects it was worse *after* the shooting and bombing stopped. The dying continued; now, though, the victims were mostly women, children, and the old, and the causes of death were different. For me, war was not just the shooting of guns and the dropping of bombs. It was all the other things . . . fear, hunger, disease, exploitation and abuse, and rape of women of all ages by force and through circumstance.

—Wolfgang W. E. Samuel, *German Boy: A Refugee's Story*

Werner was taller and thinner than I, and not very strong. The lack of proper food seemed to affect him more than me. On one occasion as we walked to one of the villages to trade saccharin for eggs, a village only six kilometers away, he fainted four times before we got there. He lay in the road as if he was dead. Each time I cradled his head in my arm and spoke to him, Werner, what's the matter with you? Wake up. We must move on. When he finally came to he muttered, "I am so ill. I don't feel good." Then he lay in the road for ten more minutes before we continued on.

—Dieter Hahn

I was born on the fourth of July, 1938. I have two brothers. Werner is two years older than I, and Jürgen is two years younger. My father, Kurt, worked in the technical department of the *Reichsbahn*, and my mother, Else, was a *Hausfrau*. My father's last assignment with the *Reichsbahn* transferred him to Posen, where we lived when he was

---

Previous page: Dieter, Jürgen, and Werner, 1944

239

War on the Ground

drafted into the Wehrmacht. Eventually he was captured on the Russian front and remained a prisoner of war until 1948.

War came to my family and to Posen in 1944. I was six years old. Against the dire threats and warnings of the adults I ran out of the basement shelter during an air raid, up to our front door, to take a look at the planes passing overhead. As I stepped outside I saw a huge, brightly burning bomber heading directly toward our house, toward me. The bomber crashed behind the house. The air raid warnings became more frequent. When I heard the sirens, fear entered my body. If no one was around I got into my swing, which was mounted on the frame of the kitchen door. In the swing I felt secure until someone came to take me into the dark, dank basement until the all clear was given. By January 1945 the Russian army was on the move, and the word was *rette sich wer kann*, he who can save himself. One January morning my mother rapidly packed two suitcases, grabbed us three boys and ran into the street. There were no more trains running. My mother saw a fleeing farm family and their horse-drawn wagon approaching. She waved the farmer down and pled with him to take us along. The farmer finally relented, saying, "In God's name, come with me. But two suitcases is one too many." Mutti left one of the suitcases standing by the side of the road, shoved the other onto the back of the wagon, and then assisted Jürgen onto the wagon. Mutti, Werner, and I followed behind the wagon. If we ever made it out of Posen, my mother's goal was to reach her sister Paula who lived in a tiny village called Erzingen, up against the Swiss border. I recall traveling for some time with the Posen farmer. Eventually we ended up on a train, and after several days' travel we arrived in Erzingen. By the time we arrived I was totally exhausted, and I don't remember anything about the trip.

In May 1945 Erzingen was occupied by the French. My younger brother, Jürgen, and I accompanied our mother on an errand which took us past the border station to Switzerland. There a French soldier stood guard armed with a rifle. Jürgen, five years old, planted himself in front of the French soldier, raised his right arm and said loudly, *Heil*

Hitler. The enraged soldier took the rifle off his shoulder, chambered a round and aimed his rifle at my little brother's head, as if he was going to execute him right there. Frantically my mother pulled Jürgen behind her and attempted to excuse my brother's behavior. The Frenchman apparently spoke no German. Slowly he lowered his rifle, removed the bullet from the chamber, shouldered his rifle again, and turned away. The atmosphere between Germans and French was tense. Once we got home my mother gave us boys precise instructions of how we were to behave in the future. "In no case," she said, "will you ever again say *Heil Hitler*. You saw, yourself"—and she looked at Werner and me—"they nearly shot Jürgen."

Occasionally we listened to the news on a radio my mother's sister had lent her. One day the French authorities ordered that all radios were to be turned in on a specified morning. Mutti, along with everyone else in the village who owned a radio, dutifully delivered their radios to the village school. When the French soldiers had collected all the radios, they carried them up to the third floor of the school building, dropping them onto the cobblestones below. I stood there open-mouthed, watching the soldiers dropping the radios to the pavement. Then an officer announced over a loudspeaker that the owners of the radios could have their radios back.

A road led through our village directly to the border crossing. As children we quickly discovered that the people who crossed over from Switzerland to Germany were foreigners, not Germans. Switzerland was a land of plenty where everything imaginable was available. Now and then, depending on how miserable we appeared to the visitors, they threw something toward us children. We collected cigarette butts for those fathers who were at home. The French smoked cigarettes down to nothing. As the cigarette was near its end, to keep from burning their fingers, they inserted a needle into the cigarette butt and smoked the last bit until nearly nothing remained. What did remain they spit upon, and then they ground the butt into the dirt with their heavy boots. The cigarette butts we collected were those discarded by foreign visitors, frequently Americans. Things changed drastically when American soldiers came through our village. They nearly never smoked more than half of their cigarettes and then threw them away. A real find.

One day I had a wild experience. American soldiers passing through the village threw us the usual Hershey bars and chewing gum, but what was so exciting that day, they also threw us giant oranges. The oranges were more yellow than orange, but they were huge. We children scrambled for them. My brothers and I proudly took our haul home. Each one of us took one of those giants and peeled them like we would an orange. The first taste was as disappointing as their size had been impressive, bitter. That's how we were introduced to grapefruit.

Food was rationed, of course. Each family, based on the number and age of children, was given a specified allotment of meat and bread. My older brother and I stood for hours in food lines, lines which frequently were over a hundred feet long. My mother was a person who always managed to master a situation. She frequently forged our allotment on our ration cards by making a four out of a two so expertly that no one would have noticed the change unless they took a magnifying glass to it. So we got two additional loaves of bread. Many times we stood in one of those long lines, and when we finally reached the counter the butcher or grocer announced, "Everything is gone. Come back tomorrow." After standing in line for three hours or longer, such an announcement was devastating. Frequently Werner and I got faint standing in line, from being hungry and standing up for such a long time.

I recall standing in line at the bakery for some *Kommissbrot*, army-style rye bread. The bread was baked in pans, and the overflowing dough on the side where it touched the loaf next to it in the oven was soft, not crisp like the top of the loaf. After standing in line for an hour I finally got one of those coveted loaves. The smell of the fresh bread nearly drove me insane. I put the bread in my shopping bag and started for home. Occasionally I reached into the bag and broke off a little of the soft rind. I did this more often the closer I got to home. When I arrived home and took the bread out of the bag I saw that I had dug a hole through the loaf all the way to the other side. No one said anything. My mother knew how hungry I was.

Mutti found a job in Schaffhausen, Switzerland, the nearest large town. She received a special pass which allowed her to travel to her job on a daily basis. She worked on an assembly line manufacturing fittings and connectors for gas and water lines. She walked into Switzerland and then caught a train to her destination. The people were hostile toward anything German, and as a guest worker she was accused of taking away a job from deserving Swiss citizens. None of it mattered to her, her family's well-being came first. Although she heard it, she didn't respond to provocation. Her boss was fair-minded and understanding. And when on occasion she arrived late for work, mostly because of weather, border crossing or train delays, he understood her predicament. From her pay, which was in Swiss francs, she could buy anything she could afford in Switzerland. She was, however, allowed to bring very little into Germany. One hundred grams of sugar each week, a fifth of a pound; fifty grams of coffee.

She frequently purchased saccharin, a sweetener, and smuggled it across the border. Werner and I then went to the farmers in neighboring villages and traded saccharin for eggs. Werner was taller and thinner than I, and not very strong. The lack of proper food seemed to affect him more than me. On one occasion as we walked to one of the villages to trade saccharin for eggs, a village only six kilometers away, he fainted four times before we got there. He lay in the road as if he was dead. Each time I cradled his head in my arm and spoke to him, Werner, what's the matter with you? Wake up. We must move on. When he finally came to he muttered, "I am so ill. I don't feel good." Then he lay in the road for ten more minutes before we continued on. Once we got to the village the farmers were all very friendly. When I said, We have sweetener. Can we have eggs? They replied, "Of course, my boy," and we made the transaction. At one of the farms I looked into the kitchen. The table was set. A large loaf of farm bread, butter, cold cuts, and a huge pot of soup stood ready for the noon meal. I was close enough to the end of the table to be able to look into the soup pot. Of the soup my mother made, we always said that more "eyes" were looking into it then out of it, referring to the floating splotches of fat. From the farmer's soup there were only "eyes looking out" at us, out of that soup pot. After we left I said to Werner, Let's go back and ask the farmer if he can spare a bowl of soup. "Yes, let's do that," Werner replied excitedly. We went back, and when I politely asked the farmer's wife for a bowl of soup she replied, "Children, why didn't you say you were hungry. Now sit down and eat all you like." Quickly she brought out two large soup bowls and served us. We had seconds and thirds. By the time we left I was feeling queazy in my stomach, but I didn't get sick on the way home. Werner threw everything up. He just couldn't hold it down. It was too rich for him.

Jürgen also was hungry, just like Werner and I. We had a bowl of tallow which we used for frying things. Jürgen looked for food around the kitchen, and the only food he could find was the beef tallow. He stuck his finger in the tallow and licked it. He kept doing it until he had eaten the entire bowl of tallow. He didn't get sick. Hunger was a permanent condition in our family in the immediate postwar years.

While my mother was away working in Switzerland we boys assumed the responsibility of maintaining our home. First Werner did the chores, but as his health deteriorated I helped until I did nearly everything. Jürgen, the youngest, gave us to understand that he had two left hands and would cause more problems than his help was worth. We had only castoffs for furniture. In the kitchen we had a cabinet with three legs. The fourth leg was a Goethe. All of our dishes were in that cabinet. Once Werner was cooking the evening meal and said to me, "Dieter, give me a plate for the omelets." I walked over to the cabinet to get a plate and accidentally hit the poetry book with my foot. The cabinet tipped over, and all of our dishes fell to the floor. Nearly everything broke. I was heartbroken over my clumsiness, but nobody got angry with me. Mutti said when she came home, "It can happen to any of us." We stuck together as a family. We didn't blame each other for anything, least of all for things we had no control over.

My mother was a communicative person and easily made friends. That's how she managed to get the border crossing permit to Switzerland. Such permits were difficult to come by. Women from our village came to her asking for her assistance to obtain such a permit which would allow them to get work in Switzerland. She helped some of them. But her kindness was not always repaid with a thank you. To the contrary. One woman whom my mother helped to obtain a permit and for whom she also obtained a job in Switzerland approached her one day on the Swiss side of the border crossing and said, "Frau Hahn, I have learned that today I will be searched for smuggled goods. You know they make you take off all your clothes. Would you be so kind and take the items I have on me, because I know for sure that I am going to be checked today."

My mother agreed. The woman crossed the border ahead of her and wasn't stopped. But for reasons only known to her, she informed the Swiss border guard that the woman following her, my mother, was carrying contraband. My mother was taken into a large room where she had to wait for another woman to exit the examination room. By the time the guard took her into the examination room she had managed to slip the items she had on her behind a bench. Had they caught her with the smuggled items, the Swiss guards would have confiscated her border crossing permit, she would have lost her job, and our family would have had its livelihood taken away.

Another time she tried to smuggle coffee beans across the border. The small packet of beans she stuck in the upper part of her stocking, high up on her thigh. As she passed through customs, the Swiss customs agent said to her, "Please step aside and go into that room and disrobe." Women had to remove all of their clothes and then were frequently searched in the most intimate ways, depending on the customs agent. As she stood in front of the agent in the process of undressing, the bag of coffee beans suddenly broke, and the beans, one at a time, dropped to the floor—plop, plop, plop. . . .The agent turned around, and as he stepped outside he turned and said to her, "Well, I changed my mind. This is your lucky day." She quickly put her clothes back on and left.

Smuggling was difficult, and to be successful one had to have skill. My mother purchased a pair of ski boots for Werner, boots which he could wear every day, not just for skiing, and which could be passed down to me as Werner grew out of them. She got one boot across the border, and then the Swiss customs controls were made so difficult and thorough it took months until she was able to get the second boot across. When my brother finally tried on the precious boots, they didn't fit anymore. So I got them, and later my younger brother, Jürgen, inherited the boots.

We lived in an old, half-timbered house in Erzingen. The house had rats. When we three boys were in bed and alone in the house, we could hear the rats running around above us and in the walls. All three of us were scared of the rats. There was no heat in the house and no running water. In the kitchen we had a wood-fired cast-iron stove with four burners. The burners had concentric iron rings which could be removed to accommodate various sizes of cooking pots. During the cold season a large part of our family life played itself out around this stove. Every morning my mother heated a kettle of water and poured it into a basin, and that's where we three boys washed up. One morning as I was washing up, I had just removed my shirt and was standing over the wash basin, my mother said, "Oh, Dieter, why don't you take the milk off the stove, it is boiling." The day before we had the great luck to receive two liters of milk from a farmer. I reached over without looking, took the milk off the stove, and, as I passed it across the stove to set it down, I got tangled in one of those iron rings which when not in use hung above the stove. The boiling milk poured over my chest and back. I was soon covered with blisters. My mother took me to the local doctor and he cut open every blister. Today I know I received treatment with a high risk of infection, but I healed nicely. When I spilled the milk I didn't make a sound. Later I cried, not because of the pain, but because of the milk I had spilled.

My mother, Else, was tall, five foot eight. I liked her very much, but, like many people, I didn't realize what I had in her until after her death. We were good friends. She was the key person in my life before I met my wife. My name is Hans-Dieter. She would call me Hanse-Vogel. I don't know how she came up with that name, but she had a unique way of expressing her affection. "Hanse-Vogel," she would say, "this afternoon we both are alone. You go into the pantry and get a nice piece of cake for the two of us." And then we would sit and eat cake and drink coffee. She treated each of us like that. She was a true mother, only concerned for the well-being of her children. When I had problems I could talk to her about anything.

My father was released by the Russians in 1948. It took him a long time to find work. He was an honest but stern man. I never felt from him that special warmth and affection which I so valued in my mother. Our mother was the central figure in our lives. He recognized that after his return, and if there was a problem when she was not around he would defer a decision or discussion until she returned home.

In school the crimes of the Nazis were taught to us. My father didn't want to talk about it. I recall my mother saying to me, "There were many awful things done by that regime which we only slightly perceived, but didn't really understand." With that I let it go. The war years themselves didn't leave any lasting impression with me, at least I don't believe so. I was very young. The time after the war strongly influenced me. On a recent visit one of my grandchildren had his mother cut the crust off his bread or he wouldn't eat it. I said to my grandson, "Do you understand that there are many hungry children in this world? I cannot understand why you cannot eat the bread crust." To my great surprise, my little grandson replied, "I will eat it from now on." And he did. When it comes to food, and I see it wasted, I realize that my reaction is a result of my experiences in my early youth. In those days, when my mother asked, "What would you like to have for Christmas?," my brothers and I replied, Just once we would like to be able to eat as much as we can. Just once we would like to experience what a full stomach feels like.

As the weeks, months, and years passed, our relationship to the French occupiers improved. One result of me living in the French zone of occupation was that I learned French in school. In 1952, when I was fourteen, we moved into the American zone, to Karlsruhe, and there I needed English. I was two years behind in English and somehow had to make it up. I continued to attend the *Gymnasium* at the urging of my mother. My father didn't think I needed more than the conventional eight school years, or at most *Mittelschule*, for another two. Our family had nothing, and the additional income of three sons could be significant in acquiring furniture, utensils, or even a new apartment. My mother, however, insisted that I continue with my education, and so I did.

My uncle Bertl, my mother's brother, was fluent in English. He tutored me for two years, and my English improved sufficiently to pass my *Abitur*. Then my uncle encouraged me to enter the *Bundeswehr*, where I would have the opportunity to continue my education at a university. Without his support and guidance I would never have thought of going into the military. Uncle Bertl had been a navy pilot in the war, and he thought the new German *Bundeswehr* offered a unique opportunity to advance my education without me having to worry how I was going to pay for it. When I took my officers' examination to get into the Luftwaffe, I had to meet with a selection panel of officers. They asked me what I would do if I were not given the opportunity to obtain a college degree. "What career would you like to pursue as an enlisted man?" they asked. I rose from my chair, came to attention, and said to them, Gentlemen, I want this to be absolutely clear. In such a case I will remain a civilian and obtain my education some other way. I was selected and served a full career in the new German Luftwaffe.

Dieter Hahn retired as a lieutenant colonel from the Luftwaffe and now works as a software consultant, a skill he acquired while serving in the

Dieter Hahn

Luftwaffe. He lives with his wife, Ulla, in a picturesque mountain village an hour's drive east of Cologne. From his large living room window he can watch cows grazing tranquilly in a meadow while he works on software solutions to his customers' problems. The war of his youth seems like a distant shadow to Dieter, recalled only reluctantly, and then in terms of his mother's sacrifices.

Arnim Krüger

{Age 11}

Potsdam, Brandenburg

Nineteen forty-five was the worst year in human history. More people were killed violently, more houses burned, more buildings destroyed and more high explosives set off in 1945 than in any other year. Indeed, more people were killed in that year than in all the previous five years.

—Stephen E. Ambrose, "What We Owe Them," *The Wall Street Journal*

Dead Russian and German soldiers with swollen bellies lay in the streets, in foxholes and trenches. Men with their legs shot off, run over by tanks and crushed into nothing. The Russians ordered "everybody" out of their houses in our neighborhood. "Everybody" meant women and us children. . . .We pulled the corpses into piles—Russians and Germans in separate piles. Then the bodies were carted away and buried.

—Arnim Krüger

I was born in November 1934 in Potsdam, a town straddling the Havel River to the southwest of Berlin, the second oldest of four boys. My older brother, Günter, was killed in the battle for Berlin at the age of seventeen. As a young man my father had worked for the city of Berlin as a civil servant, a *Beamter*. To be a *Beamter* was held in high esteem because it bestowed job tenure for life. At some point he joined the *Reichswehr* and in 1933 became a member of the newly formed Wehrmacht. I remember him as a soldier in the finest Prussian tradition—honest, correct, decent. He was in the infantry. For a time he commanded a coastal artillery battery in Holland. Later in the war he was the commander of a security detachment for V1 and V2 launch

Previous page: Arnim behind the wheel barrow and author on the right, 1949

facilities. I remember as a young boy watching the launch of a V1. I thought it was very exciting. My father began his military career as a simple soldier, progressed to the rank of sergeant, was commissioned a lieutenant, and when the war ended in 1945 he was a major. My mother's family came from Stettin, where my mother, Grete, and my father, Julius, met and married.

We lived near the old palace of Sanssoucie, built by Frederick the Great, *Der Alte Fritz*. My father's family owned a large property in Potsdam which included our living quarters, a restaurant, and a *Café*. I think 1945 to 1946 was the worst year of my life. There was the constant bombing by the English and the Americans—the Americans by day, nearly every noon, and the English at night. We children watched the American bombers pass overhead on their way to Berlin, dropping their aluminum chaff, which frequently landed on us. At night we watched the nearby German antiaircraft batteries firing at the English bombers.

In 1944, when I was nine years old, the most important thing in my life was to be able to join the *Jungvolk*. I anxiously anticipated the arrival of my tenth birthday in November when I would be old enough to join. I looked forward to wearing a uniform. Wearing a uniform was the greatest, I thought. I was notified by the authorities to join the *Jungvolk* on April 1, 1945, and was deeply disappointed when the first meeting didn't happen. My older brother, Günter, had been in the *Jungvolk* and in the Hitler Youth before he was drafted. I was in awe of Günter whenever I saw him in uniform, and of course I wanted to be just like him. My mother was very nationalistic. Whenever the *"Deutschland Lied,"* the national anthem of the Third Reich, was played on the radio, we boys had to stand, raise our right hands, and say Heil Hitler. In contrast my father didn't like the Nazi Party. He saw himself as a Prussian soldier, and I believe the party was incompatible with his concepts of soldiering and officership. While he was away though, my mother raised us boys in her image.

In March 1945 streams of refugees from the East came through Potsdam, on foot or with horse and wagon. They looked tired and bedraggled. Day after day they came. Then came the Russian *Tiefflieger*, who attacked them with their cannons and machine guns. The next thing I knew the ground war came to Potsdam. I heard the artillery for days, then the shells began to fall in our neighborhood. Very young German soldiers moved into our house. From my window I watched the battle as it moved down our street. I was peeking out of my window when I saw one of those young soldiers running out of our house, crouching forward, his rifle in his hand. Suddenly there was a loud bang, the soldier's head exploded, and he fell forward, dead. I looked to the other side and saw a Russian sniper in a tree. Everyone else was in the cellar hiding, seeking protection. When it was quiet outside I ran into the street and into trenches where dead soldiers lay. I went through their coat pockets and removed the bread they carried. They no longer needed it. The bread was fresh and tasted good.

Women tried to make themselves look old. They smeared ashes on their faces, wore head scarves and the oldest and most unattractive clothing they could find. They had heard about the Russian soldiers and what they supposedly did to German women. The Russians raped all of them, young and old, regardless of how they looked. I could hear the women screaming in the street behind ours as the battle raged through our area, seesawing back and forth for two or three days. Then there were only Russians. I clearly remember the Russian soldiers coming into the air raid shelter where we sat hiding, looking for German soldiers. Then they took us children outside and went back into the shelter and raped the women. Two days later I saw the Russian army come through Potsdam heading into Berlin. There were some tanks, but mostly they came on little horse-drawn *Panje* wagons. They were Asian troops. They called out to us children, "Hast du Uri? Hast du Uri? Hast du Frau?," gesturing with their fingers. As I saw them pass by me I wondered how an army arriving on horse-drawn wagons could have beat our Wehrmacht. It was inexplicable to me as a ten-year-old boy.

A Russian captain moved into our house. He chose one of the women, a waitress who had stayed with us for safety, to be his companion, and in return provided protection for our family from marauding soldiers. In the days that followed I frequently observed Russian soldiers raping women on the side of the street, out in the open. One woman, many soldiers. When they finished some of the women couldn't get up and walk away. I knew many of them. I can describe them to this day. They were our neighbors. I felt lucky we had the protection of the Russian officer.

Dead Russian and German soldiers with swollen bellies lay in the streets, in foxholes and trenches. Men with their legs shot off, run over by tanks and crushed into nothing. The Russians ordered "everybody" out of their houses in our neighborhood. "Everybody" meant women and us children. There were no men. We pulled the corpses into piles—Russians and Germans in separate piles. Then the bodies were carted away and buried. We children saw all the mayhem, but at the time it made no impression on us. It was our world. We ran around the neighborhood looking for food. I wandered into a German antiaircraft position once. I looked around and saw a German soldier sitting behind the gun, smiling at me. I went over and touched him. He was long dead. Stiff.

For a time dead horses littered our streets. People went out and stripped the skin from the carcasses and cut out sections of meat. Not until years afterward did I find out where the meat came from for the good-tasting *Boletten*, hamburgers, my mother served for several days in succession about that time. People had to eat. Within a short time after the fighting stopped, a black market sprang up. Women and children traded the suits of their husbands and fathers for whatever food a Russian soldier might give them. One morning my mother traded my father's suits for what she assumed was cooking oil. The Russian soldier carried the large canister of oil on the back of his *Panje* wagon. We had no fats at all. Once at home we drained the oil into bottles, and then she and I went out and traded bottles of the much-coveted cooking oil for other foods. Then we had potatoes, bread, and sugar to eat. That afternoon my mother made potato pancakes for us three boys, myself and my younger brothers, Eckart and Manfred. It was the first meal we had in a long time where we could eat our fill. I ate until I thought my stomach would burst.

Toward evening word reached us that a shop down the street was selling bread. I rushed out with a shopping bag in hand and joined the already-long bread line. Suddenly I felt a pain in my stomach which made me double over, accompanied by the immediate need to relieve myself. I ran home, wetting my pants. There I found everyone else occupying the lavatories. The house stank from our many-hour-long ordeal. We had traded one bottle of the oil to our doctor for medication. He analyzed the oil and determined it was mineral oil used in submarines to lubricate torpedo tubes.

My mother was very good at making deals. She always found something to put on the table for us children. She made sausages out of suit material, butter out of coffee, so to speak. She was always on the lookout for food. During the entire period in Potsdam from late 1944 until we fled to the West in 1946, my mother, with my help, kept the family fed. My two younger brothers were much more timid than I and mostly stayed inside while I roamed around town. I don't recall us ever going really hungry like some of my friends' families. If my mother and I were not looking for food, I was collecting coal and wood, carrying it upstairs, always doing something.

Besides being a good provider my mother was also an accomplished piano player. She taught me to play the piano. I played by ear, without sheet music. It came naturally to me. When she saw Russian soldiers approaching our house she often made me play the piano. Some of the soldiers came into the house and up to the second floor where we lived. They marveled at what a young boy could do on that magic instrument. They promptly wanted the piano for themselves. My mother negotiated with them behind my back and they left, to soon return in a *Panje* wagon. They unloaded three hundred-pound sacks of flour and carried off the piano. My uncle had a piano shop in Potsdam which had not been damaged by bombs or robbed. He replaced the piano for us, and we went through the same routine again, sharing the flour with him. We bartered away three pianos. To stay alive such things as pianos didn't matter any longer, only food was important. My mother traded the flour, a kilo at a time, for other foods. In this way we stayed alive from one day to the next.

I recall when the Americans first came into Berlin, around the time of the Potsdam Conference in July 1945. The Russians blocked off the main road when the Americans came through. Their guards stood ten meters apart with submachine guns slung across their chests. An American unit camped near us in a forest. My mother went to meet the Americans. When she came home the next day she was loaded down with food, including lots of chocolate. She didn't talk about how she got the food, but I knew she had to give something in return. It didn't matter. What I remember most about the Americans though was something very different. A German Tiger tank had sat in the middle of the main road since late April when the battle for Berlin ended. The Russians just drove around the tank. When the Americans first came, they too drove around the tank. But only hours later two Caterpillar tractors equipped with huge blades showed up, dug a large hole in the middle of the road, pushed the Tiger tank into the hole, covered the tank with dirt, and leveled the road again. That's how I remember the Americans. That one act was very impressive to me, and in a way demonstrated for me at least the vast differences between the Americans and the Russians. I had no personal contact with the Americans, only with Russians. When the Americans passed by me on their way into Berlin they threw chocolate and chewing gum to us children. To me they looked cleaner and more organized than the Russians I had watched coming into Potsdam. They roared down the Alte Heerstrasse toward Berlin in their motorized convoys day and night. I felt relieved when I saw the Americans. It made me happy. Unfortunately they didn't stay. My family remained behind in the Soviet zone of occupation.

The black market was ever present. You couldn't buy anything, everything was traded. One time an appreciative Russian soldier gave me four chocolate bars for playing the piano for him. I took the chocolate to the black market and traded it for cigarettes. The cigarettes, which were much more valuable than chocolate, I could trade for butter. Suddenly at the black market we were surrounded by Russian soldiers, loaded on trucks, and driven to a prison. As an eleven-year-old I sat amongst women and men crowded in a small cell. In time I was led into a room and interrogated by a German who worked for the Russians. He wanted to know what I was going to do with the cigarettes. I told him a heart-wrenching story of an invalid father whose birthday was coming up. They let me keep some of the cigarettes, not all, and let me go.

Although we still lived in our apartment, the Russians occupied our bakery, the *Café*, and the restaurant. In the bakery, which once provided the bread and cakes for the *Café* and the restaurant, they baked bread for their soldiers. They built a chute from a window in the bakery out into the street. A *Panje* wagon was driven below the chute and the bread thrown down the chute into the wagon where a soldier stacked the bread like bricks. We children collected the bread crumbs which accumulated in the chute after the wagons drove off. Those fresh bread crumbs really tasted good.

When the S-Bahn trains began to run again I took the S-Bahn into Berlin to the Bahnhof Zoo to trade suit material for food. It took about an hour to get there. At the zoo station was the really big black market where you could trade anything and find anything. It worked this way. My mother obtained suit material for flour which she had obtained from the Russians in exchange for our pianos. For 350 centimeters of material, enough for a suit, I could get a kilo butter. I did this often. On the way home I had to walk from the train station through a forest. After dark, people were frequently robbed as they passed through that forest. One day when I and several friends were playing war in that area, we found the people who robbed us living in an empty water tank on top of a hill overlooking the forest. We reported them to the police, and after that it was again safe to walk through the forest.

School started and of course we had Communist teachers. I frequently took issue with their interpretations of history and told them that they were wrong, and that my father was not a brutal murderer. As a result I was kicked out of school for being a troublemaker. I was allowed to attend another school, further away from where we lived. When we children played, we still played war with our wooden rifles. That's all we knew—war.

In early 1946 we learned that my father was alive. He wrote that he would be released soon from a British prisoner-of-war camp. When he arrived, clothed only in rags, I didn't recognize the man who claimed to be my father. Soon afterwards he was arrested by German secret police. They came at night just like in the old days. No one knew where they took him and why. My mother learned by talking to neighbors that the newly formed German secret police had arrested him because he had been an officer in the Wehrmacht. I borrowed a bicycle from my uncle and rode to the prison where I had learned they kept him. I told the German guards that my father was a driver for the Russian commanding general and that I had a book for my father to read. They let me pass. I entered a building, having no idea where I was going. I saw someone I knew from our neighborhood. I said, Herr Forster, have you seen my father? He didn't answer, but instead pointed to a door, and hurriedly mounted his bicycle and rode off. I knocked on the door and opened it. My father sat on a chair facing two powerful lamps aimed at his face. Two policeman behind a table were interrogating him.

That they were surprised by my arrival is an understatement. I told them bluntly, I am here to visit my father. We are worried about him. Why are you doing this? I asked them to their faces. I tried to give my father the book I brought with me, but the two secret police wouldn't let me. Instead, one of them grabbed me by the shoulders and ushered me outside, closing the door behind him. He sent me on my way with a strong admonition, threatening punishment and jail if I returned or said anything to anyone. After a week they let my father go. Twice a week thereafter, in the evening, I saw my father going somewhere, but he wouldn't tell me why and where he was going. My mother sent me after him; she thought he was having an affair with some other woman. Her jealousy was always easily aroused. I followed him to the main entrance of Schloss Sanssoucie. At the obelisk in front of the Schloss my father waited until out of the dark three men appeared. I saw them whispering to my father. When the clandestine meeting broke up I quickly ran home. This went on for four weeks. Then he told my mother that the secret police wanted him to spy on people in the neighborhood. "I can't do it," he simply said. "I am a Prussian officer. We don't do things like that." He packed a few things into a rucksack, and took a train to Magdeburg that night. Several weeks later we received a letter reporting his safe arrival in the West. He went to work at the Royal Air Force base at Fassberg, near Hannover.

The *Volkspolizei* soon learned what had happened and began to pressure my mother. One or two secret police in civilian clothes watched our apartment around the clock. My uncle found us a furnished apartment in another section of Potsdam. We feared those silent watchers. My two brothers, my mother, and I left our old apartment one day and never returned. We went to our new place and immediately started to plan our escape to the West. But we hadn't eluded the police after all. I noticed two men constantly looking from across the street through thin window curtains at our small apartment. I think they were waiting for my father to return. We decided it was time for us to leave.

The day my mother decided to make our move, we each took only a few things, not to appear different, and individually left for the train station. We took a train as far as Magdeburg. No passenger trains went any farther than that. The border was about thirty kilometers further west. Freight trains ran in both directions. So, my mother, I, and my two brothers crawled onto an open railroad car of a passing freight.

When the train stopped near the border we jumped off. A man we ran into pointed us in the direction of the border and said, "Once you cross the small stream you are on the other side." It was rapidly getting dark. As we approached what we thought was the border we could see the outlines of a hut, and we headed for it. We thought the hut was in the West. The stream was shallow, and we boys crossed it easily, first taking off our shoes. I carried my mother across the stream on my back. She was a slight woman, only five feet four, and she weighed maybe 120 pounds. As we climbed up the slight embankment toward the hut, its outline barely visible in the dark, two flashlight beams were suddenly directed into our faces. We stopped, not knowing what we were facing. Two policemen came toward us. My mother immediately began to babble in her exuberance. She joyously greeted the two, expressing her happiness to be in the West and telling them how awful the police were in the East. The two policemen came closer. She kept on telling them that my father was already in the West. She was getting ready to continue with her excited litany when one of the two police interrupted her and said, "We are *Volkspolizei*." My mother was speechless. I nearly peed in my pants.

It was raining slightly. The two *Volkspolizei* had sought shelter in the hut to stay out of the rain and have a cigarette. The hut was actually in the West. We were totally confused and stood there undecided, not knowing what to do next. We saw lights of an approaching car, and the two *Volkspolizei* hastily took off across the stream for the other side. The car passed, going slowly down a dirt road near the hut. It didn't stop. We saw more lights in the distance and decided to head for them. In the village we found the mayor's office, and to our delight he was still there. My mother went in hoping to find a place for us four for the night. A barn and some straw would be just fine, she told the mayor. He refused to help. "Anybody could make up a story like yours," he said. "Where would we be if we handed out food and shelter every time riffraff like you comes through our village? In the poorhouse." He chased us out of his office. My mother was furious. Outside she made us wait until the mayor locked up his office and left. We watched him walk away, giving us a last disdainful look. When the street was quiet and empty, my mother squatted in front of his office door and relieved herself. "Come, children," I recall her saying calmly when she finished, "now we can go." We were so exhausted, we couldn't go on. That night we slept in a ditch.

A West German policeman came by at first light on his bicycle and woke us. He pointed us to the next village and a train station. My mother always was a good storyteller, and without inhibition she told everyone we met that morning of our plight: that we had no food or clothing, came from the East and had slept that night in a ditch. I didn't have enough pockets into which to stuff all the cookies, cakes, and bread people spontaneously shared with us. We took a train to Müden, a small village near Fassberg, and then walked the rest of the way to find my father. He had found us three rooms in a former Wehrmacht barracks, and that became our new home. We started new from scratch like many others.

The school in Fassberg was very good. Another refugee boy was in my class; he lived in a village several kilometers away from Fassberg. His name was Wolfgang Samuel. We became good friends. The English at the air base were very reserved. There was little contact between them and us. We couldn't go anywhere on the base. Once the Americans came in 1948 during the Berlin airlift, everything changed. Everything was open, and the Americans were very approachable. They brought life into our staid and reserved community. My father led a section of loaders on the base, loading coal onto trucks and into the American C-54 transports which flew the coal to Berlin.

We built a small shed behind our barracks to house several pigs, and when the pigs reached the right weight we sold them to the local butcher. That provided both meat and money for our family. It also led to my future job. I apprenticed at the Fassberg butcher shop and eventually went to Switzerland to complete my training. There I met my wife, who was also German, and once we returned to Germany I opened my own butcher shop in Stuttgart.

Those were wild, interesting, and challenging times. There was always something new to do or see. We had to provide for the next meal, search for wood and coal. We experienced German, Russian, American, and English soldiers. We saw war, we saw its aftermath, we saw the Berlin airlift. It was a very exciting childhood. Today's youth doesn't have such experiences. I don't mean to say that there is a need for war, I am just talking about the intensity and variety of life, and the responsibilities I assumed as a very young boy.

Arnim Krüger suffered a stroke several years ago which forced him to give up his butcher shop. He has undergone a remarkable recovery, rejecting pity, and taught himself to speak and walk again, although he still has a slight limp. His right arm is forever useless. Like many self-made men he tries to do everything himself, doesn't suffer fools, and rejects assistance. We took the streetcar into Stuttgart when I visited, he hobbling behind me, finally getting on with some difficulty. I knew better than to give him a hand. It was morning, and a man at the other end of the streetcar shouted, "Isn't this something. Drunk already at this hour of the morning." I was aghast and stood speechless. Arnim simply shrugged his shoulders, saying to me, "Sit down. Don't let him bother you. It happens all the time." Arnim Krüger is as courageous a man as I have ever met, and in spite of much adversity and hard work in his life, he has not forgotten how to laugh.

Helgard
Seifert

{Age 10}

Berlin

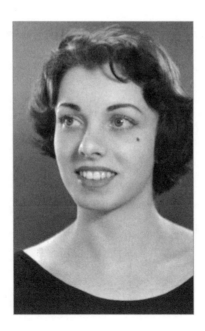

In December 1944 the Berlin Philharmonic Orchestra gave its last con‑
cert of the year. Wilhelm Furtwangler had invited me to come to the con‑
ductor's room. With disarming unworldliness he asked me straight out
whether we had any prospect of winning the war. When I replied that the
end was imminent, Furtwangler nodded; he had come to the same conclu‑
sion. I felt he was in danger since Bormann, Goebbels, and Himmler had
not forgotten many of his frank remarks as well as his defense of the
blacklisted composer Hindemith, and I advised him not to return from an
impending concert tour in Switzerland.

—Albert Speer, *Inside the Third Reich*

My father was never a party member. How he managed to stay out of the
party I don't know. I remember him saying once while we still lived in
the city, "I have to go to this damn dinner again with Göring and all
these people. I have to be so careful. I have to be so careful." He was
fearful of saying the wrong thing as a comedian. He had quit drinking by
then, but at those parties he was obliged to have a drink, and that wor‑
ried him because the alcohol might induce him to say something he
would later regret.

—Helgard Seifert

I was born in Berlin in 1935. My sister, Evelyn, arrived two years
later, in 1937. We called her Evy. The registrar of births told my moth‑
er that Evelyn was an English name. "Yes, indeed it is," she replied.
The registrar, still trying to get her to change her mind, said, "We
would prefer a German name of course."

Previous page: Helgard, 1955

"Of course you would" was my mother's curt reply, then she turned away from him and walked out. My own name, Helgard, is Swedish, which was acceptable to the Nazis.

My father, Kurt, was a stage and screen actor, as well as a director in his later years and a first-rate comedian. In his early years he performed on stage in Luxembourg, Hannover, and Magdeburg. After 1932 he played Berlin exclusively, including the Metropole Theater. Berlin was the "big time." Berlin meant he had arrived. Concurrently with his stage acting career my father became a screen actor as early as 1934, performing in three movies that year. By the time he died in 1950 he had performed in forty-five movies, including *Der Gasmann, Frau Luna, Eine Nacht im Separee, Schwarzwaldmädel,* and *Hochzeit im Heu.* Kurt Seifert was a well-known name in Germany.

My mother, Irma Fust, was a beautiful singer and dancer. She came from Hamburg. Kurt and Irma fell in love and married—a somewhat incongruous couple, as my mother was slender and thin, and my father was large and heavy. He looked very much like Jackie Gleason. She gave up her acting career soon after they married and devoted herself to making a home for her husband and two daughters. That's the way it was done in the early 1930s—the man worked and the woman stayed home. My father's appearance was very important to him, it determined the roles he got to play. He was a character actor, and a very funny comedian. He got this huge contract in Berlin about the time I saw the light of day. My parents were able to afford a nice house in the Berlin suburbs, employed a *Kindermädchen* for us children, a maid for the house, and a fancy Horch convertible. They had come into the good life and lived it in a grand style as *Schauspieler* were expected to.

The good life lasted until about 1943. Then the bombing became very heavy, the Americans appearing during the day and the British at night. Our cellar, although inadequate for the purpose, served as our shelter. Frequently my father came home around one o'clock in the morning. After a strenuous performance he was hungry and wanted to eat. He never ate before a performance, always afterward. This one night he was up in the kitchen frying potatoes when the alarm sounded. He ran downstairs into the cellar with the hot skillet in his hands. "Damn," I heard him exclaim to my mother, "I have to go back upstairs again. I have to eat. I am so hungry," and with that he turned around and ran back upstairs. Nearly every night there was a scene between him and my mother over the air raids and his *Bratkartoffeln*. The alarms upset me greatly to the point where as soon as the siren howled I had to go to the bathroom.

My father was also the air raid warden in our area. During a raid he had to go outside to ensure that people had gone into their shelters and no light was coming through the *Verdunkelung*. Recognizing the depth of my fear, he took me outside with him when a raid was in progress. It calmed me down and made me feel better to be out in the street rather than sitting in our cellar worrying about being buried alive. As the intensity and frequency of the raids increased my father decided we would seek shelter in the Siemens' bunker. The Siemens family's palatial home was next to our house. They had built a real air raid shelter in the basement of their house. There the children were separated from their parents and put in their own room which was equipped with beds. We children were supposed to go to sleep in our shelter beds like good German children. Of course we couldn't. The adults sat on chairs and benches in their own shelter room. I didn't do well in that environment and became even more anxious.

I especially dreaded the night raids. I had to run through the darkness to the Siemens' bunker holding my sister Evy's hand. They dropped phosphorous bombs on us. The burning phosphorous ran like rivers of liquid lava all over the street. "Don't touch it, don't touch it," I remember my mother yelling at us. I was scared to death and wanted to run even faster, but my little sister with her short legs couldn't go as fast as I wanted to. I was responsible for Evy because mother carried our survival suitcase. My father was usually somewhere in the middle of Berlin doing a performance or on his way home.

A bomb hit the caretaker's house adjacent to the Siemens' mansion. As the bomb exploded I went crazy. I thought we were hit and I had been buried alive. I couldn't stop screaming. My mother ran over from the next room to calm me, but it took a long time for me to regain my composure. For years after that I had dreams that I would be buried alive. My father decided it was time for us to leave Berlin.

A man by the name of Heinrich Specht, my father called him Heini, had a farm in the small village of Dolgenbrodt, about twenty miles southeast of Berlin, at the shore of the Dolgensee. Heini adored my father and came into Berlin to the theater frequently to watch him perform. I always suspected that Heini Specht came to Berlin to have a good time, which may very well have been true in the beginning. But over time their relationship changed. I suspect Heini was in the resistance and recruited my father. Of course the resistance movement at that time was Communist. I remember an occasion late one evening when I looked into my sister Evy's bed and saw a man lying in it. The man's eyes filled with terror when he saw me looking at him. He was afraid, like a dog with its tail between its legs. Seeing him there made me feel a little sick. He said, "Don't say anything." He pulled a brief-case out from under his blanket, opened it, and gave me money. He slept in my sister's bed that night. Evy slept with Mutti. In the morning he was gone. Our house was frequented by actors at all hours of the day and night, many of them in various stages of intoxication. It was their way of relaxing after a strenuous performance. People didn't expect anything else from actors, so they didn't say anything. But I knew the man in Evy's bed was not an actor. I think my father provided a safe house for the resistance.

Heini Specht encouraged my father to build a house on his property in Dolgenbrodt, on the shore of the Dolgensee. The village was a place where many prominent people had their country homes. When we moved out there in late 1943 there were no windows in the house, no doors, no light, no heat. Only the bare walls and a roof. While we waited for the men to finish the house, we slept in the village sports center. We had our own household goods, beds, and linens, and were allowed to sleep in the center because my father was Kurt Seifert. By that time he had lost his Horch convertible, it had been requisitioned by the Nazis, and he drove a little propane-powered car. Once a week he and Heini Specht continued to meet and have their cognac, smoke big cigars, and have their little talks.

My father was never a party member. How he managed to stay out of the party I don't know. I remember him saying once while we still lived in the city, "I have to go to this damn dinner again with Göring and all these people. I have to be so careful. I have to be so careful." He was fearful of saying the wrong thing as a comedian. He had quit drinking by then, but at those parties he was obliged to have a drink, and that worried him because the alcohol might induce him to say something he would later regret. I know he didn't enjoy going to those dinners, but he couldn't say no. He was part of the entertainment for the evening, and Göring was especially fond of him.

My parents always spoke openly in front of us girls. As I got older they had to be careful around me, because at age seven I had a big mouth. I was being indoctrinated in school about Hitler. I couldn't wait to meet someone on the street so I could say *Heil Hitler* to them. To me saying *Heil Hitler* meant being grown up, being important. I wanted to brag that my father went to dinners with Hermann Göring, so my parents began to watch what they said around me.

My father always put in his contracts that he'd give his first three performances before wounded soldiers. No party officials, only wounded soldiers and their doctors and nurses. A smart move on his part, because it endeared him to the public. And I suspect this may have been one of several reasons why he was not forced to join the Nazi Party. My parents shunned politics. I can remember Mother and Father sitting on the balcony in Berlin having coffee before the war started. There was a parade going down the street led by a martial band. They both got on the balcony floor, sat under the table, and continued to drink their coffee— they didn't want to stand and salute and say *Heil Hitler*.

Early in the war I recall people walking around with a yellow star on their coats—a *Judenstern*, my mother said. My mother explained to me,

"Those wearing the yellow star are Jews. They are being recognized that way. Be very careful, be very careful," she cautioned me. At that age I didn't know what she meant, because she didn't explain in what way I was to be very careful, nor did she ever explain why they had to wear that star just because they were of the Jewish faith. It was obviously difficult for her to talk about such things, not knowing if she could trust a child of seven. She and my father frequently mentioned *Konzentrationslager*, commonly just referred to as KZ (pronounced Kazet). We knew about concentration camps, at least my parents did, and I knew the words. I had no idea what a concentration camp was. I remember my father saying more than once to my mother, "Remember, Irma, if anything goes wrong, we are all going together. The four of us. It is in the medicine cabinet," I heard him say. There he hid a stash of pills; he had many doctor friends. "They are not going to get us," he said. Again, I didn't really know what he meant when he said, "They are not going to get us." Strangely, his comments gave me a feeling of security, knowing that we as a family would always be together.

By late 1944 most of the theaters had closed in Berlin because of the bombings. It was too dangerous to collect that many people in one spot. So my father stayed with us in Dolgenbrodt. Here we were able to sleep through the night. Life became calmer, more relaxed. Berlin colleagues of my father's visited frequently just to be able to get a good night's sleep. We fished and rode our bikes around the lake, tended to our chickens, but we couldn't kill them because we were all animal lovers. We just collected their eggs. At night we could see the glow emanating from the city. Berlin was burning, we were safe.

Living in Dolgenbrodt was a group of Russian forced laborers. Whole families. There were four Russian children with whom I played frequently. Tanya and Hanya, Shurik and Stefan. Tanya was the youngest. Her job was to watch the geese on the farm where her mother worked. I often sat with Tanya watching the geese, playing with her, getting lice from her. I remember playing with Stefan on the ice when the lake froze over in winter. He would ram a pole into the ice, tie a rope to the pole, a sled to the other end of the rope, and then push us around the pole in dizzying circles. I also learned some Russian while playing with them, as did Evy. I remember the birthday party we had for their grandmother. We ate potato plinzes, rolled pancakes filled with sour cream and other tasty things, until we couldn't walk anymore. I still know how to say "Give me more plinzes" in Russian.

The Red Army came in March 1945. As the Russian soldiers entered the village, German soldiers were still out by the lake. The soldiers started shooting at each other. Our house was between the Germans and the Russians. We heard a machine gun firing, and suddenly I heard something go clatter-clatter-clatter in the walls of our house and my mother cried out, "Oh, my leg, my leg, my leg." She had been hit in her thigh by one of those machine gun bullets, shattering her hipbone. She never could walk very well after that. My father dragged her behind the fireplace, and we sat there panic struck.

My father's sister, Tante Teddy, was with us at the time. To this day I don't know why she was with us. Tante Teddy lived in Essen, where she and my father were born, and she also was an actress. I don't even know her last name. Tante Teddy was in the silent movies in Hollywood and was an American citizen. I remember her running around yelling to the Russians after they occupied the village, "Amerikanski. Amerikanski." She had papers to prove that she was an American. She had dyed red hair and always smoked cigarettes. She quickly became buddy-buddy with the Russians.

After three days, Mother's wound became infected—she had a fever, and the bullet started wandering in her body. By then the Russians had established a field hospital in Dolgenbrodt. My father put Mother in a little wagon and pulled her into the village to the Russian hospital tent. Evy and I followed behind. He went up to a group of Russian surgeons and spoke to them. My father, with all his many talents, spoke only German. One of the Russian surgeons spoke a little German and immediately tended to my mother and removed the bullet from her thigh. When he finished, the doctor pressed the bullet into mother's hand and said to her, "Keep the bullet. It is your good luck charm." My father wheeled Mother back to our little house the same way he had delivered her to the hospital, in the little handwagon. Mother recuperated slowly. Later my mother gave one of the Russian doctors, a woman, some silk scarves and silk stockings to thank the Russian doctors for what they had done for her.

I know my father saved many people from ugly fates. Many neighborhood women sought refuge in our home, fearing the worst from the Russians. One woman was nine months pregnant, I remember. Eventually she was raped several times, I heard my parents say. I didn't know what rape meant. I just knew it was something bad. The minute the Russians entered our village my father went into his act. As they came into our house he told them he was an artist and sang for them and played the balalaika. I had no idea he could play the balalaika. He danced, did funny things, and made the soldiers laugh—common soldiers and officers alike. So instead of rape and killing, we had my father's daily and nightly performances. But in other parts of the village the mayhem went on without mercy. I recall Herr Resemann, a farmer who sported a huge, red handlebar mustache. His cats always swam behind his boat when he went out on the lake fishing. When he stopped, the cats clambered on board and waited patiently for him to throw them a small fish. His two daughters were raped so many times that he finally couldn't take it any more. He killed them. Then he shot himself.

More and more Russian soldiers came to our house to see my father perform. They came like a wave. None of them threatened us. Two Russian majors visited with us frequently. They gave my father a letter which stated that our property was off limits and that we were under their protection. Most of the soldiers were able to read the letter when my father showed it to them, but not all. One day two soldiers came who apparently couldn't read. As our dog, Rex, a young stray German shepherd my father had rescued from a bombed-out house in Berlin, came playfully bounding out of the house to greet the soldiers, they shot him right in front of Evy and me. The two majors came later in the day. When they saw the dog and heard what had happened they wanted to know the details about the killing. Tante Teddy, the Amerikanski, then described the events of the dog's shooting in vivid detail. The two majors went off looking for the soldiers, promising to shoot them if they found them. I don't think they found the offending soldiers, but they felt so guilty over our loss that they brought us food— sugar and flour in pillow cases and a pile of fish. They threw hand grenades into the lake and had soldiers collect the dead fish floating on top of the water.

When we moved to Dolgenbrodt my panic attacks had subsided. When the Russians came and the shooting started my attacks came back. We had dug an air raid bunker in back of our house. We sat in that bunker many a night to stay out of the line of fire. Once I spent an entire night in the bunker with only my sister and Teddy. I didn't know where my parents were. The fear of losing my parents drove me nearly mad. Teddy smoked throughout the night, but eventually ran out of cigarettes. In the middle of the fighting she ran back to our house to get more cigarettes, leaving Evy and me alone in the bunker. It seemed like an eternity until she returned. When the firing finally let up a little we three crawled on our hands and knees to Frau Vetter's house, at the end of the village—she had the only house built of stone which could offer us some protection from the bullets.

The war seemed to last for a long time around our area. Before the Nazis finally left, at the very end, they came into the village to settle things. I didn't see that for myself, but I heard my parents talk about it. They came to Heini Specht's house, my father's friend, and said to him that they understood he had a Russian wife and that she was Jewish. His own son had turned him in. Heini admitted to it, offered them cognac and cigars, and made them comfortable in his study. Then he excused himself, saying he would be right back. Heini went into the next room and shot himself. The Nazis didn't think that was very funny. They didn't just burn Heini Specht's farm, they blew it up. From that point onward I recall my parents being extremely worried. There was for the first time deep fear for our lives in our house. I believe they thought we would be next.

"The war is over. The Russians have Berlin," I remember my father saying. "I know the Russians are going to carve up the city. We need to get back there. Our house is still standing. We need to get into the American sector." Don't ask me how he did it, but he came up with a truck and gasoline, and we loaded the family on the truck. My mother could hardly walk because of her wound. She sat up front. We children were in the back with our possessions, the chickens, and our cat, Moritz. I suspect that my father and one of our neighbors who owned several cars, and who had hidden them on our property, buried some gasoline for future use. When we got back to our house in Berlin everything was pretty much in order. A couple had moved into the house in our absence and had taken care of things. They told us that Russian soldiers had come through the house and looked at our pictures of Caruso, Lehar, and Rastelli, saying, "Artist, artist" as they looked, touching nothing. Two months later, in July 1945, the Americans came and told us to get out. They only let us take our clothes, everything else we had to leave behind. My parents' bedroom was turned into a barbershop, Mother's room into a tailor shop, and the living and dining room into an officers' mess, using our china, silver, table linens, and Persian rugs. All of which disappeared slowly but steadily into different officers' houses.

The Americans gave my father a piece of paper, assuring him that the document would help him obtain a room or an apartment for his family. But we never found the people who could perform such miracles. My father finally located one room for Mother and us children, and a bed for himself somewhere else. No kitchen privileges, no laundry facilities. I don't know how my mother did it. Our mattresses were infested with bedbugs. There was no heat in the room. When it got cold, "ice flowers" formed not only on the windows, but also on the walls. I could see my breath as I lay on my mattress. In the mornings there were ice crystals on my covers from my breath. There was talk about wolves having been spotted near Berlin. It was the worst of times. We had little contact with the Americans.

I went back to school. Not only was the school unheated, but the teachers were old, had been called out of retirement, and didn't want to be there. They were starving just like the rest of us. The boys constantly fought amongst themselves. Nobody learned anything. Then I was transferred to another school. To get to that school I had to climb across the debris of blown-up bridges—down one side of the bridge, into the river, up the other side. I remember the long walks to and from school that year, and men exposing themselves to us girls. We girls didn't know what to do when the men did that. We just turned our heads and continued on our way. I never told my parents. I became very sensitized to my immediate environment and possible signs of danger. Going past bushes or rounding a corner I always put myself in a position not to be surprised, to be able to run away. It was a dangerous time. That year I learned nearly nothing. For us Germans the war just went on.

At this time I started growing again, and my mother gave me some of her clothes to wear. I had no shoes that fit. None were to be had anywhere. So I wore my mother's galoshes, which were designed to be pulled on over a pair of ladies' shoes. I stuffed the hollow heel of the galoshes with newspaper, but every step I took the heels would collapse and bend to the side under my weight. One day when I came home from school, as I passed a house, I was confronted by the sight of a decaying corpse laid out on an open wagon. I was shocked. The corpse had been dug up from the small garden fronting the house—someone who was killed in the last days of the war and buried where he or she fell. I had to go by the corpse to get to my house. Nobody cared about the effect of corpses on children. The stench was nearly unbearable.

My father and his fellow actors started presenting little plays on their own just to get things going again. He quickly received a permit from the Russians, but it only lasted for a year. People had no money. They paid with goods. Then my father got very ill. He, like the rest of

274

us, suffered from malnutrition. My mother didn't know how to cook the dehydrated carrots and potatoes we got on our ration cards. It was 1948, the time of the Berlin airlift. In school we children received a watery soup. Our teacher made us feel guilty eating the soup. She would say, "Did you eat well? I didn't have anything." Everything seemed to have a downside. My father, once a big man, became a thin man. He lost his teeth and became diabetic. I remember him saying, "I can't make a living anymore. I have to be big for my roles. Words just aren't funny coming from the mouth of a thin man."

Around Christmas of 1948 my father obtained some beef stewing meat. I don't know how he obtained the meat. He came into our room cradling the meat in his hands like it was a treasure. My mother burned the meat. I had never seen her so down. She couldn't handle the deprivations anymore. About that time Father found a house for us where we could all live together again as a family. The house had no heat, and the owner's name was Frau Doctor Frost—it was a frosty house all right, but what mattered was that we were together again.

After the airlift was over and with new money, in 1949, we suddenly had more food. My father made many movies and we regained a measure of prosperity. He had an offer to go to Hollywood, but turned it down. He couldn't speak English and didn't think he could make a living there. Earlier in 1948, after the blockade had started, he had received an offer from the Zürich Schauspielhaus. That offer he had also declined saying, "The Berliners have always been loyal to me. I can't leave them now when times are bad." He was still ailing and became addicted to morphine. The money he made went for his drug addiction. He died in 1950 at age forty-seven, leaving us in debt. We lost everything again, and my mother was on her own.

As for myself, my father had taken me out of school at age fourteen. I went to work for him in his film studio as a gofer. He enrolled me in a ballet school. He planned for us to work together on stage as a father-daughter act: dance, comedy, a little singing. When he died the only thing I knew was dance. I got a job in the national circus of

Switzerland, Zirkus Knie. They played fifty-two towns every year. I danced, carried snakes, sold programs, cleaned seats, did whatever they told me to do. After my contract expired I signed on with an Italian circus, which led me to the Hiller Girls. The Hiller Girls, a famous European dance group, happened to be in Bologna when I was there with the circus. I was tall, a good dancer, and they hired me. We danced all over Europe. Two years later I auditioned at the Lido in Paris and was hired. I became part of the Lido travel group. We danced all over Europe and South America.

While in Berlin I occasionally baby-sat for an American army major and his wife, an attorney, Maxwell McKnight. I met them through my father. His wife was a great supporter of Berlin artists. After my contract with the Lido expired in 1955 I contacted the McKnights. They lived in Scarsdale, New York, and had stayed in touch with us. They sponsored me to the United States. In 1956, at the age of twenty-one, I set sail on the *United States* for a new life in America. The McKnights suggested that one way for me to get acquainted with my new world was to work in a family setting. They helped me find a job with a Jewish family as a *Kindermädchen*. The woman had lost all of her relatives in the Holocaust. I was scared out of my wits when I first went to them. But they were very good to me and helped me to understand my new country. In time I married and had two children of my own, Micheline and Daniel.

I don't know what happened to Tante Teddy. We weren't close. Evy stayed in Berlin and became a successful editor for *The Third German* TV program. She married late in life and had no children of her own. As for my mother, who had been left nearly destitute by my father's drug addiction and untimely death, fate was kind to her. In 1951 an admirer of my father's in the Berlin housing authority signed over an apartment to her which had been vacated by the British. The apartment was modern with central heating and electricity. My sister and I supported Mutti after that. She died in 1997 of a stroke at age ninety-two.

Helgard Seifert

Helgard nurtures the memories of her youth as a dancer with the Lido group. Her eyes sparkled when she showed me colorful Lido posters with long-legged, plumed ladies kicking up their heels. "Dancing is a business for the young," she said wistfully, "but it was so much fun while it lasted." Helgard lives with her husband, John, in Seattle, Washington.

Erich
Abshoff

{Age 9}

Wuppertal, Northrhine-Westfalia

Then gradually the Russian army began to cross the bridge [across the Elbe River]. The army came in like a sort of tide; it had no special shape; there were no orders given. It came and flowed over the stone quay and up onto the roads behind us like water rising, like ants, like locusts. It was not so much an army as a whole world on the move. . . . But it came on and on and on, inchoate, formless and amazing. It was very noisy and slightly mad and it knew exactly what it was doing.

—Martha Gellhorn, *The Russians, Reporting World War II, Part Two: American Journalism 1944–1946*

An interesting hindsight is that at the time I viewed my own relationship to the Russian soldiers as normal. I went to their campsites and watched them build their fires. They gave me some of their food, mostly canned goods. Different Russian soldiers even presented me with three ponies. I was pretty proud of owning three ponies at age nine. I kept them on a meadow near the farm, and soon two of the ponies were stolen by other soldiers. It was give and take.

—Erich Abshoff

I was born in 1936 in Wuppertal, not far from the Bonn area where I now live. Soon after I entered school in 1942 at age six we lost our house in a bombing raid. It was the first big raid against Wuppertal. The old town was totally destroyed. My parents owned an old half-timbered house which burned like a candle. It sat right next to the Wupper River. I recall someone throwing me bodily up the stairs from

Previous page: Erich (center) in his office on the Hardhöhe in Bonn at the German Defense Ministry

our cellar, and whoever caught me put me down outside on the river bank. Someone put wet blankets over us children to keep us from dying. Every ten minutes someone dipped the drying blanket in the river again and spread the wet blanket over us children. That's how we survived that terrible night. Our entire street was in flames. One after another the houses collapsed, sending up a shower of hot ashes which settled slowly upon us.

My father, Erich, was in the Luftwaffe and stationed in Vienna, Austria, with an antiaircraft battalion. My mother's father came and found us after the air raid—Mother, my younger brother, Gerd, and I. He took us to his home in a nearby town. Within days my father came up from Vienna. We returned with him. We lost everything in that raid except the clothing on our backs. In Vienna we first lived in a small garden shack; then my father found something a little larger, and finally we moved into an apartment. Every time we moved I had to change schools. I very quickly learned the Viennese dialect. Because of my language ability I became the one who did most of the talking with Austrians. The Viennese didn't seem to like Germans. If there was anything of importance where we were dependent on the good will of others—for instance, grocery shopping—it was I who was sent to the store because I sounded like an authentic Viennese boy.

In Vienna I don't recall how many bombing raids there were or when they occurred. I recall our neighbor's house was hit by a bomb. In October 1944 my mother gave birth to my youngest brother, Jürgen, and about the same time my father was wounded during a bombing raid. In the military hospital he met a farmer's son who came from Bodin in the province of Mecklenburg, in northern Germany. The Russian army was getting closer to Vienna, and my father was concerned about our welfare. He arranged for my mother and us three children to take the train to Bodin, where we were to wait out the end of the war on the farm of a casual acquaintance. In retrospect of course that move had all the trappings of jumping from the frying pan into the fire. Within weeks the Russian army occupied Mecklenburg and Bodin.

I remember the closing weeks of the war very well—jumping into a ditch more than once when I was attacked by *Tiefflieger*. I don't know if they were Russian, American, or English planes. All I know is that they were planes which came very fast and very low, and I jumped into or behind the first thing at hand, preferably a ditch or a large tree. As a little boy I thought for sure they were attacking me. Today I can't imagine that was really the case. I just happened to be there.

In Bodin I attended school. I won't forget that experience as long as I live. Children from age five to age fourteen sat in one room together trying to learn. Of course at that age I saw everything in terms of how much trouble I could cause, how many pranks I could get away with without getting caught, rather than from the perspective of how much I might learn. It was at that time when I began to comprehend the nature of what I was caught up in. As the Russians entered the village, my teacher, who was also the NSDAP chief for the area, the top Nazi, shot his family and himself. I saw their lifeless bodies lying on the floor of our classroom in a huge pool of blood. That was a powerful shock to a nine-year-old boy.

My parents told me in later years that I always wanted to join the Hitler Youth. I had this vision as a little boy of wearing a uniform, sitting around a campfire with others my age, singing and doing exciting things. It seemed all so fascinating. Untold numbers of German boys must have had visions similar to mine. My father, I believe, would have let me join the HJ (pronounced Hayot). My mother, however, said firmly, "You will not go into that." She came from a devout Catholic family and believed there was no compromise possible between her religious upbringing and the Nazis. The discussion with my mother about religion and the Nazis was the immediate result of my teacher's suicide and his murder of his wife and two children. In 1993 I had to attend a meeting in a town not far from Bodin. I stopped at the schoolhouse and looked at the scene of that long-ago crime with horror. I can still see the scene before my eyes just as I saw it that day in 1945, the four bodies lying there and the pool of blood covering much of the floor.

The Russians occupied Bodin, a village with less than two hundred souls, the day of my teacher's suicide. I watched some of the women on the farm where we were staying hide under hay and straw in the barns. I was the one who brought them food and drink. Soldiers came and went continually. That very night I experienced my mother's rape by a Russian soldier. It was dark and I couldn't see anything; I only heard her fearful whimpering as she lay under the soldier on the floor of our room. Only years later did I fully comprehend what I had heard and seen that night. My baby brother who was born in Vienna was about six months old at that time. During the day we kept him near us. When Russian soldiers entered and saw the baby, they recoiled, and whatever they had in mind they did not do. On one occasion after seeing my little brother, a soldier even gave him a can of meat, placing it on his bed, and then he left.

An interesting hindsight is that at the time I viewed my own relationship to the Russian soldiers as normal. I went to their campsites and watched them build their fires. They gave me some of their food, mostly canned goods. Different Russian soldiers even presented me with three ponies. I was pretty proud of owning three ponies at age nine. I kept them on a meadow near the farm, and soon two of the ponies were stolen by other soldiers. It was give and take.

Several weeks later I saw a strange man bending over the baby carriage of my brother. I ran to my mother and pointed out the presence of the stranger to her. It was my father. He had been taken prisoner by the Russians and escaped, walking all the way from Austria to Bodin. Within days our family walked through field and forest to the east-west border, my mother pushing the baby carriage, my brother lying on top of the little we owned. We knew the Russian soldiers would most likely not touch the baby or anything in the carriage. At the border as expected we were stopped by a Russian soldier. My father gave him his wristwatch, and the soldier let us cross unmolested. It was late in 1945 as we crossed into the English zone.

Our house in Wuppertal was a ruin. My father and I built a small hut from lumber we found lying about. That's where we slept. My mother and two brothers stayed with her parents. My father located a house ruin, its lower floor burned out, the upper floor covered knee-deep in debris. He decided we would make the upper floor liveable. For six months my father and I worked to remove the debris from the second floor. I returned to school. My father, with the help of acquaintances, dug machine tools out of the debris of a former machine shop, which he then installed on the lower floor of our house ruin. He started to do simple jobs for others—everything that had to do with pipes and threading pipes. With that, the war was over for me.

I found a home, so to speak, in a Catholic youth organization until 1948. I went into a missionary program at age twelve because I thought I wanted to become a missionary. I don't remember if that choice was my own, or if it was the result of a comment made by my priest, who said that if you become a missionary you may attend the university without cost. Since my parents had no money, that may have been the incentive that got me interested in the program. On the weekends our teachers went to nearby villages where they heard confession and conducted church services for a sack of potatoes or other food. Things got better in 1948 with the introduction of new money. In 1952 I decided to leave the missionary school. When I went home on vacation I discovered a continued interest in girls and decided that becoming a priest probably was not such a good idea, at least not for me. At age sixteen I returned to the Humanistische Gymnasium in Wuppertal, where I made my *Abitur*.

There is a nearly comical conglomeration of reasons why I ended up in the *Bundeswehr*. After the *Abitur* I entered a machine tool apprenticeship, as my father wanted me to become a machine tool engineer. It was a prerequisite to have six months' experience before being accepted to the university. As I was in my apprenticeship in 1956, the *Bundeswehr* came into existence. About that time I clearly understood that my parents had no means to support me during my studies. I was mulling things over when the Hungarian uprising occurred. My mind was made up for me. I joined the *Bundeswehr*. I intended to leave after six years to continue my studies. My inclination was to become a teacher in the humanities with emphasis on Greek and Latin, rather than becoming an engineer as my father wanted me to.

No one could believe that I of all people would go into the new German military, certainly not my Boy Scout leader. He said to me, "There is no future in that, Erich." My teachers and classmates gave me to understand I was throwing away my education. Someone who studied Greek and Latin had no business going into the military. One of my former classmates corresponded with me for weeks to dissuade me from what he viewed as an unfortunate decision. In basic training in the *Bundeswehr* I continued my education in Greek and Latin. I had a Bible which was printed on one side in Greek, the other side in Latin. If I got stuck in Greek, for instance, I could continue my readings in Latin. I continued to expand my vocabulary in both Greek and Latin, with the intention of preparing myself for my future university studies. I never became a teacher; instead I made the *Bundeswehr* my career, because I found it to be an interesting and challenging occupation.

In spite of everything that happened in my youth, I didn't permit the past to influence my future. As a matter of fact, I viewed my experiences as no better or worse than what others of my age group had experienced. I think we all took it as a slice of life, and let it go at that. We were alive, and that was enough.

Hans-Erich Abshoff flew as a navigator in the Luftwaffe, and spent much of his professional career as a staff officer on the Hardhöhe in Bonn, the German equivalent of the Pentagon. He retired from the Luftwaffe in 1996 in the rank of colonel. He and his wife live in the greater Cologne-Bonn metropolitan area.

Johann Koppe

{Age 9}

Wollup, Brandenburg

[It was] one of the biggest and bloodiest mass migrations in history, the flight of the German people from the Red Army. The year 1945 was the worst in the world's history.

—Stephen E. Ambrose, foreword, *German Boy: A Refugee's Story* by Wolfgang W. E. Samuel

On the first of February the sun shone brightly. We made it as far as Heinersdorf, where we stayed overnight with a generous farm family. Our horses were visibly tired and desperately needed the rest. The following day we heard the sounds of battle again from the direction of Seelow. Time to move on. Wagons of refugees from the East were everywhere. Our going was slow.

—Johann Koppe

I was born in 1936 in Frankfurt-an-der-Oder, which lies about thirty miles south of Wollup. I was the oldest of five children. In January 1945 I was eight, my youngest brother, Dieter, was not yet two years old, my brother Eberhard was seven, and my sisters, Ingrid and Heide-Marie, were five and three years old respectively. All five of us came into this world in the Frankfurt military hospital. This curiosity of our birthplace—most children then were delivered at home by a midwife—can be explained by the fact that my grandfather, my mother's father, was a medical doctor and the chief of medicine of the Frankfurt military hospital. He personally delivered each of his grandchildren at the request of my parents. Not only was my mother's father a medical doctor, but so were both of her brothers.

Previous page: Johann (second from left) with his mother Edith and siblings

286

My father, Walter, managed the Staatliche Domäne of Wollup, a large agricultural estate, which had been in our family for nearly 150 years. Wollup lies about ten miles north of Seelow, where the Wehrmacht made its last desperate stand against the Red Army in April of 1945, and about fifty miles east of Berlin, in the *Oderbruch* region. The *Oderbruch* is a floodplain along the Oder River which flooded to some degree nearly every spring until the erection of dikes damming the river under Frederick the Great. My great-great-grandfather, Johann Koppe, the first manager and trustee of the *Domäne*, was not only a well-known farmer in Prussia, but also acquired a measure of fame for the authoritative books he published about agricultural practices in the province of Brandenburg. In 1944 my father was unexpectedly drafted. Until then men with large families and in war-essential positions were exempted from the draft. Times had become more desperate. A replacement manager was provided, but he knew little about farming and about our particular needs.

Wollup was an estate of four thousand *Morgen*, about twenty-five hundred acres—large for that area of Germany, but not in comparison to the estates further east. It included a sugar refinery, brickworks, forge, five large storage barns as well as barns for sheep, cattle, horses, pigs, and for the numerous wagons and agricultural implements. We had our own pumper wagon and a tavern on the premises which served our many employees. As for animals, the estate had at any one time about a hundred working oxen and forty horses, one hundred ten cows and calves, over a hundred pigs, eight hundred sheep, and hundreds of chicken, geese, ducks, and pigeons. Additionally, there were twelve houses for our help. We lived in a large manor house with three kitchens, three bathrooms, and twenty-nine rooms, many of which were occupied by the help.

By 1944 there were no young or middle-aged German men remaining on the estate, only French, Russian, and Polish prisoners of war. After my father was drafted in September 1944, my mother,

Edith, had to manage the estate, take care of us five children, as well as look after my father's mother who lived with us. My grandfather had died in 1943. It was a heavy load for her. As a result of her workload and the deteriorating military situation in the East, in December 1944 she considered sending us children to a friend's farm south of Berlin, both for our safety and to gain more free time to devote to managing the estate. When the mayor of Letschin, the nearest little town, heard of her plans, he immediately called and dissuaded her from sending us away. "You can't do that," he told her. "If you send your children away everyone else will get nervous and start to move out. Our *Volkssturm* will defend you," the mayor declared optimistically. Although my mother did not believe in his promise of safety and protection, she didn't send us away.

Eberhard and I attended the *Volksschule* in Zechin, which was only three kilometers from Wollup. It was a two-room school, accommodating grades one through eight. There was no school in Wollup. Wollup lay in an isolated region of Germany, and the world largely passed us by. The war had not been much in evidence to any of us and influenced our lives relatively little. The estate employed many French and Russian prisoners of war, as well as Poles, replacements for the German men who had been drafted into the Wehrmacht. It was typical around harvest time, from midsummer until late autumn, for large numbers of Poles to be brought to the estate to help with the beet, grain, and potato harvests.

We children had a very good relationship with the French. As prisoners of war they lived in their own house, surrounded by barbed wire and guarded by one or two soldiers. But access was casual, and as children we often visited with them. One of them was a very good cook who introduced us to superb French cuisine. We children had to go out looking for snails which he prepared and served to us and the other Frenchmen. He introduced us to foods and methods of preparation which were totally unknown to us. On a farm like ours we usually ate plain food, which our French cook upgraded significantly. I don't remember having any contact with the Russian prisoners. When the time came and we fled the Red Army, the French soldiers chose to remain behind to await the Russians. My mother invited them to come along with us, but they declined.

I remember playing war with the children of our employees, but mostly I played by myself. I had a little pony, and before my father was drafted I rode with him into the fields. We had two nannies who took care of us. The nannies pretty much ran our lives from early morning until we went to bed. They made sure we washed up, were there on time for breakfast, lunch, and dinner, left for school on time, did our homework. After all that was done they would decide how much time we had for play. The two nannies totally ran our lives. My parents focused on running the farm. Although farm life was mostly hard work from early morning to late at night, there were a fair number of festivals in which everyone participated, such as the *Ernte Dank Fest* after the harvest had been brought in. My parents invited the neighbors to join us on such occasions, and we were in turn invited to their festivals. It was great fun for us children. An acquaintance of my parents was in the Luftwaffe and he would arrive in a *Fieseler Storch*, a three-seat observation plane. That was very exciting for us children. He would land the plane in a meadow and then take us up for short rides.

In all this time I had little exposure to Nazi ideology as such. One reason for that may be that our farm was so remote. There was really no one else around except family and our employees. Although my family had more than one member in the military, including the husband of my mother's twin sister who was a general in the Wehrmacht, and other family members who had been drafted, there was no one who was a really enthusiastic National Socialist. I believe that many of the adults were National Socialists in the early days, even my parents. They were initially impressed with Hitler's achievements, if I correctly remember conversations I overheard. Hitler provided work; the streets again were quiet. People who earlier experienced unemployment and lawlessness on the streets were very much impressed when those issues were resolved. Although my parents supported the National Socialists in the early days, they did not become party members. It wasn't common for anyone around Wollup to say *Heil Hitler*. We children always liked seeing German soldiers though; it was exciting to see a uniform.

1945 was a very cold winter. The Russians came closer and closer to the Oder. My mother made preparations for an evacuation. She frequently called her father in Frankfurt to find out what was really going on. One day she told us that he informed her that Frankfurt had been declared a *Festung*, a fortress city, like so many other German cities further east. It was a worrisome development. On top of that he told her that the section of the Oder abutting our farm was to be defended by *Volkssturm*, old men and young boys, which did not bode well.

Refugees from the East streamed through Wollup on their way west throughout the month of January. It was a pitiful sight to watch these tired, hungry, and dispirited people passing through, frequently in wagons without covers, totally exposed to the elements. We provided them fodder for their animals and food for the children, milk for the young ones, bread and hot soup for the others. Naturally the sight of the refugees made us very uneasy too. Would we be next? The wind blew incessantly, whistling loudly as it turned the corner of our house. I watched as Mutti had wagons prepared for our own flight. The wagons were covered with heavy tarps and loaded with food and fodder for the horses. Mutti offered everyone on the estate the opportunity to accompany us, but many people wanted to remain in Wollup no matter what happened.

Several small German army detachments were stationed in Wollup. On the thirtieth of January we heard artillery fire in the distance. A German army officer told Mutti, "*Wir setzen uns ab.*" They were leaving. Our milk wagon taking milk to the dairy was stopped by German soldiers and sent back. The guards assembled the Russian prisoners and marched off with them toward the west. The French prisoners stopped working and refused to leave; they wanted to be liberated by the Red

Army, they told my mother. Their two guards left along with the Russians. I could tell the adults were getting more and more restless. On the afternoon of the following day we heard rifle and machine gun fire. Mutti called one of our neighbors, a relative with an estate next to ours directly adjacent to the Oder River. The woman told her that as she was speaking on the telephone she could see Russian tanks driving into her farm's yard. "The Oder is frozen over," she said to my mother, "and their tanks have crossed the river. You must leave immediately, before it is too late."

My mother notified everyone who wanted to go with us that we would leave right away. The five wagons which she had prepared for the occasion were four covered, flatbed wagons equipped with automobile tires which made for quicker and easier riding, or so she thought, and one wagon to carry feed for the horses. Our wagons carried twelve children and fifteen adults. Our nannies had dressed us children warmly in furs and layers of sweaters. Each person was allowed to bring a small suitcase and some food. We loaded the baggage in the back and covered it with feather beds. There we children lay. The adults sat on crude benches along each side of the wagons. Mutti had covered the floor of our wagon with a thick oriental carpet for warmth, and in addition we tied two oriental carpets across the tarp covering our wagon. The cold wind blew hard from the east, and a thin layer of freshly fallen snow covered the road. Mutti dressed us children in fur coats and fur jackets for extra warmth. As we harnessed the three horses to our wagon, bullets began whistling past us. We moved out quickly, with our old and trusted *Kutscher* Hanisch leading our small trek. It was dark, and when I looked back I could see some of our barns erupting in flames. I wanted to cry. I was very afraid.

We headed west, towards Berlin. Our five-wagon trek didn't get far before we ran into trouble. Our rubber tires didn't give us very good traction on the ice-slick cobblestones. The last wagon with the feed for the horses was overloaded. The horses were unable to get sufficient hold on the icy road with their hooves, and the wagon slowly slipped into a ditch. A Wehrmacht medical unit, seeing our plight, lent us their horses to pull our wagon out of the snow. Then the soldiers led us through the forest to the village of Gusow to make sure we were able to continue on our own. All around us barns and houses burned fiercely. As we approached the road from Seelow to Berlin I could see the silhouettes of Russian tanks moving toward us. They were outlined by the eerie light given off by burning villages. Overhead German Stuka dive bombers appeared, and they attacked the Russian tanks. We were in the middle of a tank battle. Mutti headed for the forest and we continued southwest on narrow *Feld-* and *Waldwege*. We didn't have brakes on our wagons, so when we got to an incline we used tree branches to keep the wagons from rolling backwards. On the way down, the heavily loaded wagons forced the horses into a gallop. We were fortunate that none of the wagons overturned. The horses labored through the night into the early morning hours. We left behind the sounds of battle, but the bitter cold was still with us.

On the first of February the sun shone brightly. We made it as far as Heinersdorf, where we stayed overnight with a generous farm family. Our horses were visibly tired and desperately needed the rest. The following day we again heard the sounds of battle from the direction of Seelow. Time to move on. Wagons of refugees from the East were everywhere. Our going was slow. Mutti decided to move off the main road and follow narrow *Feld-* and *Waldwege*. After dark we reached Fürstenwalde. We slept there in our wagons. My brothers and sisters huddled together quietly, not saying a word, confusion and fear showing in their eyes. Hanisch parked us for the night in the exercise yard of an army barracks. All night long I could hear the sounds of shouted military commands and marching troops leaving for the battle we had left behind us. We left early the following day, the second of February, heading south to get around Berlin. We made it as far as Grabendorf. The people of Grabendorf were not very friendly and offered no help of any kind. It was storming again, bitter cold, and the horses were exceedingly restless. We kept on moving until we got to Mittenwalde, where a very helpful *Bürgermeister* found us a place to stay. As the oldest I tried to help Mutti as much as I could.

The next day, the third of February, we kept on moving around the southern fringes of Berlin, again caught up in the huge wagon treks from the east. It was a cold, beautiful day. The sun shone brightly, and before us lay the once-beautiful city of Berlin. Then, as if on parade, came a huge formation of American bombers. We passed by an anti-aircraft gun firing one round after another at the bombers. The horses didn't react to the firing. My little sister Ingrid began to cry and hid under the bedding in our wagon. My brother Eberhard and I watched as the bombers released their bombs, which looked like raindrops falling on the city. Smoke and fire billowed high into the sky. My mother began to cry at the sight. I heard her say in a tear-choked voice, "The poor women and children. The poor women and children." The raid lasted fifteen minutes.

On the fourth of February we reached Beelitz, just south of Potsdam. We were directed to park our wagons on the *Marktplatz* along with hundreds of others. It was total chaos—children crying, men and women screaming. Mutti and I tried to calm my brothers and sisters. We stayed in the wagon most of the time. Our destination was a farm family, friends, near Gatterstedt west of Leipzig. They had no idea we were coming. We kept on moving day after day, eventually leaving behind the refugee treks from the East, which made our movement a little easier. As we passed through Halle-an-der-Saale we witnessed another bombing raid, this time against the oil refineries at Leuna, just south of Halle. After twelve long days and nights our small trek finally arrived at one o'clock in the afternoon on our friends' farm in Gatterstedt. Everyone was exhausted and cold, the horses were exhausted.

Of course our friends were taken by surprise with the unexpected arrival of so many people. Achim Beyling and his wife managed to find room for all of us, and soon my brothers and sisters and I sat around their large farm table for a belated dinner. For us children it was delightful to be able to leave the confines of our wagon and run around again. As we say in German, *wir Kinder musten uns austoben*, we children had to get rid of our built-up excess energy. In the days that followed, some of our people found shelter in a nearby village. We settled down and found a routine.

Those of us of school age enrolled in the village school. That lasted only for a short time before the school closed down. The frequent presence of *Tiefflieger* made our walks to and from school too dangerous. I helped around the farm as Mutti did—thinning beets, planting the garden, helping in the kitchen. The air attacks against Leuna and Berlin continued. I could see the bombers passing overhead when we were in the fields. It seemed there were more and more air attacks of incredibly large bomber formations. Then the *Tiefflieger* came, shooting at anything that moved. Wounded people lay in the fields, often without help for a long time. Retreating German soldiers were everywhere.

Sometime in late April I heard American tanks coming down the road. Several of the tanks rolled into our farmyard, and infantry jumped off the tanks with submachine guns at the ready. I was playing with my siblings in the garden when several soldiers jumped across the garden wall. They smiled at us children. My mother came out of the house. She spoke good English. The soldiers wanted to know if German soldiers were in the house hiding or if there were weapons and munitions stored in the house. She told them, neither. The tanks and most of the soldiers moved on. A small group stayed behind and occupied our village. The soldiers moved into the main house, and we moved into a smaller house.

No one could complain about the behavior of the American soldiers. What was troubling though was when we learned the Americans were going to leave the area and hand it over to the Russians. Mutti was very upset at that unwelcome news. There were stories going around about what Russian soldiers did to women. Mutti decided it was time for us to move on. We had friends near Frankfurt on the Main River, in Bad Silbel. We prepared to move out. Our friends who owned the farm had already departed when we moved out on the morning of the twenty-third of June. There were only two wagons left of our original trek of five. The others had dropped off along the way. We also lost one of our horses to the Wehrmacht just before the war ended. Our second trek proved to be as difficult as the earlier trek from Wollup. The cobblestone roads were slick with the oil from passing American tanks and trucks. The horses had great difficulty getting up the many hills we had to pass over. Mutti decided to get off the main roads again, and we took to *Feldwege*. There we got mired in a swampy area. Farmers were working in the fields, but not until they finished in the evening would they give us a hand to free our wagons. Our progress continued very slowly, hampered by continuous rain. After four days and nights we reached the new American line. An American soldier stopped us and inquired if we had weapons with us. Mutti said, "Yes, I have a small-caliber rifle." My father had once given it to her as a birthday present. The rifle was inscribed with her initials on the stock and had a telescopic sight. The American soldier was visibly delighted when Mutti handed him the rifle, and he let us pass without further delay.

Our second trek took us ten days, nearly as long as the first. When we arrived at our destination we stayed with our friends until autumn. Then we moved on to Freinsheim in the Pfalz with friends of my father's. Those people lived in a large house, took us in and were most generous. Only Mutti and us five children remained. Everywhere we stopped, someone from our trek had stayed behind. For us children our new location was a paradise, because our host family also had four children. The difficult part was to find enough food to feed everyone. Rations were meager. Fortunately we were in the country. We children went to neighboring farms to see what we could beg. We stood in lines for hours for our meager rations. We did the usual things, searching for remains on harvested fields, looking for berries and mushrooms.

In August 1946 my father was released from a French prisoner-of-war camp. I don't know how he located us, but he did. He eventually found work as a manager of a vineyard, since we were in a wine-growing region. I entered school and in time was admitted to the *Gymnasium*. Since we lived in the French zone of occupation I had to take French. The French military offered a limited number of scholarships to German children to attend their schools, including room and board. My mother thought that would be a good thing for me. "First, you get enough food to eat. Second, you have a nice room. Third, learning French may be advantageous to you in the future," she said. So I attended the French school in Neustadt. Later I transferred to the school in Mainz, and eventually completed the French baccalaureate in Baden-Baden.

I finished school in 1956, about the time when the new German army was being formed. In 1957 I decided to join the *Bundeswehr* as an officer candidate. I ended up in air defense, training on American anti-aircraft guns, M-42s. In 1959 I was transferred to the Luftwaffe and spent much of my military career in the air defense business, commanding Nike and Hawk surface-to-air missile units. I retired in 1994 in the rank of major general.

Looking at my mother's role throughout this period, I must say that she took her responsibilities very seriously. She made certain that each of us children got as good a start in life as the times permitted. That included the full spectrum of life, from finding a place for us to live to providing food. She alone organized and orchestrated our escape from the Russians the first and second times. She determined where we were going, what routes to take, what to take along. She did all that herself. It was an incredible responsibility for her which I didn't recognize until later in life. My mother, without doubt, became my role model, and she strongly influenced every one of my brothers and sisters. She was the leading persona in our household. My father made his contribution, of course, but in those critical days at the end of the war he wasn't there. Without exception, all of us children were more focused on our mother than on him.

As for war itself I don't recall much fear—except when we fled the Russians in January 1945, and when the German Stukas flew overhead and attacked the Russian tanks. That's when I became aware of war and what it really meant. At that age, one takes life as it comes, even finds the unusual interesting. My brother and I watched the huge bomber formations flying toward Berlin. We thought it was interesting to see so many airplanes together in the sky. I never thought they were a threat to me personally, nor did I think of the consequences of their being there.

After we escaped from Wollup in January 1945 the front stabilized until April 1945, when the Russians made their final big push for Berlin. Many of the people who initially accompanied us returned to Wollup after the fighting in late January and early February died down. The Russians retreated back to the Oder. The Wehrmacht breached many of the Oder River dikes, flooding the countryside. I returned to Wollup for the first time in 1990. Under the DDR the farm had been turned into a collective. It was a touching and emotional reunion with many people whom I had last seen in 1945. The farm looked pretty much the way I remembered it, with few changes, only everything was fifty years older and badly maintained.

Johann Koppe retired in the greater Bonn area, not far from where he worked on the Hardhöhe, the German Pentagon.

Part III

Other Dimensions of War

It seems possible that a million Germans died in the flight from the east in the early months of 1945, either from exposure or mistreatment. In the winter of 1945 most of the remaining Germans of eastern Europe—who lived in Silesia, the Czech Sudetenland, Pomerania and elsewhere, numbering some 14 million altogether—were systematically collected and transported westward, largely into the British zone of occupation in Germany. . . . Of those who failed to complete this terrible journey, it is calculated that 250,000 died in the course of the expulsion from Czechoslovakia, 1.25 million from Poland, and 600,000 from elsewhere in eastern Europe.

—John Keegan, *The Second World War*

Felix von Eckard, Adenauer's press chief, reported about the [September] 1955 negotiations in Moscow: Suddenly, according to Adenauer, Bulganin said, "Let us come to an agreement. Write me a letter about opening diplomatic relations and you get all your prisoners-of-war. In one week! We give you our word of honor!" Adenauer then asked if that also included the others, the abducted. Bulganin repeated: "Yes. All! All!" Then Bulganin pulled over Khrushchev.

He confirmed the offer: "We can't give you written guarantees, but you have our word." The chancellor didn't hesitate to tell the gentlemen that their words raised his spirits. . . . Nine days after Adenauer's return from Moscow the Bundestag voted unanimously to resume diplomatic relations with the Soviet Union. Still the same year, four days before Christmas 1955, the first Soviet ambassador arrived in Bonn. The release of the prisoners-of-war began on October 7, and ended three months later.

—Wolfgang Hug u.a., *Unsere Geschichte*

The war from the sky in the west of Germany and the war on the ground in the east generally defined the experiences of German children as the conflict came to an end. The situation of German children living outside the boundaries of the Third Reich, such as in the Sudetenland of Czechoslovakia, was somewhat different. German families had lived, thrived, and worked in the Sudetenland for generations. Neither war from the sky nor war on the ground was extensive in this part of Europe. The experiences of these children, therefore, are principally defined by their postwar world and by subsequent expulsion from their homes.

Additionally, two new situations arose for German children of that time. The first was the apparent permanent division of an already truncated Germany into the communist Deutsche Demokratische Republik in the east and the Bundesrepublik in the west. This division translated politically into the continuation of a totalitarian regime in one segment of Germany and a free democratic form of government in the other, with resultant educational dichotomies children had to learn to deal with when moving from one political entity to the other. Usually that movement was from east to west. Germany after 1945 turned into a country with a politically split personality, and such a situation obviously had consequences for Germany's children.

The second situation which defined life for many of Germany's children after the war was the continuing imprisonment of their fathers by a number of countries, long after the war had ended. The Soviet Union was especially known for prolonged imprisonment of Germans, but so were France and Yugoslavia. The last German prisoners of war were not released by the Soviet Union until January 1956, over ten years after the war had ended. For many German children their fathers were merely pictures—men who were at first simply away in the war and who later, if they had not perished, were held for years as prisoners and cheap labor. The children grew up without ever knowing a father. Once the fathers returned, children suddenly had to adjust their lives and make room for these strangers. In some cases adjustment came easily; for others it was a problem. Regardless, the consequences of war continued to haunt German children far into their teenage and adult lives.

Heinz
Loquai

{Age 7}

Komotau, Czech Republic

On entering the heart of the Czech lands, for example, even hardened Soviet tank commanders expressed their shock at the cruel punishments they witnessed being meted out to the Germans by vengeful Czechs. . . . Where Germans did not leave voluntarily, they were forced out, beaten, or starved, and their homes were sometimes burned to the ground. In some towns, Germans were required to wear white armbands and to engage in forced labor.

—Norman M. Naimark, *The Russians in Germany*

I don't know how the men on board the train determined that we had crossed into the West, but as soon as we did the men tore off their white armbands, which they had been ordered to wear, and threw them out the doors of the moving train. My family was in one of the last cars. When I looked outside the door of our boxcar, there was a band of white alongside the tracks from the discarded armbands.

—Heinz Loquai

Komotau lies about eighty kilometers northwest of Prague, fifty kilometers northeast of Karlsbad, at the foot of the Erzgebirge. My family was German as was everyone else living in Komotau and in the surrounding villages. Komotau had about twenty thousand inhabitants, most of them employed in the local factories producing military goods. Very early in the war my father, Josef, was drafted into the Wehrmacht, but his employer soon asked for his return, which was granted by the authorities. He worked as a skilled machine tool operator in an iron and steel processing factory of about two thousand workers. There was

Previous page: Heinz in Komotau, Czechoslovakia, 1942

also a large Mannesmann factory in town, and as a result Komotau became a bombing target. I recall several air attacks. Usually we were given timely air raid warnings allowing us to walk to a nearby mountain cave about twenty minutes from where I lived. The large, man-made cave was secure, but my mother always worried about my father, who was working in the exposed factory down in the valley.

On one occasion after my mother, Maria, my grandmother, Anna, my brother, Franz, and I returned from the mountain cave, my father came home—his face white as a sheet. A *Bombenteppich*, as the mass drop of bombs from a large formation of bombers was called, had come down that day, missing his factory by only a narrow margin. Although the bombs exploded in an adjacent field, their lethality was clear to the factory workers. Several days later a time-delayed bomb exploded nearby. The tremendous explosion shook the entire valley.

On a dark night in February 1945 I heard the adults excitedly saying, "Dresden is burning," and they all rushed outside. I followed. Dresden lay about seventy-five kilometers northeast of Komotau. In the distance I saw a huge red light. It was a frightening experience for me—the red light given off by the burning city was like an omen, an unseen, god-like power exercising its violent ways. Would I be attacked next by this evil thing which could burn whole cities? Although the adults understood what was happening, my perceptions were less precise. At age six, I was unable to give the monster that was burning cities a face.

Although my father was not away in the war, he was most of the time at his place of work. I didn't see him often. My mother, Maria, carried the major burden of assuring the survival of our family of five. My father brought home the money; my mother had to see that she got something for it so we could eat. In 1944, as the result of the air raids, my mother, my younger brother, Franz, and I moved in with my grandmother in a small village six kilometers from Komotau. There we felt relatively secure. Here the war seemed remote and intruded little into our daily lives. People in our family, however, continued to die in remote lands. A cousin was killed in the war as early as 1942. An uncle, a train engineer, was reported missing in 1944. There were tears, I recall, and their pictures appeared in prominent places in my grandmother's house. Still, I didn't really know what war was. To me it was airplanes and bombs, to be awakened by my mother at night, and to be running up the mountain into the cave.

As the war approached its end adults started talking about who would occupy our town, the Russians or the Americans. One day the adults shouted, "The Americans are coming." I ran outside to see the Americans. I could hear a rumbling noise in the distance. Then I saw tanks coming down the road; as they came closer I noticed that they had red stars on their turrets. They were Russians. Everyone was in shock, because we heard stories about the Russians and what they did to people. The tanks drove through the village without stopping. Soon after the tanks passed through, a Russian officer moved into my grandmother's house. I recall him taking me onto his lap, but I soon saw him change from a kind, caring man into someone brutal. He threw me off his lap as he jumped up, screaming at a soldier who had come into the house, telling him something he didn't like. The officer pointed his pistol at the soldier as if he was going to shoot him right there on the spot. After that experience I feared the man.

At night the women hid. I saw fear in their eyes and heard it in their voices. I began to understand that at night things were happening to women which made them fear for their lives. I didn't know specifically what these things were, but of course today I do. My mother and the other women went to a barn and hid in the hay. In the barn lived several French prisoners of war. They were free to go, but had stayed for the time being. The Russians didn't go where the French stayed, so every night the women in our village went to the French for protection. A few weeks later the French left, and people had to find new ways to provide for their safety. I have no resentment against Russians today, but I found them frightening as a child, because they threatened my mother. I found them unpredictable. An indirect fear of the Russian soldiers was passed on to me by the adults in my life. They were afraid of Russians, so I became afraid of Russians too.

The adults were even more afraid of the Czechs. The Russians didn't kill anyone; they only raped the women and took jewelry and watches. But the Czechs came to our village and systematically robbed us, evicted us from our houses, and beat people brutally, killing some at random before my eyes. My family was given an hour to leave our house. My mother and grandmother packed a few things, and we walked to a house where twenty people were living in two rooms. A few days later, my mother found a single room in another house for us. Throughout that period my father continued working in the Komotau factory. Although the war had ended, the factories continued to produce. My father was asked by the Czech overseer if he would consider staying on, because of his skills and experience. My mother refused; she didn't like the Czechs and foresaw that nothing good would come of it. As a result we were moved by the Czech authorities into a former school to await transportation to Germany. My father continued working.

My mother's major fear was that we'd be shipped into the Russian occupation zone. One day Czech militia directed us to go to the railway station for transportation to Germany. We could take what we could carry. My mother wanted to take our feather beds. They were of course bulky. Then my mother wanted me to take a small can in which we kept our money. I was the designated money-can carrier, because she thought I would probably have a better chance of not being searched. I clearly recall the Czech guard who searched me, confiscating with glee my money can as if it contained a small fortune. It was September 1945. We were loaded at night into boxcars, and the train moved out, heading west. Then the train stopped, and rumors immediately began to circulate that it was being diverted to the Russian zone. My impression of the Russians was one of total fear. I had never met Americans, but I knew the adults saw them as saviours. No one seemed to be afraid of the Americans. The train continued its movement westward, and suddenly we were in the West. I don't know how the men on board the train determined that we had crossed into the West, but as soon as we did the men tore off their white armbands, which they had been ordered to wear, and threw them out the doors of the moving train. My family was in one of the last cars. When I looked outside the door of our boxcar, there was a band of white alongside the tracks from the discarded armbands.

In the American zone we came to a camp where we were fed American food. Spam and pork and beans. The food really tasted good. Much better than eating dry, sour rye bread. We were deloused. Sprayed with a choking white powder. The train then continued on to Bamberg where we stayed four weeks in a refugee camp. Then we learned we were to be moved to our final destination. There was no choice of where we were to go. We ended up in a small village near Coburg, about five kilometers from the Russian zone border. About seventy refugees from various places in Czechoslovakia were put up in the dance hall of a *Gasthaus*. There I celebrated my seventh birthday. My mother baked my first carrot cake for me, red and a little bit sweet. I loved it. The men went into the forest and cut wood to heat the dance hall. There were no jobs, and food was becoming really scarce. Just before Christmas my family was assigned a room in someone's house. We lived there for the next nine months and were finally assigned a two-room apartment.

American soldiers were abstract to me in the sense that I saw them pass daily in their jeeps, coming and going to a post at the border, but I never had any personal contact with them. The soldiers were *Schokoladenwerfer*, candy throwers, as we children referred to them. Whoever of us children saw the soldiers first would call out loudly, "*Die Amis kommen, die Amis kommen*," and we would bolt outside to be there when they passed by, because they always threw us some candy bars or chewing gum, or both. One day several black soldiers stopped their jeeps in front of the *Gasthaus* where we stayed, pulling up under the large linden tree and dismounting. It was exciting for me to see such exotic-looking men up close. The soldiers distributed pieces of chocolate to us children, smiling all the while, making jokes only they understood, and then laughing loudly at their own jokes. To me they seemed to be warm and gentle men. Americans for me were black and white. I don't know where I got that from, but when I thought of Americans I didn't just think of white soldiers. Black soldiers embodied the very concept of what I as a child thought was the American soldier. White or black, Americans were not threatening, in contrast to the Russians and the Czechs.

The years 1946 and 1947 were the very worst for my family. People can't imagine today how we lived. Our own children believe we exaggerate when we speak of those days, so we mostly don't. We went into the forest and picked up tree branches and pinecones to heat our room. We were not allowed to cut down trees. The German forest at that time was absolutely clean. Every twig, every pinecone, anything combustible lying on the forest floor was picked up and burned. We scoured the potato fields after they had been harvested, looking for potatoes which had been missed. The height of success, similar to a gold digger in California unexpectedly finding a nugget, was to find a small corner of a field where they had missed two or three potato plants. That was a euphoric experience. We did the same in the wheat and rye fields, picking up every single ear of grain which had dropped to the ground. The one thing available in relative abundance was beer. Beer became a food for the adults. Every village seemed to have a small brewery.

My family also kept chickens and rabbits. Some of the grain we gleaned from the fields we fed to the chickens, but mostly the chickens fended for themselves. We also received ration cards. Whatever was provided in that manner we took. But it was never enough. My father found work with a coal distributor. Occasionally he received a few cigarettes as part of his pay, and since he didn't smoke we traded the cigarettes for something else. Altogether life was a constant struggle for each day's meal. Not for tomorrow's meal, but for today's meal. Once we found out that a dairy in a nearby town had whey available for whoever wanted it—water, mostly, that remained after making buttermilk or cheese. My mother and I walked six kilometers to the train station, then we took the train to the town of Rodach where the dairy was. Even before the train came to a stop everybody jumped off and ran as fast as they could toward the dairy, accompanied by the sound of clanking milk cans. All that for three or four liters of a watery substance which farmers normally fed to their pigs.

Our life was improvisation. We acquired a small plot of land and planted potatoes and vegetables. Occasionally we got work with local farmers. In the beginning the farmers didn't want to have refugees working for them, fearing we would steal from them. On the other hand, at harvest time, when the farmers needed help the most, we preferred not to work because that was the time when we as a family went out to scour the fields. We picked berries and mushrooms in season, cooked nettles into a fine-tasting spinach, and young dandelions made a tasty salad. To this day I have an instinct for where to find mushrooms in a forest. We children fully participated in the acquisition of food and heating materials. Our eyes were constantly open to find these two essentials of life. The situation improved dramatically with the issuance of new money in June 1948. The *Währungsreform* turned everything around. Before there was plenty of money and no goods. After the *Währungsreform* there was little money and plenty of goods. Goods appeared overnight on empty shelves once the new money appeared. We could look, but not touch, because we had no money.

The most important person in our household, as I saw it, was my mother. More important than my father. He always was away working while she was at home managing the family. My father died relatively young. That was sad for us. But I know if my mother had died it would have been a catastrophe. That is how I saw her. I must say we were fortunate. At the end of the war and in the years afterward we didn't really find ourselves in a hostile environment as many others did. The locals viewed all of us *Flüchtlinge* with a degree of hostility, that is true, and is also somewhat understandable. After all, there were many refugees, and we took from them some of their living quarters. Also there were religious differences between refugees and locals. The village we lived in was Protestant. Many refugees from the Sudetenland were Catholic. That led to a degree of friction. Still, locals and newcomers adapted to each other relatively quickly. The town council added two refugee positions, one of which was occupied by my father. That helped to alleviate problems. Also sports clubs, especially soccer, played a role in helping to integrate the community.

In school the problem was rather one of differing skills. Those of us who came from larger towns were generally better educated than the village children. The schoolhouse was simple, accommodating four grades in one room. I recall crying terribly when my mother took me to school in early 1947. I thought I was being separated from her and would be taken away. Prior to that time I had no formal schooling, although I had turned six in November 1944. I lost two years of school because of the war. But my mother taught me the alphabet, and to read and write. She read stories to me, and I read them back to her. She taught me numbers and arithmetic. Her teaching was very important, because it allowed me to eventually enter a class which corresponded to my age. Our teacher first put me in the first grade, because I had no formal schooling. But my mother continued to push the teacher, insisting that I had all the necessary skills, until she relented and accepted me into the third grade, but only on probation. Of course I didn't want to disappoint my mother after all she had done for me, and I worked very hard not to get sent back to a lower grade. Reading and writing was not a problem. I had problems in arithmetic—my first grade was a *drei*, a C. By the time the school year ended, though, I had worked myself through those problems and received what I considered an acceptable grade, acceptable to my mother, that is.

My mother grew up near Komotau in a village deep inside a forest. People went there on pilgrimages to visit the St. Marienkirche. In this region religion had mythical overtones. People believed in miracles, and that deeply influenced my mother. We prayed at dinner and attended church, but religion remained only one of many factors in our family life. It didn't become dominant. Since there was no Catholic church in Coburg, we attended a provisional church in a nearby factory.

Although religious, my mother was constantly in conflict with others, including my father. My father was just the opposite from her. That constant state of conflict between Mother and Father was difficult on me and my brother. As a child I often didn't know how to behave. I didn't want to take sides, but somehow I was pulled in one direction or another. In spite of that internal family conflict, my mother represented existence. She was the central person in our household. In the battle for food she was the one who knew which field to go to, which forest to visit to find berries and mushrooms.

Politics played not much of a role in our household, although it was there. My mother initially was enthusiastic about Hitler. By the time I became aware of symbols and related things, such as the swastika, it meant to me the coming of the bombers. I never saw my father in a uniform nor with a swastika armband. I was not aware of the National Socialist regime as such, being as young as I was. How did my past influence me in future life? I am sure it did, but I don't know how. I am certain that the fight to stay alive, to have enough food from one day to the next, influenced me.

Being a *Flüchtling* all on its own marked a person. Being a refugee, coming from a village school and going on to higher education was something considered most unusual at the time. Before me maybe one or two youngsters had passed the examinations from our village to enter the *Gymnasium*. None of the ones who passed were *Flüchtlinge*. My mother wanted me to attend the *Gymnasium*. My father was against it. When I went to take my examination, the question asked by many locals was, What does that *Flüchtling* want? He isn't capable of something like that. The children who had preceded me to the *Gymnasium* were the daughters of the coal wholesale distributor, a prosperous family living in a villa. I was only a poor refugee and looked upon as being presumptuous, even offensive, I think, to aspire to higher education. To the longtime residents of our village, higher education was something reserved for finer people, for the children of nobility or successful merchants. Three of us took the examination to enter the *Gymnasium*. One was the son of the accountant of the coal merchant. He failed, but was accepted anyway. He didn't last a year in the rigorous school environment.

What drove me in the *Gymnasium* to succeed was not to disappoint my mother. Secondly, as a student with good grades from a poor family, I was entitled to a monthly stipend of fifty marks. Fifty marks was a substantial amount of our family's income. After the death of my father in 1950, my mother received 150 marks widow's compensation. His death was catastrophic for my family. It was routine for me and my brother to go to the grocery store and have our purchases *angeschrieben*, to buy on account. For us children it was difficult, disgraceful, to stand behind the counter and have to ask the clerk—in the presence of others—to please let us have our purchases on credit. I have to say that without exception the merchants did give us the credit we needed to stay alive. And we always paid them, frequently much later than we should have. Around Christmas my father usually received an extra payment, and that's when we paid off our debts. With his death times became really hard again.

I chose to leave the *Gymnasium* and entered an apprenticeship at Siemens in sales. My teachers at the *Gymnasium* were disappointed in my decision, but there were no aspirations on my part or on the part of my mother for me to go to the university. My training at Siemens was practical and excellent, allowing me to go to work and contribute to the support of my mother. I wanted to make my *Abitur* in night school in Munich, which I did. In 1958 I entered the new *Bundeswehr*, mostly because I viewed it as a physical and intellectual challenge, and I needed something like that.

While in the *Bundeswehr* a political representative from my district came and lectured us soldiers on opportunities provided by the federal government for young men to enter the university. I applied, but the personnel department wrote me back that I was ineligible. So I thought I would ask that representative just what he meant at that lecture. I wrote him, and I included the letter from my personnel department which informed me that I was ineligible to attend a university. It only took a week for my personnel officer suddenly to notify me that I was, after all, qualified and eligible to attend the university under government sponsorship. It was pure chance which led me into my subsequent career. That one lecture I attended provided information and aroused my interest in a future I had never even contemplated.

Heinz Loquai subsequently obtained his Ph.D. in political science and retired from the Bundeswehr in 1998 in the rank of brigadier general. He now lives with his wife in the greater Bonn area. The Loquais have three daughters, all of whom have professional careers.

Hans-Peter Haupt

{Age 5}

Prague, Czech Republic

On May 4 Eisenhower finally authorized the Third Army to cross the Czech border, but there was to be no advance beyond Pilsen, which Huebner's V Corps easily occupied before halting. . . . Eisenhower, whose sole concern was to end the war as rapidly as possible, could see no strategic benefit to the allied capture of Prague. . . . Instead Eisenhower left the decision to take Prague to the Red Army, which predictably requested no American advance beyond Pilsen.

—Carlo D'Este, *Patton: A Genius for War*

On a beautiful day in May there approached a seemingly endless convoy of American trucks and tanks. The trucks had large white stars on their doors, and on the fenders of the trucks sat black soldiers cradling guns in their arms. For us few remaining children it was an exciting event, and we ran out in the street to watch the Americans. There, for the first time in my life, I saw black people. Negroes. I only knew about Negroes from an old children's book I had, *Der Struwwelpeter*. I didn't know that people actually existed who looked other than I. The black and white soldiers threw chewing gum and chocolate at us children. It was all so exciting.

—Hans-Peter Haupt

My father, Johannes, was born on April 20, 1912, in Ostrau, a small town southeast of Leipzig. My mother, Frieda—everyone called her Friedel—was born three years later, on February 21, 1915, in Alt-Rohlau, a small community near Karlsbad in the Sudetenland. At age five my mother lost her own mother to blood poisoning during the delivery of her second child. The child also died. Friedel then lived

---

Previous page: Frieda, Hans-Peter, and Johannes in Prague, 1944

with her aunt Frieda and her uncle Rudolph in Karlsbad whom she de facto adopted as her parents. As a result of my mother's close relationship with her aunt and uncle I referred to them as my grandparents. In 1925, when Friedel was ten, her father remarried and took a job in Berlin. Friedel moved to Berlin reluctantly. The happy days of her youth, she confided to me many years later, were spent in Karlsbad with her "parents." For many reasons my mother never succeeded in establishing a good relationship with her stepmother. Once Friedel finished the eighth grade she entered an apprenticeship in Berlin as a tailor and successfully completed her training after three years.

In contrast to my mother's somewhat unsettled childhood, my father's youth was what one considers normal. He apprenticed as a coppersmith in the family business, making all sorts of copper vessels, including the large vats required by breweries. At age twenty-one he chose to join the army. He went through cadet training in Berlin and upon commissioning as a lieutenant was assigned to the signal corps of the Luftwaffe. In 1937 he met my mother, Friedel. They married in 1939, just before my father's transfer to Prague. In Prague my father was in charge of a Wehrmacht communications site at the headquarters of the Reichsprotektorat Böhmen und Mähren. My mother soon joined my father in Prague, and I was born there on August 20, 1940. After I was about six months old, I understand, my mother obtained a job in the classified documents office in the headquarters of the Reichsprotektorat.

I had a *Kindermädchen* care for me while my mother worked, a young Czech woman, Ruscha, who lived with us in our apartment. In 1941 my father, along with his communications unit, was transferred to the *Ostfront*. I only saw my father twice during the war years—once when he came to visit on military leave from the East in 1944, and again in 1945, a week before the heavy air raids on Dresden, on the occasion of his father's death. My mother and I met my father at the funeral in February 1945, coming by train from Prague through Dresden. At that time I was nearly five years old. On the return trip to Prague we again traveled through Dresden, only one or two days before the fateful air attacks. After the funeral my father returned to his unit near Riga, Latvia.

I remember my mother best as a businesswoman, a woman who went to work in the morning and came home in the evening. From my birth until 1945 I practically didn't exist for her. In the evenings she would try to exert her authority and tell me to do this or do that, or not to do this or not do that. The woman who raised me, however, and to whom I looked for guidance was my *Kindermädchen*, Ruscha. I remember Ruscha as a kind, charming, and beautiful woman. She cooked for me, took care of me, played with me, did things with me when I wasn't in kindergarten. She was my de facto mother. Ruscha married a German soldier, Tommy, in 1944. She didn't have much of a married life because her soldier husband only occasionally came home on military leave. But when Tommy did come home I played second fiddle. I didn't like that at all. I became quite jealous of Tommy. One day early in 1945 Ruscha received the awful news that Tommy had been killed in action. Ruscha cried for days, and even as a four-year-old I could feel her sadness and her loss.

Prague of course was similar to Dresden before the air raids in February 1945; it was considered an open city. At least we thought it was an open city. Prague wasn't bombed, and no one expected it to be bombed. I remember that at precisely twelve o'clock every day a huge German aircraft, a Gigant, flew over our house. I believe it had twelve engines. I waited for it to come over every noon. In the spring of 1945 I was in a city park with Ruscha. Suddenly there was an air raid warning. Since there were no shelters in Prague, we hid behind a bench in the park. I saw a huge formation of bombers passing overhead. It took a long time for them to pass. They glistened high up in the sky, and the sound of their engines made things vibrate around me. Otherwise there was no war in Prague that I was aware of. We lived in peace, isolated from everything that took place around us.

In early April 1945 when the last German troops moved out of the city, my mother lost her job, and Ruscha left. My relationship with my mother changed. Suddenly she became the focus of my world. In late April my mother's intuition told her that as Germans we had to get out of Prague for our own safety. When she saw the first Czechs walking around with red armbands, carrying red flags, she knew it was time to go. We saw red pieces of cloth hanging from windows everywhere. The Red Army couldn't be very far away. The *Reichsbahn* still ran its regular train service, so my mother decided to take me by train to Karlsbad, to my grandparents, her pseudo adopted parents. During the trip our train was attacked by *Tiefflieger*. The train stopped abruptly, we hurried outside in panic, throwing ourselves into the bushes near the tracks. I remember Mutti covering me with her body. Although many of the coaches were damaged in the attack, the train continued its journey. I recall opening the door to the toilet. I tried to step inside, and I thought my heart would stop of fright—there was no floor in the toilet. A cannon shell from one of the attacking *Tiefflieger* had taken out the floor. All I saw was a large hole and the railroad ties passing swiftly below me. We arrived in Karlsbad without further incident. My grandparents owned a coffeehouse, Conditorei Rudolph Heimrath Café, in Karlsbad, and there I soon felt at home. My mother, though, became restless, having no real responsibilities now, and within days she returned to Prague to retrieve additional clothing and valuables from our apartment. Her return trip was much more difficult, because her train was attacked by *Tiefflieger* more than once. She later told me that she completed her trip hitching rides on passing Wehrmacht trucks.

My grandparents' café sat in the middle of Karlsbad, very near the mineral springs. The German troops once stationed in Karlsbad had departed. Karlsbad, like Prague, had not suffered air attacks. At the very end of April 1945 several German munitions trains ended up in the railroad yard at Karlsbad, and I believe just by chance an aircraft dropped several bombs near the trains. The day my mother returned from Prague a fire started to blaze near the munitions trains, and I saw trucks with loudspeakers coming through town ordering all adults to come to the *Bahnhof*. My grandparents hurried to the *Bahnhof*, where they helped push the munitions trains, one boxcar at a time, away from the fire. The people saved the town, because Karlsbad lies in a valley, and an explosion would have caused incredible damage. My grandparents and Mutti returned that night exhausted and dirty.

We had plenty to eat, though. The café was closed, so I played in the bakery or among the tables in the winter-garden. Soon our German neighbors began to leave. Some packed their things and left. Others just left without taking anything, always leaving at night. My mother felt insecure again. On a beautiful day in May there approached a seemingly endless convoy of American trucks and tanks. The trucks had large white stars on their doors, and on the fenders of the trucks sat black soldiers cradling guns in their arms. For us few remaining children it was an exciting event, and we ran out in the street to watch the Americans. There, for the first time in my life, I saw black people. Negroes. I only knew about Negroes from an old children's book I had, *Der Struwwelpeter*. I didn't know that people actually existed who looked other than I. The black and white soldiers threw chewing gum and chocolate at us children. It was all so exciting. The soldiers looked relaxed and smiled at us as they passed. I saw the Americans as totally nonthreatening, even though they held weapons in their hands.

The seemingly endless convoy went on and on. First came the tanks and armored cars. Then the trucks. Everything shook as the tanks rumbled past. It took two to three days for the column to drive through Karlsbad. At night I had difficulty going to sleep because the house shook from the passing trucks and tanks. I also was very excited. I wanted to be outside to get more chewing gum and candy. The soldiers were always throwing something to us children—if not candy bars, then powdered milk and all sorts of canned rations. After the Americans finally passed through town it was quiet again. Karlsbad was almost like a ghost town. Our family continued to have plenty to eat, because the bakery was stocked with flour and sugar and other staples. Two weeks later the Americans came again, this time heading west. After three days it was quiet again for another two weeks. Then still another convoy came from the same direction as the departing Americans. But that convoy was different. There was no rumble of tanks, no noise of truck engines, no grinding gears. Instead I heard the clip-clop of horses' hooves. Small *Panje* wagons pulled by equally small, shaggy-looking horses moved through town. Next came long columns of marching soldiers carrying their weapons. In between the soldiers were more horse-drawn wagons and an occasional truck. The Russians had arrived.

I watched the Russian soldiers march through town as I had watched the Americans before them. They were orderly, but they threw no chocolate or chewing gum to us children. Their faces looked grim, in stark contrast to the smiling American soldiers I remembered. Soon after their arrival the Russians opened a *Kommandatura*. They appointed a city commander and established a governing structure. There were no attacks or other infringements by the soldiers against us. I can't even recall seeing drunken or rampaging soldiers in the streets of Karlsbad. The Russians I saw were disciplined troops, and they left us alone. At times when Russian soldiers passed by our house they even waved at me. It made me happy, and I waved back at them.

My mother and her parents then decided to move on to Alt-Rohlau where my mother was born. Alt-Rohlau was about five kilometers out of town. She thought we would be safer there. In Alt-Rohlau my grandparents had a second, smaller coffeehouse. When we left Karlsbad we only took what we could carry—important papers and the family jewelry, which my mother sewed into a towel and wrapped around her waist. Once we got to Alt-Rohlau there was little food for us. For the first time I experienced hunger. My mother decided to walk the five kilometers back to Karlsbad, where she knew there was still food in the bakery of our *Conditorei*. She took me along as security, I suppose. On the way we passed through a huge Russian bivouac area where the troops lived in tents. I recall how nervous and afraid she was. She was thirty years old at the time, young and attractive. No one bothered us. By the time we began our walk back to Alt-Rohlau it was getting dark. We entered a forest, and suddenly, about twenty meters ahead of us, we saw a Russian soldier. I could feel my mother's tension through her hand. She stopped briefly. We saw the soldier kneeling in front of something. As we got closer I could tell it was a small religious roadside shrine, a *Marterl* of Maria holding the Christ child. It was twilight, nearly dark. The soldier knew we were approaching. I had seen him turn his head briefly to look at us. I could feel the hesitation in my mother. She whispered, "Quiet. Come." As fast as we could walk, not run, still walking, we passed the soldier. He appeared to be in deep prayer. He didn't move.

Several days later we again returned to Karlsbad to fetch more food. We blundered into a group of three Russian soldiers. They came toward us when they saw us, shouting, "*Uri. Uri.*" They wanted watches. My mother had a watch on her arm. One soldier took the watch. Another held out his hand for her purse. She had another watch in her purse, and he took it. I saw my mother was visibly agitated, probably fearing what might come next. Then one of the Russian soldiers reached into his knapsack and took out a piece of bread spread with margarine and sprinkled with sugar. He smiled broadly as he handed it to me. It was coarse, brown bread. I remember it vividly. I took a bite out of the bread, and it tasted good. I was very hungry. While my mother was dragging me by the hand away from the scene I kept looking back at the nice Russian soldier. As we came to a railroad crossing a train suddenly appeared out of a hollow around the bend. My mother grabbed me around the waist and ran with me across the tracks. In the confusion I dropped my piece of bread. I had only eaten half of it. The bread fell on one of the rails. I felt terribly sad about losing my bread. I looked for it after the train passed, but there was nothing left but a smear on the track. I cried.

That was the last time we were able to return to Karlsbad for food. A period of hunger followed. My grandparents were innovative and went out and collected berries from which they made jelly. From nettles they cooked a spinach-like meal. Still we were hungry. That period of hunger has influenced me to this day. I have an incredibly high regard for all kinds of food. I always clean my plate no matter what the food or how it is prepared. Later in life when I had my own command in the *Bundeswehr* nothing infuriated me more than seeing my soldiers taking heaping portions of food and then throwing much of it away. I know it all goes back to that piece of bread and the Russian soldier in 1945.

In the meantime the Russians and the Czechs established a jointly occupied *Kommandatura* in our village. One day my mother was ordered to come to the *Kommandatura* to have her identification papers checked. As usual she took me along for protection. She later told me that she had purposely left her papers behind in Prague because they showed that my father was an officer in the Wehrmacht. We entered the *Kommandatura*. My mother was ushered into a room while I was kept in the reception area. Several Russian soldiers and Czech policemen sat there. One of the soldiers had a bowl of straw-berries in front of him. He saw me looking at the berries and motioned for me to come over. I walked over, and he promptly started to feed me strawberries. Then I heard my mother screaming in the room next door. The soldier continued to feed me strawberries while my mother screamed in the next room. I don't remember what I thought or felt at the time. All I remember is the strawberries. I was five. About fifteen minutes later she came out, walking gingerly. Her face was streaked with tears. In later years she told me that the Czech police wanted information about other people, and when she claimed she didn't know or refused to answer, they took off her shoes and stockings and beat the soles of her feet with a wooden ruler.

We exited the *Kommandatura* quickly. As we came outside, I saw my first intoxicated Russian soldiers. They were trying to learn to ride bicycles and obviously had never ridden bicycles before. They fell down frequently, laughing loudly, taking no notice of their falls. They just kept it up and ignored us. My mother grasped my hand firmly, and walking as fast as she could, pulled me past the laughing soldiers and out of their sight. I didn't know at the time, but my mother had heard rumors that in Prague and in other nearby towns Germans were being killed and mutilated. It was June. She decided it was high time for us to move on.

Before my mother could put her plans into action, Czech authorities directed all Germans to report to the riding school in Karlsbad—a school similar to the famous riding school in Vienna, Austria. My mother went there with mixed feelings, she later told me. She had no idea what we were facing. When we got to the riding school—mother, me, and my grandparents—the place was jammed with trucks and horse-drawn wagons. People were herded onto the wagons and onto the trucks, and when a vehicle was full it drove off. My mother intended to get on one of the trucks, but I, at age five, wanted to ride on a horse-drawn wagon. I begged my mother to get on a wagon, not on a truck. It looked like so much more fun to me to ride a horse-drawn wagon than standing up in the back of a crowded truck. I stomped my feet and cried out loud, *Ich will auf den Pferdewagen fahren*, and attempted to pull her toward one of the wagons, away from the trucks. She finally gave in, and all of us climbed on a horse-drawn wagon and sat down in the straw. In time, we ended up safely with a Czech farmer, friends of my grandparents, in Grossenteich, a small village still in Czechoslovakia.

In Grossenteich I remember again seeing men with red armbands carrying red flags. We stayed on a potato farm. When we arrived they were harvesting their first crop. My mother and I could go *nachstoppeln*, meaning we could look for potatoes where they had already been harvested. We had plenty of potatoes to eat. Another farmer in the village had milk cows and willingly gave my mother milk for me. He spoke German and showed no animosity toward us. The potato farmer had a young boy my age, his name was Karel. Karel and I couldn't understand each other very well, but we could tell that we liked each other. Right away we started to play together from early morning until late at night. With him I smoked my first "pond" cigar. We made the cigar from last year's dried cattails still standing around a pond. We both got sick.

One afternoon late in the summer of 1945, my mother and I had just gotten our daily can of milk and were walking back to the farm, when suddenly on the road ahead of us appeared a huge tank. The tank moved at a high rate of speed, taking up most of the narrow farm road. Three soldiers sat on the tank. Water-filled ditches were to the left and right of the narrow road, a low-lying, swampy area. We stopped and watched the approaching tank carefully. The tank stayed to the right of the road and could have passed with ease, but just a few meters ahead of us the tank turned slightly and headed straight for us. My mother dropped the can of milk and both of us jumped into the ditch. The tank drove on; the inebriated soldiers sitting on the tank laughed loudly at our predicament. After that my mother desperately wanted to leave and find some place where there were no Russians. My grandparents decided to stay with the farmer in Grossenteich who didn't mind having them. We two set out toward Hof in Bavaria where my mother had an aunt. She had heard that the Amis were in Hof, not the Russians. That made up her mind.

That night the potato farmer drove us to the nearest train station. There were no passenger trains running, only freight trains. The train my mother chose to ride was supposed to go to Komotau. One of the cars had a small brakeman's house attached to one end of it. My mother lifted me into the brake house. We carried with us a bed sheet tied together at its four ends holding our clothing and other possessions. My mother shoved the bundle in front of me so I couldn't move and closed the door. She whispered just before closing the door, "Stay real quiet. Real quiet. Don't talk. I'll be right back." It was pitch black outside. I was terrified that the train would leave before my mother got back. She didn't come back and didn't come back. It seemed like eternity to me; all the while I was stuck in this brake house, unable to move. I heard the engine puffing at the front of the train and whistles blowing. And then there she was. As soon as she squeezed herself into the brake house with me the train began to move. She later told me that she went to the station and gave one of the guards some of her jewelry so he would conveniently overlook our presence. All trains had guards to keep them from being plundered.

The train went to Pilsen. There we switched to a coal train. My mother carried me up the side of a coal car and dumped me headfirst into the coal. I was immediately covered with coal dust from head to toe. Together we dug a hole in the coal to hide. The train was long, and once it began to move, it moved slowly. By morning I crawled over to the side of the coal car and peeked over the edge, only to see Russian soldiers lining the railroad tracks, standing about fifty meters apart. They were facing away from the tracks guarding the coal train to keep people from emptying it before it got to its destination. The train continued on its slow journey, stopping briefly, then moving again. When I next looked over the side of the car, I saw old friends. Black friends. Americans. I knew we were in Germany. As the train passed the American soldiers I could hear them talking loudly. They always talked loudly. We got off the next time the train stopped. When we finally arrived at my aunt's in Hof, Mutti and I were still covered in coal dust. My aunt was not pleased by our arrival, or by the prospect of us staying with her. I could feel the tension between my mother and my aunt.

My mother had no idea where else we could go, but at least for the time being we were safe, away from the Russians. We stayed in Hof for two winters, until 1947. Both winters were very cold. My mother continually tried to find my father, using the Red Cross and other search organizations which tried to reunite families. In March 1947 my mother learned that my father was a prisoner of the English in Kiel, a port city on the Baltic Sea. My mother couldn't figure out how that had possibly come about when his last duty station was in Riga, Latvia. My father later told me he left Riga on the last ship. The ship was already moving away from its mooring when in desperation he jumped for it. The ship made it to Kiel, where it was intercepted by a British destroyer, and he was put in a prisoner-of-war camp. As soon as my mother learned where my father was, we two left Hof. Trains were running again, and we didn't mind walking when we had to. We slept on benches in train stations and once in a barn. After several days' travel we arrived in Kiel.

I didn't recognize my father at first. I hadn't seen him in two years. He was thin and had grown a beard. The English didn't release him right away, but allowed him to leave the camp in the morning as long as he returned by six in the evening. Kiel itself was a pile of rubble. In the camp my father met a local woman who was employed in the kitchen. She had an apartment, and, although it was bomb damaged, it was habitable. She agreed to let us move into one room of her apartment. My father still slept at night in the camp. There was little to eat in 1947 except for turnips. Rations were meager. My father brought us most of his camp rations—toast, cheese, some sausage. That's how we got by. The English then organized the GCLO, the German Civil Labor Organization, which later was renamed GSO, German Service Organization. My father was made commander of a GCLO truck unit, issued a dyed dark-brown British uniform, and released from the camp. Things definitely began to look up when one day my father came home with a can of English tobacco and cigarette paper. That evening he and my mother rolled cigarettes until late into the night. The cigarettes they traded the next day to sailors on ships passing through the Kiel Canal locks in exchange for coffee and food.

In the summer of 1947 my father located a small garden shack in a *Schrebergarten* outside Kiel. The shack was just a simple one-room structure of boards nailed to a frame, with no insulation at all. As a result of his GSO connections he was able to get tar paper, lumber, and cement. He made a deal with a contractor, who then, while we continued to live in the shack, built a small house around the shack. When the house was finished we tore down the old shack, which was on the inside of the new, larger house. We lived in that tiny house for many years. That's where I grew up. I loved the garden and the trees and the berry bushes.

One day in 1952 while riding the streetcar on his way to work, my father noticed a man sitting across from him. The man was thin to the point of being bony. His face looked old, although something told my father that the man wasn't all that old. The man stared back at him. Finally my father said to him, "We know each other, don't we?"

The man replied, "Yes, we do."

"Johannes Haupt," my father said, extending his hand.

"Stefan Eggert," the stranger replied. They had been cadets together in the officers' training academy in Berlin in 1934. Eggert recently had been released from a Russian prisoner-of-war camp, weighing just over one hundred pounds, still recovering from double pneumonia. Eggert said, "Hey, I have a business opportunity which might interest you. There is a publisher by the name of Bertelsmann giving out distribution franchises in a new business called book clubs. I am helping them develop the concept and I could use someone to help me. Does that interest you? We could do it together. How about it?"

My father jumped at the opportunity. "I can't work in the GSO forever," he told his old friend. That's how my father got in on the ground floor of what turned out to be a very lucrative book distribution business. When my father got too old he sold his franchise back to Bertelsmann, but retained the rights to a percentage of all sales in his region. To this day my mother lives very comfortably off the proceeds of a chance encounter between two former German soldiers on a streetcar in Kiel in 1952.

Looking back, I can't help but admire my mother for what she did back in 1945. She had good intuition and a sense for danger. She acted upon her intuition. That's what made my mother unique, I believe. In what could have been a truly life-threatening situation for us, such as the riding school incident—which we know today was the beginning of a seven-day pogrom of brutal revenge by Czechs against Germans— she could sense the danger. She relied on her intuition, on her finely honed sense of detecting hidden danger, and then she acted on it. Many of the people who boarded the trucks in the Karlsbad riding school instead of the horse-drawn wagons, we later learned, were killed. Ruscha, my *Kindermädchen*, was killed by a mob in Prague because she had married a German soldier. After we escaped the pogrom in Czechoslovakia, my mother continued to incrementally move us away from danger until we two finally arrived safely in Bavaria, in the American zone of occupation.

Hans-Peter Haupt apprenticed as a banker in Kiel, but soon took advantage of the university education offered by the new Bundeswehr. He became a logistician in the Luftwaffe and in 1996 retired in the rank of colonel. He now is the regional director of a prominent Germany-based nonprofit organization, putting to good use the organizational and leadership skills he acquired and cultivated in his military career. His mother, Friedel, still lives near Hans-Peter in Kiel. His father died at age seventy, in 1981, of Hodgkin's disease. As for Peter's adopted grandparents who had stayed behind with the Czech potato farmer in Grossenteich, no harm came to them. On their own they crossed the border into Germany in the early summer of 1945. German authorities resettled them in Breidenbach, a small town north of Giessen, in the American zone.

Etta
Krecker

{Age 5}

Eilenburg, Saxony-Anhalt

The subject of contemporary studies became a compulsory course in all schools, including the trade schools. Like civics in the American class-room, contemporary studies was decidedly political in its goals. . . . The course also placed a strong emphasis on the individual's role in society, his or her obligation and responsibility for the entire society, and the moral obligation to take an active role in the antifascist democratic transformation.

—Norman M. Naimark, *The Russians in Germany*

In the East I grew up under a system that surrounded me like a cocoon from morning to night. In the mornings I had attended school with its constant emphasis on the tenets of Communism and the evils of the West. In the afternoons I was involved in complementary organized activ-ities such as choir, dancing, and stage acting. We children constantly were under someone's supervision and influence.

—Etta Krecker

I was an only child, born in 1940 in Eilenburg on the Mulde River. My father, Erwin, was drafted into the Wehrmacht in 1941, and then the war swallowed him up. For much of my early life he was the man in a picture my mother kept by her bedside. In 1945, at war's end, I still lived in Eilenburg, thirty kilometers southwest of Torgau, where American and Russian troops first met on April 25, 1945. My mother, Edith, and I, and my mother's parents who had joined us from East Prussia, found ourselves hiding in a factory on the east side of the

---

Previous page: Etta and her mother Edith, 1953

Mulde when the Russians arrived. We tried to escape the approaching Russians and had left our apartment on the west side of town—only to run directly into their arms. Then the Americans appeared on the west bank of the river and occupied the only bridge across the Mulde. With the Russians occupying the east end of the bridge we couldn't get back across. That night my mother tried to cross the river to get to our apartment, but she soon was caught and sent back. I only saw the Americans from a distance. I never had any contact with them.

Several weeks later in July, after the Americans had evacuated the west side of town, we returned to our apartment and found it pretty much as we had left it. My grandparents, my mother, and I only had two hours in our apartment before we were evicted and the apartment was occupied by Russian soldiers. As a five-year-old I could feel the fear of Russians radiating from the adults around me, but no violence was done to any of us. As long as I lived in the East, however, I was always afraid. I never walked past the Russian army barracks or the *Kommandatura* without fear—an unspecific type of fear, but fear nevertheless. And of course we all heard things, and my mother made no effort to keep anything away from me.

Putting food on the table soon became an all-consuming activity for my mother. I was very thin as a child, suffered from malnourishment, and had severe problems with my spine. I recall my mother taking the peelings from boiled potatoes out of the trash and grinding the peels into a mush and baking the mush into cookies. A compassionate farmer's wife often gave my mother pieces of sausage and ham and bacon trimmings from their smokehouse for her ailing child. Sometimes we found wormy fruit that had fallen off trees prematurely. If it was eatable we took it.

My mother was notified by the *Arbeitsamt* that she had to go to work. In the new Communist state that was taking shape everyone had to work, she was given to understand by a Communist functionary. First she was assigned to clean a park. Later she worked in a bank and at other office jobs.

When stores did have food to sell against our ration cards, I had to do the shopping. I would grab an *Einkaufstasche* and assorted glasses, in case there was marmalade or jelly for sale, and off I went. The store often was several kilometers from where we lived. On the way home I was of course very hungry. I remember sticking my finger into a glass with marmalade, and when I got home I had eaten half of it. The ration had to last us for a long time, and I had eaten most of it already. My mother was terribly upset that evening when she saw what I had done. She gave me a good spanking. Whenever my mother went to work, she locked the cabinet where she kept the little food we had. She didn't trust me.

My father finally returned from a Russian prisoner-of-war camp late in 1949, around Christmas. He had been a prisoner for four years. I met my father for the first time at age nine. Before he was drafted into the Wehrmacht he had been a teacher at a business school. Like myself, my father was an only child. His family's plan had been for him to eventually take over his parents' clothing store in Liegnitz, in Niederschlesien. The war changed all that. Liegnitz and Niederschlesien was now a part of Poland. However, he was allowed to return to his teaching profession. One day in 1954 he was invited to a meeting in a building which he knew was occupied by the STASI, the *Staatssicherheitsdienst* of the DDR—the equivalent of Hitler's gestapo. At the meeting he was asked to become an informer. My father never told me in detail what it was they wanted him to do, but he refused. Fearful of what the STASI might do to him, that same night he took a train to West Berlin. After staying in a refugee camp in Berlin he finally obtained a teaching position in Bremen.

My mother and I stayed behind in Eilenburg. I attended the *Gymnasium*. One day I was summoned to my principal's office. He spoke to me at length about my political orientation, attempting to get me to spy on my parents. He became angry with me when I didn't cooperate. I argued with him. When I got home I broke into tears when I told my mother of my experience. People we had thought of as friends came to visit my mother and tried to persuade her to get my father to return. "Nothing will happen to him," they said. "All will be forgiven." My mother took these comments as a sign for us to get out of East Germany as quickly as possible. The following day she took me first to our doctor. I was still ailing. The doctor ordered rest for my recovery and excused me from school attendance. We then went to stay with friends we thought we could still trust. That evening, in the dark, my mother and I walked to the *Bahnhof* and bought tickets to Fürstenwalde, where her sister Marie lived. Instead we got off the train in Berlin and took the S-Bahn, the elevated train that circles the city, to West Berlin. We later learned that the following day two men showed up in front of our house in Eilenburg to watch for us. Of course they didn't know we had already escaped.

For weeks my mother and I stayed in a small refugee camp on the *Kurfürstendam* in West Berlin. We were interrogated by German and American intelligence people, and given some money. Then we heard of people who lived in our camp being forcibly dragged back into the East. My mother decided she would have none of that. She planned to take the first plane we could get on out of Berlin. After making contact with my father in Bremen, we were given refugee status and flown out of Berlin on an American plane. I was fourteen years old. Once we arrived in Bremen my parents immediately enrolled me in the *Gymnasium*, where I soon ran into numerous problems, especially with foreign languages. In the East I had studied Russian. In the West I had to study English, a language in which I was far behind my classmates. I encountered similar problems with Latin and French. Although much of my education in the East had been thorough, politically the focus had been on the Communist part of the world and on our relationship with our new "brothers," the Russians. I knew all the republics of the Soviet Union and their capital cities, but I knew very little about anything in the West. History and social studies had been viewed through the lenses of our new leaders, the Communist Party.

In the East I grew up under a system that surrounded me like a cocoon from morning to night. In the mornings I had attended school with its constant emphasis on the tenets of Communism and the evils of the West. In the afternoons I was involved in complementary organized activities such as choir, dancing, and stage acting. We children constantly were under someone's supervision and influence. Once I transferred to the West I thought my new classmates often behaved superficially and were excessively silly. Especially the girls. I found little of the sense of focus and serious consideration of international relationships that I had gotten used to in the East. I suddenly had to accommodate to a differing way of life in the West, a way of life which was much less directive and without the round-the-clock schedule of activities I had grown up with. I found it difficult to adjust.

While I was trying to accommodate to my new situation in school and the lack of structured activities after school, my home life was slowly coming together again. When we first arrived in Bremen my mother, father, and I lived in one small room. Finally we found a small apartment, and life became less stressful for us. How did I view Germany and its partition once I had time to accommodate to the ways of the West? I saw the DDR as a part of Germany, the other part. Not as a separate state, although it was that. I had looked at West Germany in the same way when I lived in the East, as simply the other part of Germany. The DDR became for me the Soviet-occupied part of Germany, never another state.

After graduation from the Gymnasium Etta Krecker soon married. Her husband served a full career as an officer in the new German Luftwaffe, and she accompanied him on his various assignments, including the United States. After his retirement they settled in a comfortable home in St. Augustine, a suburb in the greater Bonn-Cologne metropolitan area. Etta had no children of her own.

Regina Demetrio

{Age 3}

Zwickau, Saxony

German POWs who had been processed in Western POW camps and cleared to return to their homes in the East . . . the healthiest among them were deported to forced labor camps in the Soviet Union.

—Norman M. Naimark, *The Russians in Germany*

My father was released by the French government Christmas 1953. He chose to go to Karlsruhe, rather than his hometown of Zwickau near Leipzig. . . . He had heard things. He didn't trust the Communists.

—Regina Demetrio

I was born in 1942 when my mother was twenty-one years old. For twelve years, until January 1954, I lived in a suburb of Zwickau, Keimsdorf, in the Deutsche Demokratische Republik, the DDR. In Keimsdorf my grandparents at one time owned several houses and businesses. Most of their properties were confiscated by the state after the war. I didn't know my father. He was a prisoner of war of the French. I met my father, Helmut, for the first time in September 1953. My mother and I were given permission to visit my father in Loos les Lille where he was imprisoned. He had seen me last when I was eighteen months old, in 1944, when he came home on a rare military leave. I only knew him from his pictures.

As a first lieutenant my father was assigned to the Brandenburg Division, and one of its units was assigned to the south of France to combat French partisans. He was a teacher by profession and spoke

---

Previous page: Regina with her mother and father, 1953

Regina Demetrio

fluent French and Spanish. At one time he taught for five years in Chile and also spent time in Madrid. His language skills were the reasons for his assignment to that unit in the south of France near the Pyrenees mountains. In September 1944 he was captured by Americans as his unit retreated toward Germany. Subsequently he was transferred to a French prisoner-of-war camp. There, a military court condemned him to death. He conducted his own defense in French, and in time the court vacated his death sentence and gave him life in prison.

I was eleven years old when I first went to visit my father. It was all very interesting for me to visit a high-security prison. We were allowed to go to his cell, and while my mother visited with him, others took me on a tour of the prison to give my parents some privacy. I wasn't so sure if I liked the new situation, with my mother and me suddenly separated because of a man I didn't even know. I had mixed feelings about our new and unexpected relationship. My father was released by the French government Christmas 1953. He chose to go to Karlsruhe, rather than his hometown of Zwickau near Leipzig. One of my mother's sisters lived in Karlsruhe. My father wasn't going to take any chances with the Communist regime, he later told us. He had heard things. He didn't trust the Communists. When we visited my father in September 1953 we didn't know that he was going to be released soon. We thought it would take several more years, if ever.

After my father's release my mother applied for permission to transfer our household from Zwickau in the DDR to Karlsruhe in the Bundesrepublik, for the purpose of reuniting our family. To our great surprise permission was granted quickly by the DDR authorities. As a result of the Berlin uprising in 1953 many previous restrictions had been relaxed. We benefited from that. In addition, the fact that my father was a French prisoner of war was viewed by the DDR authorities as positive, meriting their consideration, because it meant that not only the Russians had kept German prisoners for many years after the war ended, but also the western Allies. That was good propaganda

337

material for the DDR authorities, and with much accompanying publicity they authorized our move to the West. We moved with all of our belongings in April 1954 to Karlsruhe.

At the time I, for purely selfish reasons, thought our move to Karlsruhe was terrible. I hated it. In Zwickau my grandfather owned a nice house with a garden. I had grown up there. It was my home. I was reluctant to leave this comfortable environment. I also did well in school, where I was entitled to free meals because of my father's status as a prisoner of war. Additionally, Christmas 1953 I had been initiated into the *Junge Pioniere*, the first-level youth organization a child entered into in the DDR. My grandfather nearly fainted when he learned that I had joined the *Junge Pioniere*, but I thought it was the right thing to do. I coveted the blue scarf of the Young Pioneers, and resented that just as I had earned this sought-after emblem we were leaving for the West. I didn't want to leave behind all that that felt like home.

In spite of my youthful enthusiasm for the world I lived in, I did recognize that there were some things which made me uneasy and suspicious, at times even wonder about what I was learning. I recall an instance in the second grade. The discussion was about Karl Marx. The teacher asked the class, "What do you know about Karl Marx?" I proudly raised my hand, and when he recognized me I stood and said, Karl Marx was a Jew. Icy silence followed my pronouncement. The other children had no idea what a Jew was. Nor did I. I had never seen a Jew in my life. I only knew that my grandfather once mentioned that the great Karl Marx was a Jew. I was proud that I remembered everything I heard adults say in my presence, and here was an opportunity to show off my knowledge. I guess I was trying to show off a little.

Fortunately my teacher liked me and didn't report me. But he asked my mother to come and meet with him. He counseled her to keep me from saying such antidemocratic things in the future, or we may have great difficulties with the authorities. From then on, my mother and my grandparents no longer discussed many things in my presence. Today I know that the DDR lived with a dual morality and was nothing less than the continuation of the Nazi regime. Only their colors were different. At the time I didn't know that. As for Jews, the DDR school system was silent about the Nazi atrocities. Not until I was in the West at age fifteen did I learn from my history teacher, who was married to a Jewish woman, of the Jewish plight during the Nazi years. He showed us such gruesome pictures my entire class cried. Boys and girls were in separate classes in my school. All of the girls in my class ran home that day, and we confronted our parents. How could you allow such a thing to occur? How could you let it happen? How could your generation do this? I asked my parents. My poor parents had no answers for me, nor did the parents of my classmates have answers for them. We didn't know, they said to us. We didn't know.

In Karlsruhe my father went back to teaching and I entered the *Gymnasium.* I had good notes in my final report card from my school in the East. That was most unusual. First, few children coming from the East went to the *Gymnasium,* not to mention girls; and second, it was unheard of for someone to transfer from the East in a perfectly normal manner. Everyone else from the East seemed to have escaped without authorization, and of course didn't have a final report card. My school principal accepted my report card and transfer papers with the provision that he would have to verify their authenticity before giving me a permanent school assignment. He then asked me to take the *Gymnasium* acceptance examination, not disguising his belief that I surely would not pass. I took the examination and received all ones, A's. When the principal next spoke to me he was serious, his normally frivolous, half-joking manner toward me gone. His surprise at my achievement was obvious to me.

Although I was accepted into the *Gymnasium,* the principal continued to monitor my performance throughout the year. At the end of the first year the final grades were passed out, and those students who were in the top 10 percent received special mention in front of the assembled class, as well as a certificate of achievement. After the end of the ceremony the principal came to me and said, "Oh, Regina, you were in the top 10 percent and I accidentally overlooked you. I am sorry." I knew he wasn't sorry at all; he had done it out of spite. After that incident my parents transferred me to another *Gymnasium* where I made my *Abitur*.

It was my *Schicksal*, my fate as we Germans would say, not to have a father until I was eleven years old. On his part, he was so happy to be finally reunited with his wife and daughter after so many years. He and my mother married for love, and were in love with each other for as long as I knew them. My own relationship with my father, however, was not that easily established upon his return. To me he was kind and gentle at all times. I was in my puberty at this time, and instead of love I felt aggressive toward him. He constantly put his arms around me and hugged and kissed me. I resented that. I was used to my grandfather, not to my father. Although my grandfather was loving, he was much less demonstrative, and I liked that better. In fact my father was a stranger to me, and I felt I couldn't change that just because my mother said he was my father.

Ever since I could remember, when someone asked me, "Who is your father?," I had pointed at a picture. A picture was my father for me. Not a real, living person. My father was a picture in a picture frame who was in a prison in France. I felt pity for him, not love. At times in those years prior to his return, I even resented having to write letters to him. He wrote many letters to me from his prison cell, letters profusely illustrated with flowers and other drawings trying to convey his love for a child he had last seen as a tiny baby. Before I could read I would take my letters with me to the kindergarten and the attendant would read them to me. Or she tried to read them to me, because she always broke down in tears.

Once my father was reunited with us it wasn't that easy for me to adjust to someone I viewed as a demanding and intrusive stranger. I know now that I was selfish and self-centered, but in my teenage years I saw things differently. Although he was kind and loving, I had to give up my home for him and move to Karlsruhe. I held that against him. I had to move from a large house to a one-room furnished apartment. I had to change from a small town to a city atmosphere. I had to take a streetcar every morning to go to school rather than walk to school in a familiar neighborhood. I had to make all those sacrifices for him. For what? The more I thought about him the more I resented him. He also tried to discipline me, which I found absolutely intolerable. For instance, at dinner we only spoke French and he made me sit up straight at the table and eat properly with my knife and fork. He taught me table manners. I resented all that, as well as having to go on long hikes with him. In the evenings, he and my mother would go for walks so I could go to sleep in our one-room *Wohnung*. I cried myself to sleep more than once, certain that in addition to all the other things he had cost me, I now had lost my mother to him too. When I didn't feel sorry for myself, I hated him for all and everything he did that was different from before. Before he came my mother and I were one. Now he and she were one.

Another negative aspect of my new environment was that nearly everyone was Catholic. I was Protestant. In Karlsruhe it was the practice that whenever the church bells rang, children had to go into their living rooms, where families had a *Herrgotswinkel*, and pray. If children were outside, they were to go in. I didn't know what my friends were doing when the bells tolled and they ran away. I soon learned it was the prayer bells. Every Wednesday, Saturday, and Sunday my friends went to church. I felt estranged by the new and constant religious presence. It was just another thing I laid at my poor father's feet.

My relationship to my mother remained fairly unchanged over time. I knew what she thought, and she knew how I thought. I thought it was a nice comfortable relationship—we were a unit, so to speak. She was a direct person. When we had a problem, or I did something I shouldn't have, she would address it immediately. Then it was over and done with. She didn't carry a grudge or moralize about things. My grandfather was just like her. My father was not that way. He moralized and couldn't let go, which probably was our greatest problem. I am fully aware now that he spent ten years in a prison, often in solitary confinement. Ten years that left a mark on him. But as a young girl I couldn't see that far. He was after all the man who came and changed my life, the man who took my mother away from me. That's what I thought at the time.

It was a difficult time for me. Not until I turned seventeen did we finally have a mutually satisfying father-daughter relationship. Some of my girlfriends whose fathers returned even later—the last POWs from the Soviet Union did not return home until January 1956—had experiences similar to mine. Some never were able to bridge the gulf, especially if the parents divorced. With the return of the German prisoners of war after so many years, families who had never been families because of the war suddenly had to become one. They had to manage on their own to find the way. There was no help. Many didn't find the way. Fortunately, my family eventually worked out its problems.

Regina and her husband live in the Rheinland near Cologne. Her relationship with her father grew to encompass love and warmth, especially after she had children of her own. Her father died in 2000, a loss which Regina felt deeply, maybe even more so because of the strained relationship she had with him in her teenage years. Regina is a sharing and intellectually compelling person, teaching German to Chinese businessmen and to ethnic Germans who emigrated from the former Soviet Union. The language skills so heavily emphasized by her father provided her a much greater grasp of the world she lives and works in.

Epilogue

No statesman of the Second World War was foolish enough to claim, as those of the First had done, that it was being fought as "a war to end all wars." That, nevertheless, may have been its abiding effect.

—John Keegan, *The Second World War*

The twenty-seven women and men who tell their stories of life in Germany at the end of World War II were childhood witnesses to chaos, deprivation, and sorrow. Each was also a youthful observer of extraordinary human resilience, inventiveness, and mental toughness. So, what of those five-, eight-, and ten-year-olds who came from Dresden, Remagen, and Köln? From Landau, Königsberg, and Berlin? Prague and Zwickau? Most became the builders of the new Germany. Some found a new life in the United States. All grew up to be productive and thoughtful citizens, many of them reaching senior positions in business, academe, the military, the arts, or public service.

In the course of my interviews I learned several things. Most important to me personally was the fact that I encountered no hate, not even veiled or hidden, in the remote recesses of someone's eyes. No one wanted revenge; no one expressed a dislike of people of other nations or ethnic groups because of events that happened long ago.

To the contrary, I found a Charlie Brach who hosted Russian children at his home more than once after the tragic Chernobyl nuclear accident in 1986, trying hard to give back to the traumatized Russian children a sense of normalcy. Charlie Brach was the same man who as a child had experienced the rape of his mother and grandmother by Russian soldiers. When I queried him about his altruistic behavior he replied, "I believe the Russian soldiers who committed those acts in 1945 were not to blame. They were simple men, followed orders and were encouraged to be that way." Charlie continues to audit Russian courses at the University of Kiel, to maintain his Russian language skills so that he will be better able to communicate with his childhood nemesis.

Another of my discoveries was that even after a considerable passage of time, many of the children of '45 are still troubled by the sounds, sights, or smells that remind them of war, bringing back the dark moments of childhood. The sound of a siren, the smell of a burning tire, a scene in a movie can suddenly rekindle long-buried memories. Some remain deeply saddened by a sense of childhood denied or a family lost. Few have shared completely their memories with their own children. Those who have attempted to do so frequently encountered skepticism or an apparent lack of interest. "My two sons are not interested in the past," a father said to me. "'You exaggerate,' my sons claimed when I persisted. 'It couldn't have possibly been that bad.'" For many of those I interviewed this was the first time they had told their own personal survival story in its entirety. Tears were shed in the process, even by men who couldn't remember the last time they had cried.

A number of the men and women spoke of the empowering lift they experienced as a result of having adult responsibility thrust upon them at a very young age. "Those were wild, interesting, and challenging times," Arnim Krüger told me. "We had to provide for the next meal, search for wood and coal, deal with German, Russian, American, and English soldiers. We saw war, its aftermath and the Berlin airlift. It was a very exciting childhood." The children also developed a keen sense of awareness of danger, and of opportunity, expanding their personal space far beyond that of a child of today. Some related to me later their reluctance to relinquish that sphere of responsibility they had acquired once their fathers returned. Said Hans Herzmann, "While my father was away in the war it was I who fed the rabbits, killed them, and put them on the table. I took care of our five beehives, fed them sugar water, and later retrieved the honey. I wasn't ready to again become an obedient little boy once my father returned." The resultant friction was of course inevitable.

However, this assumption of early responsibility and the attendant development of personal initiative may have contributed to the high level of achievement and productivity of this group of German children. Although a number of them missed as many as three years of schooling, that did not prove to be an impediment to later achievement either for those who continued their lives in Germany or for the few who emigrated to the United States. These young people quickly chose to put the past behind them and looked only to the future. Catching up on lost learning opportunities, striving to achieve at the same level as peers who had not experienced interruption in schooling, and seeking opportunities for higher education were common themes in our conversations. To the German children of war and to their families, education was the way to a better future. Many of those I interviewed completed the *Abitur*, or high school, and subsequently obtained university degrees. Several received doctorates in complex disciplines. Christa Glowalla told me, "What I remember most about my father has to do with education. He would say to me, 'As long as you go to school, any school, I will work and support you.'" That was a common theme for many German parents. I too had a paternal grandfather who repeatedly told me, "They can take everything from you in life, Wolfgang, but they can't take away your education. Get all the schooling you can get." And so I did.

Naturally, with fathers away fighting, missing in action, imprisoned for lengthy periods, or killed in the war, each child's mother, and in some cases the grandmother, became the central adult in the child's life. At a time when all that was familiar seemed to vanish, the one constant was the woman called Mutti. Wherever Mutti was, that became home, no matter where it might have been—a house ruin, a rotting barracks, a ditch by the road. It is clear that German mothers rose to wartime challenges and the brutal conditions of the postwar years with ingenuity, imagination, foresight, and a willingness to make any sacrifice for their children. I too had a mother of that sort. Without her quick thinking, decisiveness, and outright bravery, my sister, Ingrid, and I would not have survived the debilitating conditions under which we lived in the postwar years. "My mother became my role model," said Johann Koppe, "and she strongly influenced every one of my brothers and sisters. She was the leading person in our household." Heinz Loquai said, "If my mother had died it would have been a catastrophe." So it was for many German children. The mothers of the children of war are remembered with tenderness for their sacrifices and their vision.

Of course foreign soldiers loomed large in the lives of this generation of German children. They saw and judged soldiers in terms of the soldiers' behavior toward them, toward their families and friends. Most of the interviewees feared the Russian soldier, although in many instances those same soldiers freely shared the little they had and often moderated their unruly and unpredictable behavior in the presence of children. In contrast, American soldiers were generally admired as the men who ended the war, and are remembered to this day for having been gentle, warm, and caring. I was surprised to learn that, contrary to the usual depiction of the American World War II GI in Europe as being white, nearly all of the women and men I interviewed remembered seeing many black American soldiers. Said Goetz Oertel, "I remember on one occasion four soldiers stopped their truck along the Autobahn, near where I was hiding. They got rations out of their truck and started to cook their meal. As they were cooking, one of the Americans noticed me. He motioned for me to come over. Three of the soldiers were black. I had never seen a black soldier before and was obviously curious, but I soon forgot about skin color. To me, they were just four American soldiers." Karl Kremer summarized his perceptions of foreign soldiers in this way: "Americans gave things; Belgians traded for things; the English did neither." White or black, American and most other Allied soldiers were not threatening, in stark contrast to Russian soldiers.

While the children clearly did not think about economic, political, and military aid and support at the time, as adults they recognize that the American presence in Germany after World War II was critical and served to mitigate the severity and trauma of the postwar years. All understood that if it hadn't been for American food shipments, the resultant famine could have been much worse than what they experienced. As adults, they understand that the Marshall Plan assisted Germany in its struggle to get back on its feet economically, and that a politically astute military governor of an occupied Germany, General Lucius D. Clay, provided an environment in which a democratic form of government could evolve and thrive. The Berlin airlift looms large in the minds of this generation of Germans. Without American generosity toward its former enemy, Germany, my own life and the lives of the Germans and German-Americans featured in this book would have been very different.

War, of course, never ends until the last witness of a conflict dies— and even then it lingers. Not only were German children left with a traumatic legacy, but their own unique experiences of war and the immediate postwar years marked each of them forever. I believe the twenty-seven women and men profiled in this book—the Ingrids and Christas and Reginas, the Wolfs and Bernds and Erichs—are fairly representative of their generation. They are unwilling to join political parties. They vote, but many choose to remain independent. Their pantries are well stocked, as is mine. I believe most could survive any combination of natural disasters for an extended period without needing to venture outside to replenish dwindling supplies. They turn off lights, a habit acquired in wartime Germany which remains with many of them to this day. Many still have a highly developed sense of their immediate environment. After all, danger could be anywhere; of course, so could opportunity.

Focusing on the past clearly is not a defining characteristic of this generation of Germans. Most, if not all, put their war-related experiences behind them and never looked back. Their defining traits as I see them appear to be resilience and an unwillingness to be pushed aside, a readiness to take on huge odds in the process of building a better future for themselves and for their families, a commitment to contribute to the greater good, and a foregoing of hatred and revenge. Courage comes in many forms. One form of courage is for children of war to move forward without hatred, leaving behind a better world than the one they entered as children. Through my conversations with these survivors of an evil war I have come to the conclusion that this wartime generation of Germans has done just that. Whether these children of war now live in Germany or in the United States, they value their German heritage. They value their contributions to their respective societies, as well as their personal achievements, often obtained in the face of great odds arrayed against them. Only with much reluctance do they look back at their distant past. After all, was it not enough just to have survived?

Explanation
of Terms

Flüchtling: refugee.

We were unwanted, although we were Germans. Villagers described us as having lice and fleas, and that we would bring desease. We were treated like dirty foreigners.
—Irmgard Broweleit

Some people callously told us to move on, saying, We don't want Flüchtlinge here. Sharing nothing with us and our tired, hungry horses.
—Goetz Oertel

I was a Flüchtling, a refugee. A lesser person. Manfred didn't come to visit me.
—Bernd Heinrich

Being a Flüchtling all on its own marked a person.
—Heinz Loquai

The residents of Adelheide were none too happy to have to accept total strangers into their homes. In extreme cases people were treated brutally by their hosts and exploited.
—Fred Rother

Explanation of Terms

Abitur Final high school examination and university entrance qualification.

Ahnentafel A Nazi document used to determine an individual's parental lineage, especially Jewish ancestry.

Autobahn The four-lane highways initially built under Hitler which became the model for the American interstate highway system.

Bahnhof Train station.

Ersatz Substitute, such as *Ersatz Kaffee* made from roasted grains.

Erzgebirge Ore Mountains running south of Dresden along the border of wartime Germany and Czechoslovakia.

Feldweg/Waldweg An unpaved path running through fields or forests.

Flüchtling Refugee. In the context of the German World War II experience *Flüchtling* refers to Germans who fled the Red Army from the eastern provinces which eventually became a part of Poland—East Prussia, Silesia, and Pomerania. The word *Flüchtling* quickly assumed a negative connotation among west Germans who did not have to abandon their homes. *Flüchtlinge* were frequently shunned; they lived in crowded substandard housing, their children were accused of being lice infested and dirty, and they were assumed to have come from low socioeconomic backgrounds, the implication being that they were probably of questionable moral character. In other words, they were considered a lower class of people—Germans to be avoided by other Germans.

Frau Woman. To many German women unfortunate enough to be overtaken by the Red Army the word *Frau* became synonymous with rape, as Russian soldiers who searched for women called out *Frau* as they went.

Front Line of combat such as the *Ostfront* (eastern front) in World War II.

Gymnasium High school in Germany.

Hakenkreuzfahne Swastika flag; the official symbol of Hitler's Third Reich.

Hitler Jugend Hitler Youth; generally referred to as HJ, pronounced Hayot. The Hitler Youth was the only youth organization authorized under the Nazis, all others having been banned. Its uniforms looked much like the Boy Scout uniform. At age fourteen German boys had to join the Hitler Youth; it was mandatory for them at age ten to join the *Jungvolk*, which became the feeder organization for the Hitler Youth. Girls had a similar setup called BDM, *Bund Deutscher Mädel*.

Explanation of Terms

Kommissar Communist political officer in the armed forces of the Soviet Union who ensured doctrinal purity and strict adherence to political orders.

Kriegswitwe War widow; a term of respect in Germany.

NSDAP *National Socialistische Deutsche Arbeiter Partei*, National Socialist German Workers' Party (Nazi Party).

Niederschlesien Lower Silesia. A former province of Germany, now a part of Poland.

Ostpreussen East Prussia, now a part of Russia and Poland.

Pommern Pomerania, now a part of Poland.

SS *Schutzstaffel*. Hitler's infamous black-uniformed personal guard. The Waffen-SS, wearing field grey, the standard German army uniform color of the time, was the combat arm of the SS and fought alongside the Wehrmacht. The Waffen-SS was not under Wehrmacht control. Many of the Waffen-SS combat divisions were manned by volunteers from lands occupied by Germany.

Sudetenland A border region of Czechoslovakia occupied by the Nazis in October 1938 as a result of the infamous Munich Conference. The Sudetenland until 1945 was mostly populated by Germans.

Tiefflieger Low-flying aircraft that strafed and bombed road, rail, and river traffic. *Tiefflieger* became a much feared scourge of the German countryside in 1945, frequently firing on anything they saw moving below.

Volkssturm Militia organized late in the war consisting of old men and young boys. They received little training, old weapons, and uniforms if available, and were used to defend their localities.

Währungsreform Currency reform instituted by the Western Allies in West Germany and West Berlin in June 1948. It replaced the valueless reichsmark and formed the basis for the economic resurgence of Germany.

Wehrmacht The collective term for the German armed forces of the Third Reich, excluding the SS.

Index

Ahnentafel (genealogical table), 113
Airmen, fate if shot down, 40
Aircraft: *Fieseler Storch*, 289; Gigant, 317; Ju, 52, 151–52; MiG-15, 47; P-38, 116; Stuka, 292
Angels, 85, 136, 304, 310

Bandits, 140–41, 144
Begging, 88, 124, 139, 219, 228–29, 233, 295
Berlin airlift, 74, 261, 275, 344, 347
Black market, 107, 109, 155, 203, 219, 231, 234, 243, 254, 257
Bombenteppich, 95, 304
Bundesgrenzschutz (border police), 175

CARE packages. *See* School lunches
Children: and fear/terror/grief, 14, 21, 89, 123, 139, 142, 168, 180, 182, 184, 189, 192, 197–99, 204, 240, 259, 266–67, 273, 291–92, 296, 305–06, 331; and nightmares, 13–14, 24, 89, 267, 272; and parental friction, 121, 123, 338, 340–42; at play, 41– 42, 83, 97, 104, 110, 181, 184– 85, 195, 212, 218, 257–58, 289
Clay, Lucius, 347
Concentration camps, 269
Curfew, 98, 215
Czechs, 306, 316, 318, 322–23, 327

DDR, 47, 50, 172, 174–75, 297, 332, 334, 336–39

Denial, 147, 176
DPs, 105, 135, 269

Education, 47–48, 73, 74, 76, 108, 110, 143, 155–59, 172, 179, 190–91, 196–97, 201, 204, 208, 219–21, 234, 236, 248, 258, 261, 274, 281, 283, 288, 294, 296, 310–12, 332–34, 339, 340

FDJ (*Freie Deutsche Jugend*), 172
Flüchtlinge, 54, 60, 61–62, 128, 133, 151, 156, 185–86, 213, 221, 290, 309–11
Food lines, 124, 242, 275, 295, 308, 332

GCLO (German Civil Labor Organization), 326
God. *See* Angels
Goebbels, Joseph, 196, 209
Göring, Hermann, 268
Gould, Gordon, 157–58
GSO (German Service Organization), 326–27
Guilt. *See* Shame

Hahnheide (nature preserve), 154, 156–57, 160
Hate, 40–41, 65, 78, 123, 129, 157, 170, 176, 343
Hiller Girls, 276
Hitler, Adolf, 7, 42, 73, 78, 115, 132, 143, 152, 168, 170, 182, 196–97, 201, 209, 227, 241, 252, 268, 289–90, 311, 332

353

Index

Hitler Youth, 114, 168–69, 196, 211, 252, 281

Identification: cards/pass 108, 167, 217, 243, 245, 322

JABO. *See Tiefflieger*
Jews, 24, 32, 65, 78, 115, 170, 268–69, 272, 276, 338–39
Jugendweihe, 46
Jungvolk, 114–15, 168, 196, 227, 252

Kohlenklau, 209, 226–27, 237
KVP (*Kasernierte Volkspolizei*), 47

Lice, 146, 202, 233, 269, 307
Lido, 276
Life, lessons in, 78, 160, 192, 222, 247, 262, 284, 322

Marshall Plan, 347
Marx, Karl, 338
May, Karl, 76

NAPOLI (*National Socialistische Erziehungsanstalt*), 167–68
NASA, 221–22
Nazis, 7, 39, 41, 59, 61–62, 81–82, 86, 93, 114–15, 123, 150, 167, 180, 204, 205, 212, 247, 252, 265, 268, 272, 281, 289, 339
Nemmersdorf, 210
NSDAP. *See Nazis*
NVA (*Nationale Volksarmee*), 47–48, 51, 174

Oderbruch, 287

Panje wagon, 43, 171, 253–57, 320
Panzerfaust, 118, 208

Peale, Norman Vincent, 221
Poles, 144–46, 153–54, 163, 165, 201, 231–32
Prisoners of war: French, 20, 196, 287–90, 305; Italian, 196; Russian, 20, 22, 37, 39, 86, 196, 217, 287–90

Rage. *See* Hate
Rape, 140–41, 145, 168, 170, 181, 199–201, 228, 253–54, 271, 282, 306, 344
Red Cross, 165–66, 182–84, 187, 189, 196, 203, 211, 325
Refugees. *See Flüchtlinge*
RIAS Berlin (Radio in the American Sector), 173

Schicksal (fate), 340
Schnitzler, Karl, 47
School. *See* Education
School lunches, 88, 98, 109, 123, 203, 234, 275
Schrebergarten, 39, 326
Secret police, 258–59
Shame, 66, 78, 158, 187
Ships: *Italia*, 220–21; *Queen Elizabeth*, 235; *United States*, 276; USNS *Ernie Pyle*, 64; USNS *General C. H. Muir*, 188; *Wilhelm Gustloff*, 179–83
Soldiers: American, 21–24, 30–31, 42–43, 62–63, 86–87, 96–97, 105, 118–22, 153, 210, 214, 216–17, 242, 256, 273, 294–95, 307–08, 319, 325, 346; Belgian, 96–97; black, 43, 87, 96, 120, 122, 216, 307–08, 319, 325, 346; English, 63, 96–97, 154, 261; French, 87–88, 108, 240–41; Russian, 13, 43–44, 70–71, 136–39, 168–73, 198–202, 228, 253–57, 270–73, 282, 305, 320–24
Sputnik, 221

Index

SS, 32, 153
STASI (*Staatssicherheitsdienst*), 332
Stoppeln, 44, 59, 97, 323

Tieffflieger, 4, 5, 28, 39–40, 58, 61, 84–86,
    95, 186, 213–14, 253, 281, 294, 318
Townes, Henry, 156
Trains, 22, 32, 63–64, 88, 151, 164–68,
    189, 192, 197, 202–03, 211, 220, 232,
    240, 243, 259, 261, 306–09, 318, 332

Volkspolizei (people's police), 173–74,
    259–60
Volkssturm, 20, 163, 197, 211, 288, 290

Young Pioneers, 172, 338

Zirkus Knie (circus in Switzerland), 276
Zones of occupation: American, 217, 248,
    307, 328; British, 146, 203, 233, 282;
    French, 248, 296; Russian, 156, 233,
    256, 306

About the Author

Wolfgang W. E. Samuel served for thirty years in the United States Air Force, retiring in the rank of colonel. During his air force career he attended the National War College and was decorated with three awards of the Distinguished Flying Cross. He is the author of *German Boy: A Refugee's Story* and *I Always Wanted to Fly: America's Cold War Airmen*, both published by the University Press of Mississippi. He lives in Fairfax Station, Virginia.